WALKING -----→
SAN FRANCISCO

 WILDERNESS PRESS . . . *on the trail since 1967*

WALKING ----→
SAN FRANCISCO

35 Savvy Tours Exploring Steep Streets, Grand Hotels, Dive Bars, and Waterfront Parks

Third Edition

Kathleen Dodge Doherty with Tom Downs

 WILDERNESS PRESS . . . *on the trail since 1967*

Walking San Francisco: 35 Savvy Tours Exploring Steep Streets, Grand Hotels, Dive Bars, and Waterfront Parks

Third edition, first printing

Copyright © 2019 by Kathleen Dodge Doherty
Copyright © 2007 and 2010 by Tom Downs

Distributed by Publishers Group West
Manufactured in the United States of America

Project editor: Ritchey Halphen
Cover design/cartography: Scott McGrew; map data: OpenStreetMap
Book design: Lora Westberg
Photos: Kathleen Dodge Doherty, except where noted
Copy editor: Kerry Smith
Proofreader: Laura Franck
Indexer: Sylvia Coates

Library of Congress Cataloging-in-Publication Data

Names: Dodge, Kathleen, author.
Title: Walking San Francisco : 35 savvy tours exploring steep streets, grand hotels, dive bars, and
    waterfront parks / Kathleen Dodge Doherty.
Description: Third Edition. | Birmingham, Alabama : Wilderness Press, [2019] | "Distributed by Publishers
    Group West"—T.p. verso. | Includes index.
Identifiers: LCCN 2018042147| ISBN 978-0-89997-909-0 (paperback) | ISBN 9780899979106 (e-book)
Subjects: LCSH: Walking—California—San Francisco—Guidebooks. | San Francisco (Calif.)—Guidebooks.
    | San Francisco (Calif.)—Description and travel.
Classification: LCC F869.S33 D63 2019 | DDC 917.94/610454—dc23
LC record available at lccn.loc.gov/2018042147

WILDERNESS PRESS
An imprint of AdventureKEEN
2204 First Ave. S., Ste. 102
Birmingham, AL 35233
800-443-7227, fax 205-326-1012

Visit wildernesspress.com for a complete list of our books and for ordering information. Contact us at our website, at facebook.com/wildernesspress1967, or at twitter.com/wilderness1967 with questions or comments. To find out more about who we are and what we're doing, visit blog.wildernesspress.com.

Cover and frontispiece: Whether you amble in its shadow or you walk its length, the Golden Gate Bridge (see Walk 17, page 117) impresses with its grandeur. Cover photo: canadastock/Shutterstock

The following artworks appear in this book with permission: **page 53:** (back) *Jazz Mural* (1988) by Bill Weber with Tony Klaas, (front) *Language of the Birds* (2006–08) by Brian Goggin with Dorka Keehn; **page 57:** Vesuvio Cafe mural by Alfred "Shawn" O'Shaughnessy (1928–2011), theartofshawn.com; **page 84:** *Where the Wild Things Are* (2015) by Sam Flores; **page 85:** *Squared* (2014) by Charles Gadeken; **page 152:** *Antepasadas (Ancestors;* 2016) by Simone Star; **page 201:** Jerry Garcia mural (2016) by Mel Waters.

SAFETY NOTICE Although Wilderness Press and the author have made every attempt to ensure that the information in this book is accurate at press time, they are not responsible for any loss, damage, injury, or inconvenience that may occur to anyone while using this book. You are responsible for your own safety and health while following the walking trips described here. Always check local conditions, know your own limitations, and consult a map.

Acknowledgments

This book would have been far less fun to write without the amazing companionship, support, and pavement pounding of people I love. I am so lucky to have friends and neighbors willing to share favorite haunts and alleyways, and a few deserve a special shout-out.

Scott Nair downed endless cappuccinos and traversed countless stairways with me, rain or shine. Rebecca Sudore laced up her shoes and provided pithy insider information about her favorite neighborhoods. Tria Cohn proved once again that she has the most amazing sense of direction of anyone in the Presidio. Leah Doherty allowed her vacation to be co-opted into direction checking and cream puff tasting.

Melanie Cantarutti and Ellen McGlynn gamely clocked many miles in search of the ideal Golden Gate Park experience. Ann Cleaveland was with us in spirit, packing extra snacks and peanut butter. Kristina Malsberger and Marisa Gierlich added humor, bourbon, and encouraging words that stretched from The Interval at Long Now all the way to Piccino. Jenn Fox and Josh Mangum provided crucial literary and cinematic inspiration.

My mom, Mary Dodge, was an entertaining (if slightly dubious) source of first-person recollections of North Beach bars and Playland at the Beach. If my dad, John Dodge, were still with us, I know he'd be wearing an Aloha shirt and enjoying a mai tai at the Tonga Room. He is incredibly missed. Johnny and Magnolia, my favorite pint-size walking companions, allowed themselves to be plied with ice cream and hilltop swings in the name of Mom's work. And I'm forever grateful to my husband, Eric, for holding down the fort when he wasn't hoisting a beer during bar-hopping research.

Finally, I want to thank the fine folks at Wilderness Press, particularly Tim Jackson, Ritchey Halphen, and Scott McGrew, for their wit, warmth, and wonderful support of this project.

—*Kathleen Dodge Doherty*

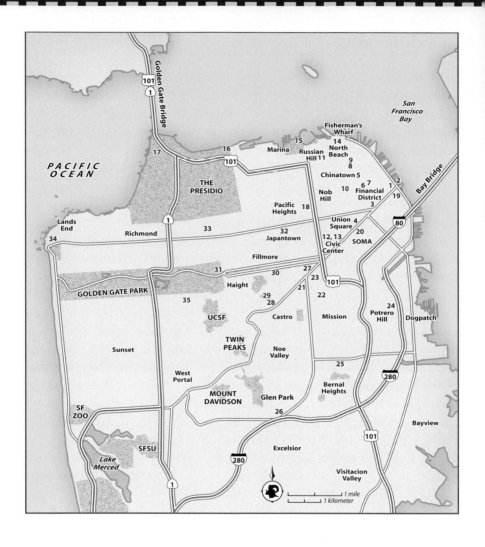

PACIFIC OCEAN

San Francisco Bay

Golden Gate Bridge

101 1

101

17

16

101

15 Marina

14 North Beach

Fisherman's Wharf

Russian Hill 11

9

8

Chinatown 5

7

6 Financial District

10

2

1

19

Bay Bridge

THE PRESIDIO

Pacific Heights 18

Nob Hill

3

Union Square 4

20

80

SOMA

1

Lands End

Richmond

33

32 Japantown

12, 13 Civic Center

34

Fillmore

31

27

30

23

101

Haight

21

22

GOLDEN GATE PARK

35

29

28

24 Potrero Hill

Dogpatch

UCSF

Castro

Mission

Sunset

TWIN PEAKS

Noe Valley

25

West Portal

280

MOUNT DAVIDSON

Glen Park

Bernal Heights

SF ZOO

26

Bayview

SFSU

Excelsior

101

Lake Merced

280

1

Visitacion Valley

1 mile

1 kilometer

Table of Contents

Author's Note

As a child growing up in the East Bay, I always viewed San Francisco as the glamorous jeweled treasure box that beckoned from across the water, the dashing urban counterpart to my quiet suburban upbringing. My family would get dressed up to have dinner in the city, where sunlight glinted off the waves, Carol Doda's flashing neon nipples made us giggle in the back seat, and untold adventures seemed to await once I got old enough.

Once I *was* old enough, the city lived up to my expectations. I watched friends' bands play at the Bottom of the Hill, danced at raves in abandoned Dogpatch warehouses, and ate more burritos than I care to admit. But my absolute favorite thing to do was to walk. I loved to pick a different neighborhood to explore each time and ferret out its distinction and charms. I delight in secret stairways, trellised gardens, windswept peaks, unexpected murals, and foggy waterfronts.

When I finally moved to the city more than 12 years ago, my walking explorations increased with fervor. These days, my favorite night out is an urban adventure with my husband, a bottle of wine in our backpack and the city stretched out before us, waiting to be discovered.

As I slip on my shoes and head out the front door, San Francisco always feels full of possibility. I love that at any one point, someone is shrouded in fog while someone else is getting a sunburn. One person is slurping noodles in Chinatown, while another is disco-dancing on roller skates in the park. Strains of gypsy jazz, Top 40, and kids practicing instruments waft down from open windows, providing the soundtrack.

More than anything, I love San Francisco's open-minded, welcoming nature and the vast variety of creative characters who make their home here. I've found that the best way to get to know them is to join them on the street and ask them their favorite places to walk. This is what I did to research this book, and this is what I invite you to do as you hit the streets yourself.

All right. Let's see where our shoes take us!

—K. D. D.

Stairways through lush gardens, like the Filbert Steps across Napier Lane on Telegraph Hill (see Walk 9, page 62), entice explorers to discover San Francisco's hidden neighborhoods.

Introduction

With its jagged coastal edges, architectural paragons, lofty peaks, and ever-shifting layers of fog and sun, San Francisco invites exploration on foot. The beauty of walking is the slower pace it affords, tempting curious travelers to the top of the next hill, past the carefully tended flowers of hidden lanes, into bars where gold miners swapped tall tales, and through parks still suffused with the patchouli of a bygone era. While the hills inarguably present a few natural challenges, your efforts are well rewarded, and there is nearly always an inviting place to eat, drink, and take a pause. Walking allows you to make unexpected detours, noticing the renegade public art, fairy gardens, and pageantry of people that make San Francisco's streets an open theater. Often the best gems are tucked away on pedestrian-only lanes.

Distinct neighborhoods, shaped by the waves of immigrants who have arrived since the city's inception, are so close to each other that you can watch fishermen pull in their nets in the misty gloom of early light, choose some dim sum in Chinatown, take a nap in a park surrounded by colorful Victorians, catch surfers carving waves in the shadow of the Golden Gate Bridge, and dance to Latin beats until morning, all in a single urban jaunt. And then you can rise the next morning and have a completely different experience.

San Francisco likes to lead the charge but also waxes nostalgic for another time. Proud of its civil rights history, unabashed about its bawdy pirate past, venerated for its Summer of Love, San Francisco is a city that rebuilds and reinvents itself constantly but never forgets its past. The city has pulled itself up by its bootstraps following earthquakes, fires, and economic booms and busts. The more you learn about the city's riotous past, the more you want to know about the footsteps that fell before yours.

All of this said, the face of transportation in the city has changed, and we invite you to explore all manner of transit options to meet our starting points. The options are plentiful: ferries, water taxis, historic cable cars, vintage streetcars, buses, BART, ride-share and bicycle services, electric bikes, and scooters.

But most of all, this book invites you to enjoy the journey. These are not purposeful walks but meandering, inquisitive strolls that focus on the story behind the buildings and the intriguing details that you'll easily miss if you're moving too fast. The philosophy of this book is to slow down, pet a dog, chat up a barista, help someone up a steep hill with her groceries, sketch a hilltop view, and become a part of the fabric of this spectacular city.

1 Lower Market Street
From Old Money to Tech-Driven Optimism

Above: *The splashing water of the Vaillancourt Fountain, once the site of an impromptu U2 concert, provides a backdrop for lunching professionals in Embarcadero Plaza.*

BOUNDARIES: Market St. from the Embarcadero to Van Ness Ave.
DISTANCE: 2 miles
DIFFICULTY: Easy
PARKING: Garage at Embarcadero 2
PUBLIC TRANSIT: Embarcadero BART station; F streetcars (street level); J, K, L, M, N, T streetcars (underground); 2, 6, 7, 9 14, 21, 31 Muni buses

Market Street slices through San Francisco's grid at a brash, oblique angle, cutting a prominent seam through the city's central neighborhoods. It's a direct conduit into the city from San Francisco's historic access point, the Ferry Building, leading all the way to Twin Peaks, where it heads skyward and disappears, having vaguely shown the way to the Pacific Ocean without actually leading there.

Market serves as the city's parade ground, but it doesn't require a parade to be interesting. To walk this graceful corridor on a weekday morning is to be urged along by the living thrum of an American city. Muni buses, taxis, restored streetcars, autos, and bicycles generate a full-throated thrum as their wheels roll up and down Market's lanes. Billions in US dollars have been earned, lost, and swindled in the high-rise and flatiron structures along blocks that hem the Financial District, and billions more have been spent in the emporiums near Union Square. West of the Powell Street cable car turnaround, Market Street once thrived as San Francisco's Broadway, with two or three grand theaters to a block. Some survive today, but this stretch of the city's main thoroughfare, up to Van Ness, has gone through quite a rough patch. The contrast from one end of this walk to the other is striking and, in some ways, baffling. Times may be changing, however, as new businesses are starting to anchor the seedier side of Market and pull it up by its bootstraps once again.

All in all, a walk along Market Street makes a fine introduction to San Francisco. This walk is as straightforward as they come.

Walk Description

Start at the foot of Market Street, opposite the Ferry Building and separated from the Embarcadero by just a few paces. (The Ferry Building is explored in greater detail in the next walk, Embarcadero North.) The open space here is ❶ **Embarcadero Plaza,** formerly named for Justin Herman, the controversial head of San Francisco's Redevelopment Agency from 1959 to 1971. (Herman is generally held accountable for the displacement of thousands of black residents in the Western Addition while that neighborhood was subjected to extensive renewal projects during the early 1960s.) For decades, this awkward plaza was marred by the elevated Embarcadero Freeway, which ran along the bayfront until the 1989 Loma Prieta earthquake brought it down. Today the plaza is a pleasant space, with palm trees, an open-air crafts market, and live music several days a week around lunchtime. At the plaza's northeastern corner is the homely Vaillancourt Fountain, described by the late *San Francisco Chronicle* architecture critic Allan Temko as something "deposited by a concrete dog with square intestines." Nevertheless, steps through the fountain's shallow pool invite you to venture behind the huge spouts, where you're likely to get a wee bit wet while enjoying a backstage perspective. The best thing to happen to the Vaillancourt Fountain was when Irish rockers U2 staged an impromptu lunchtime concert here in 1987, thrown together in less than 48 hours. Bono dubbed it the Save the Yuppies concert, as it took place less than a month after "Black Monday," one of the nation's most devastating stock market crashes, and he thought the Financial District needed cheering up. The 20,000 attending fans agreed. (Parts of this show appear in the U2 documentary *Rattle and Hum*.) This is also a good vantage point from which to view the staggered backside of the ❷ **Hyatt Regency** hotel. (The Embarcadero Center, which also towers over the plaza, is included in Walk 3, Financial District; see page 18.)

Start walking up Market Street, noting the attractive One Market building across the street. It was home base for the Southern Pacific Railroad, the enormous conglomerate run by the Big Four railroad magnates, who dominated transportation in the western United States during the late 19th century. The building went up in 1916. Southern Pacific survived until 1996, when the company was absorbed by Union Pacific.

At Drumm Street, turn right and enter the Hyatt Regency, which is merely interesting from the outside but truly spectacular from within. Head up the escalator to the atrium level, where glass elevators whiz up to tiered, vertigo-inducing balconies. Mel Brooks took full advantage of the striking setting when he shot scenes for *High Anxiety* here. Ride an elevator up and down, and get back to Market Street.

Cross to the other side at Spear and continue walking inland. After passing the Federal Reserve Bank, the next block is dominated by the ❸ **Matson** and ❹ **PG&E Buildings,** which make a perfect pair. The Matson office, home to the city's largest shipping line, was built in 1921, and the office of the local power company, PG&E, went up four years later. Scan the ledges of the upper floors of these buildings, and you might spot one of the peregrine falcons that regularly perch on them when not flying amid the high-rises. From 2003 to 2005, two falcons, dubbed Gracie and George, raised their nestlings outside the 33rd floor of the PG&E Building, overlooking Beale Street. Since then, dozens of falcons have nested on the ledge, with more than 40 chicks having hatched since 2004. So great is their popularity that they have their own live web cam (pge.com/falconcam) and hundreds of people submit names when the babies are born. (Edward, Archibald, and Hallie were the newest trio to arrive.)

If you look back across Market Street, you'll get an eyeful of ❺ **101 California,** a cylindrical glass tower that's worth a closer look. Cross over to it, and you'll see that the lower floors are supported by unclad pillars. The exposed pillars, which of course run unseen to the top of the building, look naked and suspiciously vulnerable without the glass curtain. During the holidays, impossibly large tree ornaments grace the large public space in front of the offices. At the confluence of Market, Battery, and Bush Streets, breaking office workers and bike messengers often perch at the base of the *Mechanics Monument* statue, a robust bronze by Douglas Tilden, who was educated at California's School for the Deaf, where he later taught. A childhood illness robbed Tilden of his hearing at age 4. The statue was unveiled in 1901 to some protest from those who observed that the subjects—muscular ironworkers—were not wearing pants beneath their blacksmith aprons, leaving their bums exposed to the elements. Tilden, himself regarded as the Michelangelo of the West, argued he was observing the classical ideal. The nude ironworkers may have had their hams roasted during the 1906 quake and fire, but they were little harmed otherwise.

Midway across Battery, on the little triangular island, keep your eyes peeled for a historical marker that informs us that the slot machine was invented by Charles August Fey in his workshop near this spot in 1894. For the better part of a century, Fey's three-reel, hand-cranked "one-armed bandit" was the slot machine of choice in many a Nevada casino. The green-tinted glass curtain wall that towers over the next block (between Battery and Sansome) is the Crown Zellerbach Building. Built in 1959, it's one of San Francisco's most attractive modern structures.

The exposed musculature of the *Mechanics Monument* caused some stir upon its unveiling.

Market Street's triangular corners necessitated the design of numerous flatiron buildings, so called because they are shaped like the old blockish irons long ago heated on stoves before being applied to wrinkled shirts. Modern office towers such as the Crown Zellerbach Building often flout the shape of their lots with surrounding plazas and what-not, but the next block is occupied by a traditional flatiron building of the sort that once lined much of Market Street. This tasteful flatiron dates to 1913.

On the same block, toward the wider end, stands the ❻ **Hobart Building,** an attractive 1914 Willis Polk design. Part of the building's unintended appeal comes from the fact that its design took a shorter adjacent neighbor into account. When that building was demolished and replaced by an even shorter structure, the Hobart Building's flat western flank, never meant to be seen, was awkwardly exposed. Cross Montgomery Street, and turn left and then right on Post Street to reach the ❼ **Mechanic's Institute,** a gem of a building. The institute opened in 1854, providing instructional books on trade skills to laid-off mine workers. It's the oldest library on the West Coast, and these days its collection caters more to literary circles; it also hosts the longest continually running chess club in the United States. While a private organization (you can't just check out a book without a membership), the institute freely welcomes visitors to tour the gorgeous spiral staircase and peruse the two-story library.

Backstory: Palace Intrigue

The original Palace Hotel was the center of the city's social life and the downfall of William Ralston, the banker who literally went belly-up while building it. First Ralston went bankrupt, and then he died while swimming in the bay a few weeks before the hotel's opening. Many suspect it was a suicide.

Three decades later, opera star Enrico Caruso, in town to perform in a production of *Carmen*, stayed in the old Palace the night of April 17, 1906. Just after five o'clock the following morning, Caruso evacuated the shaking building several hours before flames engulfed it. Some eyewitnesses claimed the singer was in an embarrassing state of panic, but Caruso wrote a lengthy account for a London publication refuting this attack on his character. He admitted that he and his valet had wandered helplessly about the city, as did thousands of others, as the entire downtown area went up in smoke. He slept on the ground on the night of April 18 and found his way out of town the following day. He never returned to San Francisco.

On August 2, 1923, President Warren G. Harding—remembered for the corruption in his cabinet and for his poor command of the English language—died at the rebuilt Palace Hotel after he was stricken with what was thought to be food poisoning while traveling to the city from Alaska. Mysteriously, no one Harding had dined with got sick, and conspiracy theories abounded. The official cause of death was later deemed a heart attack.

Returning as you came, cross Market and briefly retrace your steps up Market toward Second Street. Turn right on Second and walk a block and a half to reach the **8 Alexander Book Company,** an independent bookstore whose three impressive floors compose a literary sanctuary in the heart of the Financial District. Clean bathrooms, an exceedingly helpful staff, and a fine selection of postcards and greeting cards make this a favorite stop of many downtown commuters. After browsing, head back up Second Street for half a block and turn left on Stevenson. After a block, Stevenson dead-ends at New Montgomery. Cross the street to reach the main entrance of the **9 Palace Hotel.** It was built in 1909 on the site of the far-more-magnificent original Palace, which was destroyed by the '06 fire, but is nevertheless spectacular in its own right, especially the atrium with its Victorian glass roof. Go inside for a look (or for an expensive pot of tea in the atrium), and exit via a hall leading back to Market Street. On your way out, you'll pass the Pied Piper bar. If it's open, peek inside for a look at the mural by Maxfield Parrish. If you're a mite parched, you can stop for a beer as well.

Another block up, at the corner of Third and Market, is the **10 Hearst Building,** its entry marked by a big *H*. Built in 1909, it was home to William Randolph Hearst's *San Francisco Examiner*. Architect Julia Morgan designed the building's baroque entry, which was added in 1937. During the early

20th century, this intersection was home to two of the city's other leading papers, the *Call* and the *Chronicle*. The Call Building has been remodeled beyond recognition, its once-glorious dome having been removed to accommodate additional floors, but the *Chronicle*'s old home, the de Young Building (1890) at 690 Market, has been restored and resembles its former self. Designed by Burnham and Root, it originally sported a four-story clock tower, which went up in smoke a year before the 1906 quake. In the 1960s the entire building was covered with metal siding, which obscured the building's solid brick appeal. As part of its recent restoration, a modern tower was added awkwardly to the top of this graceful landmark but is set back enough not to detract from the attractive facade.

In front of the de Young Building you'll spot ⑪ **Lotta's Fountain,** a gift to the city in 1875 from Lotta Crabtree (1847–1924), a beguiling redhead who as a child entertainer worked the halls of Sierra Nevada mining towns; when she matured, she moved east and became the "Belle of Broadway." The fountain became legendary, however, for the congregations that gather here every year on April 18 to commemorate the 1906 earthquake. In years past, the festivities included a few quake survivors. (In 2009 a 106-year-old woman and a 103-year-old man were in attendance; the last known survivor died in 2016 at age 109.) In the immediate aftermath of the quake, the fountain was a meeting place for separated families.

At the intersection of Market, Grant, and O'Farrell Streets is the ⑫ **Phelan Building,** a large and elegant flatiron. Clad in white terra-cotta tiles, it's one of the prettiest sights on all of Market Street. James Duvall Phelan, the city's mayor from 1897 to 1902 and a US Senator from 1915 to 1921, kept his offices here after the building went up in 1908.

Cross Market Street and walk on the south side. Midway up the next block, enter Westfield Centre, a shopping mall fashioned from the gutted shell of the historic Emporium department store. The facade is original, as is the beautiful glass rotunda, which is the building's real attraction. You'll have to work to see it, though, as it's obscured by intermediary levels and escalators.

Across the street, the block is dominated by the gray hulk of the ⑬ **Flood Building,** built by James L. Flood, the son of silver-mining magnate

The Hearst Building is the former home of the *San Francisco Examiner*.

The Hibernia Bank Building has played host to everything from money to cops to lavish parties.

James C. Flood. It's an impressive eye-catcher with a staunch demeanor. In the early 1920s, Dashiell Hammett, yet to establish himself as the father of American crime fiction, worked upstairs for the local branch of the Pinkerton Detective Agency. Today, as you'll see, its ground floor houses the Gap flagship store.

Just past Hallidie Plaza and the Powell Street cable car turnaround (launching point of the Union Square Walk), Market Street begins to change noticeably. For years this mid-Market area has been a blight, with plywood-covered storefronts and a rather downtrodden feel. The city, however, is making strides to revive this section of Market Street, and you'll see new businesses cropping up among the shuttered movie theaters, check-cashing shops, and strip clubs. If planners have their way, this area will be transformed over the next decade. Indeed, in the 1930s this whole area was awash with twinkling white lights from the marquees of more than 20 movie theaters over five blocks that gave rise to the moniker Great White Way, a theater district touted on postcards and tourist literature. The Warfield, between Mason and Taylor, and the Golden Gate Theatre, where Taylor and Golden Gate meet Market, are still important venues for live music and Broadway shows that remain. The ⑭ Hibernia Bank Building, designed by Albert Pissis and William Moore in 1892, dominates the intersection of Jones, McAllister, and Market. The building hasn't housed a bank since the mid-1980s. Over the next decade, it was home to the SFPD's Tenderloin Task Force, which departed in 2000. A lovely building with a green copper dome, it has finally been restored after years of neglect. Hillary Clinton held a fundraising event here in 2016 following the renovation.

On the next block, the Proper Hotel's bright marquee, hanging off a historic flatiron clad in brick, is a look at what the future may hold. Sophisticated and hip, the hotel features a rooftop bar, Charmaine's, with warming firepits, strong cocktails, and decadent views from 120 feet up. But it also sits at the foot of the Tenderloin, so it's a delicate balance.

At Seventh Street the sturdy Grant Building, a steel-framed quake survivor, and the comely Odd Fellows Temple, where Odd Fellows still congregate, face off on opposite corners. A little farther down, the **15** **Strand Theater** is the latest attempt at revitalizing the mid-Market arts district. A performance space for the American Conservatory Theater, the Strand is housed in a 1917 building that opened its doors as the Jewel, offering 1,200 seats for well-dressed theatergoers to enjoy silent films. Like the neighborhood, the building went through a series of changes before falling into disrepair and disuse after being pinched in 2003 as a porn shop that doubled as a base for a drug and prostitution ring. It now has a fresh coat of shiny red paint, bears little resemblance to its historic past, and serves as a black-box theater. Past UN Plaza, the **16** **Orpheum Theatre** in 2003 has a spruced up, flamboyant facade rising above the urban grit. Built in 1926, the Orpheum was initially a Pantages vaudeville theater and then a grand movie palace. Today, it houses Broadway stage productions. Step into the covered entryway, elegantly clad in marble. It's still a beauty.

On the other side of Market, a giant pit indicates where new condos will soon rise, as well as San Francisco's largest Whole Foods. Dozens of developments like this are under way as part of the city's plan to overhaul this mid-Market area. This is not the first time that urban planners have tried to fix Market Street, but with tech dollars pouring in and the city bursting at the seams with new residents, it does seem to have a shot at success.

Past Eighth Street, a plaque beside the entrance of the Hotel Whitcomb states that the hotel served as city hall from 1912 to 1915 while the current City Hall was being built. The rest of the block is occupied by a cold office tower that from the street appears devoid of life; few people walk in or out, even during the busiest of times. Kitty-corner to that, at Ninth Street, Fox Plaza, a mix of offices and rental apartments, is similarly off-putting. Unwelcoming high-rises such as these reflect a regrettable midcentury approach to redevelopment, which all too often failed to bring renewed energy to the surrounding neighborhood. In this case, as a twist to the knife, Fox Plaza stands on the site of the sorely missed Fox Theatre, a stunning movie palace that was demolished in 1963.

Across from Fox Plaza, the block-long former **17** **SF Mart Building** is an Art Deco gem completed in 1937. These days it's known as the Twitter Building, thanks to the tech giant moving its headquarters here in 2012. (The move was incentivized by a large tax break from the city to keep the internet titan from moving out of the city.) More tech companies followed suit and set up shop in the mid-Market area, including Spotify, Square, and Yammer. And underneath the Twitter Building is Market, a foodie-oriented grocery filled with kombucha, Blue Bottle Coffee, craft beer, a wine bar, locally sourced arugula, and all the other overpriced and delicious goods that make folks roll their eyes at the tech industry's elitist tastes.

The intersection of Market and 10th Streets now boasts ⑱ **NEMA,** a luxury apartment complex. The name derives from "New Market," and it's definitely a shift from the lot's prior history as a vacant lot. The condos come with everything from dog-washing services, cooking classes, and a heated saline pool to outdoor grilling stations. The insanely priced units—some studios rented for $4,000 per month in 2018—were mercilessly mocked for their seemingly tone-deaf marketing campaign about being a "design-driven lifestyle pioneer," mere steps from the city's burgeoning homeless population. But naysayers aside, the units were also quickly snatched up. On the next block, a drab building at 1444 Market has a much more colorful history than its architecture belies. This was the home of the revolutionary ⑲ **San Francisco Cannabis Buyers' Club** and the birthplace of the medical-marijuana movement. Founded in 1984 by activist Dennis Peron and "Brownie Mary" Rathbun, who earned her nickname handing out pain-relieving pot brownies to AIDS patients at San Francisco General Hospital, this was the nation's first dispensary. *The New York Times* called it "the biggest open secret in town," and with the help of a well-crafted media push, they are credited with getting Prop 215 (a proposition to legalize medical marijuana) on the 1996 ballot. Drama ensued as the attorney general sent some 100 law-enforcement agents to raid the club shortly before the election. Despite the arrests, the landmark proposition passed. Today, you can have weed delivered to your door via a mobile app.

A few doors down is the corner of Van Ness Avenue, and the end of this walk.

Points of Interest

❶ **Embarcadero Plaza** Market and Steuart Sts.; 415-831-2700, sfrecpark.org/destination/justin-herman-plaza

❷ **Hyatt Regency** 5 Embarcadero Center; 415-788-1234, sanfrancisco.regency.hyatt.com

❸ **Matson Building** 215 Market St. (no published phone number or website)

❹ **PG&E Building** 245 Market St.; 800-743-5000, pge.com

Lower Market Street

5 **101 California** 101 California St.; 415-982-6200, 101california.com

6 **Hobart Building** 582 Market St.; 415-395-9057, hobartbuilding.com

7 **Mechanic's Institute** 57 Post St.; 415-393-0101, milibrary.org

8 **Alexander Book Company** 50 Second St.; 415-495-2992, alexanderbook.com

9 **Palace Hotel** 2 New Montgomery St.; 415-512-1111, sfpalace.com

10 **Hearst Building** 5 Third St.; 415-777-0600, hearstbuildingsf.com

11 **Lotta's Fountain** Intersection of Market, Geary, and Kearny Sts.

12 **Phelan Building** 760 Market St. (no public-facing phone number or website)

13 **Flood Building** 870 Market St.; 415-982-3298, floodbuilding.com

14 **Hibernia Bank Building (former)** 1 Jones St.; 415-291-8429, onejonessf.com

15 **Strand Theater** 1127 Market St.; 415-749-2228, act-sf.org

16 **Orpheum Theatre** 1192 Market St.; 888-746-1799, shnsf.com

17 **SF Mart (Twitter/Market) Building** 1355 Market St.; 415-767-5130, visitthemarket.com

18 **NEMA** 8 10th St.; 415-881-5060, rentnema.com

19 **San Francisco Cannabis Buyers' Club (former)** 1444 Market St. (no published phone number or website)

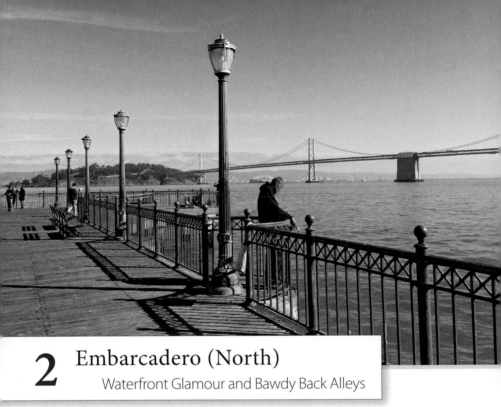

2 Embarcadero (North)
Waterfront Glamour and Bawdy Back Alleys

Above: *Pier 7's pedestrian wharf is a great place to soak in bridge views or cast a line into the sea.*

BOUNDARIES: Market St., Embarcadero, Chestnut St., Sansome St.
DISTANCE: 2.75 miles
DIFFICULTY: Easy
PARKING: Off-street parking at the Embarcadero Center and on Howard St.
PUBLIC TRANSIT: Embarcadero BART station; F streetcars (street level); J, K, L, M, N, T streetcars (underground); 2, 6, 7, 9 14, 21, 31 Muni buses

Much of the history of early San Francisco centered on the waterfront around Yerba Buena Cove, which, before it was filled in, curved into what is now the Financial District, as far inland as Battery Street. At high tide, early structures along Montgomery Street are said to have had water lapping at their steps. Most of the ground we'll tread on this tour covers the bones of rotted ships, many of which were abandoned by seamen who made a dash for the diggings in the Sierra foothills. Some deserted ships became boarding houses, while others were converted into saloons. One even served as the city jail. Eventually, their wooden hulls formed the foundation for landfill, and the wharves where they tied on became the city streets we walk today.

For the unwary sailor, a stop in this neighborhood was perilous indeed, with swindlers and crimps seeming friendly enough until the hapless seaman was drugged or slugged and sold to the next ship embarking on a two-year voyage. This practice was prevalent in other ports, but it ran rampant in San Francisco, where it became known as *shanghaiing*. We'll uncover some of that history here, so keep your wits about ye.

This tour doesn't dwell exclusively on the past, though, for the Embarcadero is returning to life after its late 20th-century slumber. Saturday morning, when the Ferry Building Farmers' Market is on, is a good time to begin this tour.

Walk Description

Begin at the ❶ **Ferry Building.** Built in 1898, it instantly established itself as the principal entryway to the city, and it remained so until bridges and airplanes made it possible to arrive in San Francisco from the east without taking a ride on a ferry boat. For a time the Ferry Building was one of the busiest transit hubs in the world, with some 100,000 passengers passing through every day. Ferry traffic began to diminish after the completion of the Bay Bridge in 1936. The building's dwindling importance was obvious by the time the elevated Embarcadero Freeway was completed in 1959, effectively concealing much of the Ferry Building from the rest of the city. That proved to be a temporary problem solved by the 1989 earthquake, which damaged the elevated freeway. The freeway was demolished a few years later, giving new life to the Ferry Building; thus, the landmark has survived the 1906 earthquake, the demise of ferry traffic, the intrusion of a freeway, and the 1989 quake.

Beautifully restored, the ground floor has been repurposed as an atmospheric marketplace with shops and eateries specializing in gourmet foods. The Ferry Building Marketplace takes the shopping mall food-court concept to a new level, with a tasteful style that appeals to locals and tourists alike. When the farmers' market is on (Tuesdays and Thursdays, 10 a.m.–2 p.m., and Saturdays, 8 a.m.– 2 p.m.), the Ferry Plaza and Marketplace bustle with vendors and crowds of people indulging in San Francisco's passionate culture of food. Walk through the building and around it, past the benches offering front-row views of the bay, Treasure Island, the Bay Bridge, and the Port of Oakland beyond. The fine ❷ **Slanted Door,** a modern Vietnamese restaurant under the direction of Charles Phan, anchors the dining scene here, and they also have a more casual to-go window called Out the Door. But for a sweet treat, it's hard to beat the scoops at ❸ **Humphry Slocombe,** where locals swear by a flavor called Secret Breakfast: bourbon ice cream with cornflakes mixed in. If you need some reading material with your treat, the well-stocked aisles at ❹ **Book Passage** offer something to suit every taste. Boasting a well-curated travel and children's section, Book Passage also hosts a bevy of literary events and book signings. In addition to all the featured shopping and dining, ferries continue to launch from the building.

Exit the front of the Ferry Building and turn right onto the Embarcadero, which is conamed Herb Caen Way to commemorate the legendary columnist for the *San Francisco Chronicle* and *Examiner*. Caen was fond of calling the city "Baghdad by the Bay," and he famously resuscitated a 19th-century edict from Joshua Abraham Norton—a local oddball who styled himself Emperor of the United States—banning "Frisco" as a city nickname. (The Baghdad tag has proved a bad fit, but many San Franciscans remain quick to upbraid anyone who uses "Frisco.") Caen wrote his anecdotal column, rife with insider knowledge and ellipses, for some 60 years until his death in February 1997.

Just past Pier 5, right before the foot of Broadway, is the wooden ❺ **Pier 7** pedestrian wharf, which extends 900 feet out into the bay. Walk out and you're likely to encounter anglers extending fishing poles over the sides. You may even see folks net rock crabs, which they are entitled to take home for dinner, or Dungeness crabs, which by law they are required to throw back. The pier, built in 1990, juts out into the bay in roughly the spot where ships docked at the old Broadway Pier. Piers extended out from Vallejo and Pacific Streets as well. Running perpendicular to these piers, Front Street stood on wooden pilings driven into the mud of the bay as late as the mid-1860s. Boardinghouses and saloons crowded around the wharves in a town still short on housing and women. You'll need to use your imagination to picture any of this today, but a few buildings from that period survive along the course of this walk.

At Pier 15, you'll find the ❻ **Exploratorium,** a hands-on, state-of-the-art science museum. Relocated here in 2013 from its original Palace of Fine Arts digs, the museum is definitely worth a visit. Even if you don't have time to explore the interior, there are a variety of free exhibits on the wharf outside, including *Fog Bridge #72494*, by Japanese artist Fujiko Nakaya.

Coming to Pier 17, you're likely to spot a few tractor tugs operated by Baydelta Maritime. On the sidewalk here, look for a historical marker labeled BARBARY COAST, which has some tasty excerpts from author Herbert Asbury and historian H. H. Bancroft, describing the rough-and-tumble entertainment district that was centered along Pacific Avenue just west of here.

A little ways down the Embarcadero, ❼ **Pier 23 Cafe** is a basic, squat wooden shack on the wharf, with seafood, a bar, and live music most nights. On warm days, you can make friends on the sun-splashed back patio overlooking the bay. Just beyond the restaurant, Pier 23 itself still functions as a warehouse for goods shipped in from overseas. If the gates are open, you'll spot pallets loaded up with imported goods, mostly from the People's Republic of China. The huge and modern glass building at Pier 27 is the new James R. Herman cruise ship terminal.

Cross the Embarcadero at Lombard or Chestnut Street and check out ❽ **Fog City,** a West Coast interpretation of the traditional East Coast diner that's been a mainstay since 1985. From the diner, follow Battery Street a few paces and detour into the small public space behind it, following the path through the little stream and fountain. This is an extension of ❾ **Levi Strauss Plaza,** corporate headquarters for the company that put blue jeans on the legs of the world. German-born Levi Strauss came to San Francisco in 1853 and opened a dry goods shop. In 1870, he and Jacob Davis, a tailor, patented durable canvas work pants on which the seams were reinforced with copper rivets, a distinguishing trademark. Cross Battery and cut through the center of the campuslike office complex, built in the early 1980s. It incorporates modern structures along with a pair of stately warehouses dating to the early 1900s. At Sansome Street turn left.

Two blocks down, in the nondescript industrial structure at 200 Green Street, Philo T. Farnsworth invented television. Farnsworth, a native of Utah, publicly demonstrated his invention for the first time in 1927. He lived until 1971, long enough to have watched broadcasts of *Mr. Ed, The Mod Squad,* and the Apollo 11 moon landing.

The corner of Sansome and Green was the northeastern extent of a neighborhood known during the gold rush as ❿ **Sydney Town,** largely inhabited by ticket-of-leave men from Australia. The denizens of this menacing little fun zone, which extended west to Kearny and south to Broadway, were known as the Sydney Ducks, and by and large were considered to be ruffians or worse by the rest of San Francisco. On several occasions large portions of the city burned to the ground, and Australians were blamed for kindling the flames or for plundering in the wake of disaster. Many were executed by vigilantes; the Committee of Vigilance of 1851 was formed in large part to contain the criminal proclivities of many Sydney Town residents.

At Vallejo Street turn left and continue to Front Street. The building on the corner, at 855 Front St., is the ⓫ **Daniel Gibb Warehouse,** built in 1855. It's a rare gold rush–era survivor built on landfill at the shore of the bay. Daniel Gibb was an importer of goods ranging from liquor to coal. The warehouse is now an office building, but it looks much as it would have when Gibb was alive.

The Ferry Building's clock tower reigns over incoming ships and Marketplace shoppers.

Backstory: Shanghaiing

Among San Francisco's gifts to the English language is *shanghai*, the verb. Sailors put aboard ships against their will were said to have been shanghaied by shady characters called crimps, who made a good living through such dastardly deeds. Bill Pickelhaupt, in his book *Shanghaied in San Francisco*, nicely explains the term's etymology. According to Pickelhaupt, during the mid-19th century, Shanghai, China, was not on direct shipping routes from San Francisco, so a sea voyage to that port necessarily involved an indirect course around the globe lasting about two years before a sailor returned to San Francisco. Sailors almost always had to be persuaded, honestly or otherwise, to accept such assignments.

In San Francisco, a perpetual shortage of seamen—often due to the opportunities and distractions available in the boisterous boom town and at the gold fields—led to an increase in crimping, or the sale of unconscious sailors to shipping companies in return for the sailors' first two months of wages. Most often the destination was not actually Shanghai. Although the practice was illegal, politicians and businessmen saw the value in looking the other way, and crimps with names like Shanghai Kelly and Shanghai Chicken Devine felt no need to hide the nature of their business. Kelly's knockout cocktail, served in his saloon, was a mixture of schnapps, beer, and a narcotic—usually opium.

Follow Front Street down to Pacific Avenue and turn right. At Battery, the **⓬ Old Ship Saloon** is a lovely old bar with a dark past. This establishment has an indelible link to James Laflin, one of the city's most notorious shanghaiers. The building dates to 1907 but stands where the business has stood since 1851. The establishment was originally in an old ship, the *Arkansas,* which was abandoned by a crew excited by news of gold strikes. The *Arkansas* docked here and her forecastle was transformed into a drinking tavern before Yerba Buena Cove was filled. Laflin sailed over on the *Arkansas* as a cabin boy and became a bartender in the Old Ship Saloon. He soon gained infamy as one of the city's most successful crimps, selling unconscious seamen to ships sailing out in the morning. A model of a ship, standing in for the *Arkansas,* hangs over the street corner, above the bar's main entrance. Have a drink here—you probably won't end up in Shanghai.

Turn left onto Battery, then left again at Jackson. Enter the old portals to **⓭ Sydney Walton Square,** now an open space but once the sight of numerous saloons. The Boston House, run by James "Shanghai" Kelly, whose notoriety circled the globe, stood at 33 Pacific, on a block now occupied by the Hyatt Regency Hotel. Pass through the square, admiring the public art and the fountain, and turn right on Davis Street. Cross Washington Street and follow paved pedestrian path through Sue Bierman Park to make your way back to the Embarcadero.

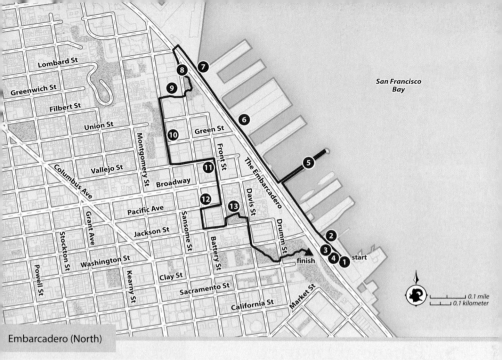

Embarcadero (North)

Points of Interest

1 **Ferry Building/Marketplace** 1 Ferry Building; 415-983-8030, ferrybuildingmarketplace.com

2 **The Slanted Door** 1 Ferry Building, Shop 5; 415-861-8032, slanteddoor.com

3 **Humphry Slocombe** 1 Ferry Building, Shop 8; 415-550-6971, humphryslocombe.com

4 **Book Passage** 1 Ferry Building, Shop 42; 415-835-1020, bookpassage.com

5 **Pier 7** Southeast of Embarcadero and Broadway; 415-274-0400, sfport.com/parks-and-open-spaces

6 **Exploratorium** Pier 15 Embarcadero; 415-528-4444, exploratorium.edu

7 **Pier 23 Cafe** Pier 23; 415-362-5125, pier23cafe.com

8 **Fog City** 1300 Battery St.; 415-982-2000, fogcitysf.com

9 **Levi Strauss Plaza** 1155 Battery St.; 415-667-9927, levistrauss.com

10 **Sydney Town (former)** Sansome and Green Sts.

11 **Daniel Gibb Warehouse** 855 Front St.; 415-323-6240, bricktimber.com/portfolio/front

12 **Old Ship Saloon** 298 Pacific Ave.; 415-788-2222, theoldshipsf.com

13 **Sydney Walton Square** Bordered by Front, Jackson, and Davis Sts.

3 Financial District
Through the Pillars of Capitalism

Above: The Transcendence *sculpture graces the plaza in front of the Bank of America Building.*

BOUNDARIES: Market St., Kearny St., Washington St., Front St.
DISTANCE: 1.75 miles
DIFFICULTY: Easy
PARKING: Russ Building Garage, 235 Montgomery St.
PUBLIC TRANSIT: Montgomery St. BART station; Muni J, K, L, M, and N trains; F streetcars; 5, 6, 9, 21, 31, and 71 Muni buses

This is where the big wheels turn in San Francisco. Looking much like a short section of midtown Manhattan or the Loop in Chicago, the Financial District is a grid of canyons formed by the high-rise pillars of capitalism. Buildings bold, stately, and conservative tell the secret that lies at the core of San Francisco's history and character, for while the cultural icons of the city are gold diggers, rainbow-flag wavers, and hippies, it was the staunch businesses of banking, stock brokering, real estate, and shipping that put the city on the map. Suitably, the Financial District resulted from a frantic scramble for well-positioned real estate. During the gold rush, each time valuable bayfront lots were sold, a little more bay was filled, creating new bayfront property.

It's not particularly comforting to consider that skyscrapers and landfill make for an unhealthy combination in earthquake country, which is why San Francisco's skyline remained relatively low until quake-resistant steel-frame construction came into vogue. The foundations of the district's skyscrapers stand on pilings driven deep into the earth, and the more modern towers are designed to sway gently in a temblor. The city's newest economic titans, tech companies, have taken up shop a few blocks farther south, and we invite you take the SoMa walk to learn more about the changing face, and skyline, of San Francisco's capitalism.

The Financial District may be cold at heart, but during workdays its sidewalks are alive with fast-paced, smartphone-driven human activity. Restaurants, small museums, public open spaces, and rooftop observatories afford the interloper ample opportunity to see the district from the inside out.

Walk Description

Start at the former ❶ **Crocker Bank Building,** now owned by Wells Fargo, at 1 Montgomery St. The curved, columned entry makes an effective statement on this prominent corner, but what's really interesting about the building is that it was once 10 stories taller: it was truncated in the mid-1960s to broaden the views from the Wells Fargo tower behind it. The building's much-diminished rooftop is an open observatory, so go inside, take the elevator up, and have a look around.

Follow Montgomery to Sutter and turn left. Note the Moroccan Arabic chandelier hanging outside the ❷ **Hunter-Dulin Building** at 111 Sutter. This 1926 architectural gem, modeled after a French château, has been impeccably restored, and it's worth a trip into the lobby to admire the hand-painted ceiling, original elevator numbers, and Italian marble floor. According to architectural historian Rick Evans, the cigarette smoke that tarnished the ceiling also ironically served as a sealant to protect it. When it was laboriously and meticulously cleaned, the paint was intact, having been preserved by a protective layer of soot. Also of note is the rounded groove in the middle of the lobby floor—for nearly half a century, an elevator captain would stand in this spot to greet people and direct them to an elevator, and his pivoting eventually wore a gentle divot in the marble. The building's most famous tenant exists only in literature, as Dashiell Hammett's Sam Spade kept his fictional office here in *The Maltese Falcon.*

Across the street at 130 Sutter is the ❸ **Hallidie Building,** notable for being among the first glass curtain–wall buildings in the world. Its glass face is supported by a steel frame—a style not at all rare today, but nearly unique in 1917 when it was built. Willis Polk designed it, and it's named for Andrew Hallidie, the cable car inventor. Note the tastefully curved fire escapes, which enhance the building's looks as well as provide a way out in the event of a blaze. The Gothic grillwork, restored to its blue-and-gold luster, was chosen to honor the colors of the University of California, Berkeley, which first commissioned the building. Fittingly, the American Institute of Architects now resides inside.

Continue along Kearny and turn right on Claude Lane, a small alley with European flair. ❹ **Café Claude** is the main draw, with sidewalk tables and the occasional live jazz wafting out. This lane, along with Belden Place, which we will discover shortly, make up the city's "French Quarter," and indeed in 1851 more than 3,000 French immigrants settled in the area, bringing with them their bistros, religious masses, and savoir faire, much of which remains.

At Bush, turn right. At the corner of Belden and Bush, ❺ **Sam's Grill** is a neighborhood institution with a traditional San Francisco menu based on seafood, pasta, and sourdough bread. The interior booths have curtains, for the privacy of patrons who need to hash out a shady deal, and black-tie waiters stand at the ready to bring you a martini. Everything about the place oozes old-school San Francisco and high-stakes deals.

Head up Belden, another pedestrian alley lined with sidewalk restaurants. During lunch and dinner hours, especially on warm days, the alley is crammed with little tables where off-duty white-collar workers enjoy mussels from ❻ **Plouf** or steak frites from ❼ **Cafe Bastille.** And on Bastille Day, July 14, the entire block is crammed with hundreds of Francophiles under the twinkling lights.

At the end of Belden Place, hook left and continue down Kearny, walking in the shadow of the ❽ **Bank of America Building,** which stands 52 stories tall and was San Francisco's tallest building until the Transamerica Pyramid went up a few years later. Look up from any perspective, and the building's striking sawtooth bays, slicing into the sky, catch and reflect light and color. Wide steps meet a raised plaza with a hulking black sculpture by the late Masayuki Nagare, officially called *Transcendence* but broadly referred to as "Banker's Heart."

Follow Kearny to Sacramento, turn right, and turn right again at Montgomery. The ❾ **Wells Fargo History Museum** is worth a quick stop to get a rosy perspective on one of the city's biggest and oldest financial institutions. (Wells Fargo opened its first office in San Francisco in 1852.) It won't require more than a few minutes to take an up-close look at the museum's old stagecoach. There's actually quite a good bit of interesting gold rush history on both the ground and second floor, including goofy opportunities to "meet" a stagecoach driver or take your picture beside one. In addition to banking, Wells Fargo initially ran a network of stages across the Western United States until the arrival of the railroads. Admission to the museum is free.

At the corner of Montgomery and California, the geographic epicenter of the Financial District, turn right. Built in 1903, the ❿ **Merchants Exchange Club** (465 California St.) was designed by Daniel Burnham and reflects his Chicago School architectural style. Enter the building and pass through the long lobby, adorned with the ceramic sculptures of San Francisco's founders. Artist Mark Jaeger made the works, and you'll recognize all the greats for whom the streets we're walking are named. Continuing, you will enter the California Bank Trust, where the glory of the building's maritime past is celebrated with huge murals by Walter Coulter and Nils Hagerup. Willis Polk tapped architect Julia Morgan to help with post-earthquake renovation and design, and she kept her offices on the top floor of the building. Morgan was the first licensed female architect in California, and the grand 15th-floor ballroom is named for her.

Exit a side door onto tiny Leidesdorff Street, a narrow lane that appears determined not to attract attention. Before the 1906 quake, Leidesdorff was known as Pauper Alley. As wild speculation on silver mining went on elsewhere in the district, Leidesdorff was lined with small-time exchanges where the nearly penniless could invest a few cents in hopes of turning their luck around. The street apparently had few, if any, rags-to-riches tales.

Return to California Street, and opposite, on the corner of Sansome, you'll spot the imposing ⓫ **Bank of California Building,** a mausoleum-like structure erected in 1908. Step inside and you'll see that the entire building is, essentially, one huge, cavernous room with enough airspace beneath its vaulted ceiling to fly a small airplane, if such a thing were permitted. It's a glorious waste of space for such a high-rent district. Down in the basement, a small museum (free admission) has a few intriguing items, including gold nuggets embedded in chunks of quartz, and some territorial gold coins and shiny ingots from the gold rush.

European-flavored Belden Place is home to celebrated sidewalk cafés and restaurants.

A replica of Stirling Calder's *Star Girl* shines in the Citigroup Center atrium.

Turn right at Sansome and right again at Pine. On the opposite corner is the former **12 Pacific Coast Stock Exchange.** Stockbrokers used to work here, and now that it's an Equinox fitness club, they work out here. The building dates from 1915, and apparently the stock market crash necessitated a 1930 remodeling job, with designs by Timothy Pflueger. The stoic sculpted figures on both sides of the broad front stairway are by Ralph Stackpole, who in the early 20th century was a central figure in the city's art scene. A side entrance on Sansome leads to the private **13 City Club of San Francisco,** in which a two-story mural by Diego Rivera graces a stairwell, which can be viewed by nonmembers on a guided tour (see sfcityguides.org for more information). Rivera was commissioned by his friend Stackpole, and the decision was not without controversy: many worried that Rivera's politically liberal leanings stood in contrast to this iconic building of capitalism. Their concern was for naught, as the brilliant fresco, Rivera's first in the United States, became a lauded symbol of the City Club.

Turn left at Montgomery, onto a block dominated by two handsome landmarks. The neo-Gothic **14 Russ Building,** at No. 235, was the city's tallest structure for several decades after it was built in 1928. It also boasts the city's first indoor parking garage. Opposite, at No. 220, the **15 Mills Building** is the city's archetypal Chicago-style office building. A Daniel Burnham–John Wellborn Root collaboration that was the first all-steel-frame structure in the city, it was built in 1892 and survived the 1906 catastrophe, though extensive renovation was required.

At Sutter turn left. At the corner of Sutter and Sansome is what remains of the Anglo and London Paris National Bank, which was built in 1910 and gutted in 1984, reducing it to an atrium for the adjacent Citigroup Center. The atrium is open to the public during business hours. Inside, beyond the café tables and fountain, you'll spot **16 *Star Girl,*** a replica of a sculpture by Stirling Calder for the Panama-Pacific International Exposition, which took place in the Marina District in 1915.

Turn left onto Market Street, and to your left is the green-tinted **17 Crown Zellerbach Building,** a glass-curtain beauty from 1959. Unlike nearly every other building in the cramped Financial

District, the Crown Zellerbach is set off the street with paved grounds surrounding it, a ground-breaking design decision at the time. It was the first tower of distinction to go up following the Great Depression, and it ushered in midcentury architecture quite distinct from the stone masonry giants surrounding it. The main entrance faces Bush, not Market, and the glass lobby is notable for its appearance of floating between the columns.

Turn left at Battery and left again at Bush, where two contrasting structures stand side by side. The elegant **18 Shell Building,** at 100 Bush, is a sleek Art Deco skyscraper clad in terra-cotta, with decorative ornamentation of gushing oil derricks that reflects its original owner. Completed right before the Wall Street Crash of 1929, this was the last Art Deco building built in San Francisco, as the Great Depression halted new construction. It dwarfs its neighbor, the pencil-thin **19 Heineman Building,** at 130 Bush. Designed by George Applegarth and built in 1910, the Gothic revival Heine-

man Building makes the fullest use of its slender, 20-foot lot. The skinny building also purposely pays homage to its original occupant, as it was once a belt, tie, and suspender factory. Its bay facade protrudes beyond the plane of the adjacent buildings, and its cornice actually overlaps them.

The venerable Tadich Grill has been serving its weekly seafood specials since 1849.

Return to Battery, and turn left and then right onto California Street. At 240 California St., half a block off Battery, **20 Tadich Grill** is a revered San Francisco dining establishment. Opened in 1849, it's the oldest continuously operating restaurant in the city, and the first to introduce the Croatian style of grilling fish over mesquite charcoal. It has occupied its present site since the late 1960s but has the atmosphere of the original—the previous location, on Clay Street, was stripped, moved, and reassembled here. Busy as ever, Tadich hasn't changed its weekly specials in decades, and it continues to draw hundreds of people daily for sand dabs, oysters, and Dungeness crab cakes.

At Front Street turn left and pass **21 Schroeder's Restaurant,** a Bavarian beer hall that's been operating in one form or another since 1893. The original building on Market was destroyed in the 1906 quake but rose from the ashes at this location shortly thereafter. The restaurant has changed with the times (it began welcoming women in the 1970s) but has remained true to its German roots in the menu and occasional polka band.

Next head into the **22** **Embarcadero Center.** This four-tower complex, with a shopping center on the bottom two floors and offices above, was loosely modeled on New York's Rockefeller Center. Walk up the winding stairs to the second level, and follow the footbridge that crosses over Battery Street. As you cross you'll get a good vantage of the **23** **Old Federal Reserve Building,** an imposing neoclassical structure built in 1924. If you enter on Sansome Street, you can walk through the lobby, graced by a Jules Guerin mural of Italian shipping merchants created for the Panama-Pacific International Exposition.

Follow Clay Street to Montgomery and the **24** **Transamerica Pyramid.** At 853 feet, it was the tallest building in San Francisco for 46 years until the Salesforce Tower took over that mantle in 2018. After it was completed in 1972, it was unpopular, mostly for being so conspicuous, but today it's difficult to imagine San Francisco's skyline without the pyramid's pointed top. The design is functional as well, as the sloped walls allow a lot of interior light without casting a shadow on neighboring buildings. Note the entrance to Transamerica Redwood Park, where 80 mature redwoods from the Santa Cruz Mountains were transplanted. As you relax in the shade, take a moment to consider that if you were sitting here in the early 1800s, the water would have been lapping at your feet. The site where the pyramid sits is essentially the former waterfront line before the shallow Yerba Buena Cove was filled in (often with abandoned tall ships) to accommodate the popularity surge during the gold rush.

Points of Interest

1 **Crocker Bank Building (former)** 1 Montgomery St. (no published phone number or website)

2 **Hunter-Dulin Building** 111 Sutter St. (no published phone number or website)

3 **Hallidie Building** 130 Sutter St. (no published phone number or website)

4 **Café Claude** 7 Claude Lane; 415-392-3505, cafeclaude.com

5 **Sam's Grill** 374 Bush St.; 415-421-0594, samsgrillsf.com

6 **Plouf** 40 Belden Place; 415-986-6491, ploufsf.com

7 **Cafe Bastille** 22 Belden Place; 415-986-5673, cafebastille.com

8 **Bank of America Building** 555 California St.; 415-392-1697, 555californiastreet.info

9 **Wells Fargo History Museum** 420 Montgomery St.; 415-396-2619, wellsfargohistory.com

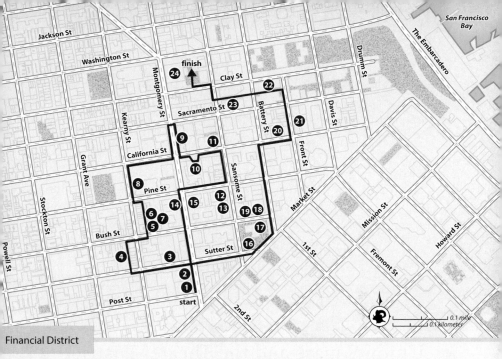

Financial District

10 Merchants Exchange Club 465 California St.; 415-591-1833, mxclubsf.com

11 Bank of California Building (former) 400 California St.; 415-986-5002, tinyurl.com/400california

12 Pacific Coast Stock Exchange/Equinox 301 Pine St.; 415-593-4000, tinyurl.com/equinoxpine

13 The City Club of San Francisco 155 Sansome St.; 415-362-2480, cityclubsf.com

14 Russ Building 235 Montgomery St.; russbldg.com (no public-facing phone number)

15 Mills Building 220 Bush St.; themillsbuilding.com (no public-facing phone number)

16 *Star Girl* Sculpture 1 Sansome St.

17 Crown Zellerbach Building 1 Bush Plaza; 415-536-1850, tishmanspeyer.com

18 Shell Building 100 Bush St.; 415-986-8880, shellbuildingsf.com

19 Heineman Building 130 Bush St. (no published phone number or website)

20 Tadich Grill 240 California St.; 415-391-1849, tadichgrillsf.com

21 Schroeder's Restaurant 240 Front St.; 415-421-4778, schroederssf.com

22 Embarcadero Center Bordered by Sacramento, Battery, Clay, and Drumm Sts.; 415-772-0700, embarcaderocenter.com

23 Bently Reserve (Old Federal Reserve Building) 301 Battery St.; 415-294-2226, bentlyreserve.com

24 Transamerica Pyramid and Redwood Park 600 Montgomery St.; pyramidcenter.com (no public-facing phone number)

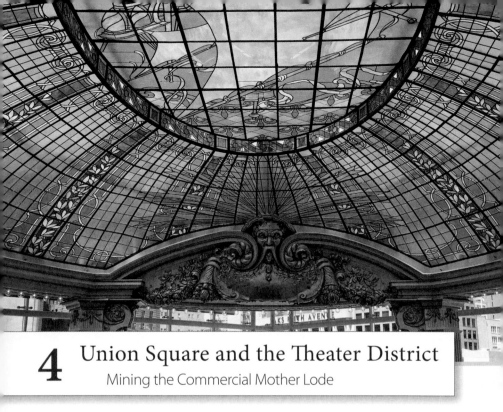

4 Union Square and the Theater District
Mining the Commercial Mother Lode

Above: Neiman Marcus's stained glass rotunda is all that remains of the old City of Paris store.

BOUNDARIES: Market St., Taylor St., Bush St., Grant Ave.
DISTANCE: 2.5 miles
DIFFICULTY: Moderately easy (one hill, some stairs)
PARKING: Off-street parking at the Fifth and Mission St. Garage, 1 block south of the start of this tour
PUBLIC TRANSIT: Powell St. BART station; underground Muni light rail, streetcars, and 5, 6, 9, 21, 31, and 71 Muni buses all stop at the starting point for this tour, as do Powell St. cable cars.

With its historical buildings, showpiece retail stores, fine restaurants, theaters, hotels, billboards clamoring for rooftop exposure, and converging public transit lines, Union Square has all the hallmarks of a commercial and cultural hub. It's a central crossroads that has a way of drawing people and traffic through it. Day and night, the area buzzes with cars and buses starting and stopping at traffic lights, the groaning of cable car brakes, the repertoire of street corner singers, the purposeful clicking of high heel shoes, and the shrill whistles blown by hotel doormen hailing cabs.

This tour will range a bit freely, proceeding from Market Street through the Theater District to Union Square itself in the least direct route possible without leaving the neighborhood. While the neighborhood takes its name from the rallies supporting the Union Army during the Civil War, this onetime sand dune is now a pulsing hive of shoppers, theatergoers, and those who cater to their whims and desires.

Walk Description

Start at the ❶ **Powell Street Cable Car Turnaround,** on the corner of Market and Powell. If it's the summer tourist season, a hundred or more people will be lined up here for a ride on the historic cable cars, and a multitude of street performers will be vying for their attention and spare change. Don't get in line, but wait for a car to come along, and watch how it's rolled onto the circular platform, then rotated 180 degrees, all by hand, as has been done for more than 130 years.

Overlooking the cable car turnaround is the staunch and impressive ❷ **Flood Building,** where the huge Gap flagship store occupies the ground floor. Designed by Albert Pissis and built in 1904, the building survived the 1906 earthquake. Dashiell Hammett worked upstairs for the Pinkerton Agency during the early 1920s, a few years before he published the novels that would make him a famous crime-fiction writer. Walk along Powell Street, below the block-long Flood Building, and hook right on Ellis Street. Half a block up you'll spot ❸ **John's Grill,** which has been operating since 1908, when it was the first restaurant to open following the '06 quake. Hammett reputedly dined at John's frequently and even mentioned the place in his best novel, *The Maltese Falcon.* Not one to rest on its laurels, John's has both changed with the times and stayed true to its roots. The waiters no longer wear tuxes, but the wood paneling remains, and the reviews (and frequent celebrity diners) attest to the high standards in the kitchen.

Return to Powell and turn right. The street is a hodgepodge of shops and hotels geared to tourists and passers-through. In the mix are some age-old establishments that seem to hang on despite the changing vibe of the neighborhood. These blocks of Powell Street not so long ago had some of the Tenderloin's flophouse atmosphere. ❹ **Tad's Steaks,** with its gaudy sign looking like a holdover from the vaudeville era, still purveys shoe-leather cuts, charbroiled and served over the counter. Turn left on Geary; at the corner of Geary and Mason stands the ❺ **Pinecrest Diner,** a 24-hour eatery that's been slinging the neighborhood's hash since 1969 but looks like it's been here longer than that. It's the no-nonsense, Edward Hopper–esque atmosphere—not the food—that draws people. The place is genuinely hard-boiled, and a little tragic: in 1997, a grill cook shot and killed a waitress here in a dispute about poached eggs.

The Pinecrest inadvertently ushers us into the Theater District, where swank hotels, art galleries, bars, and performance spaces rub elbows. Two landmark stages stand side by side on this block. The ❻ **Geary Theater** opened in 1909 and is now home of the highly respected American Conservatory Theater. The building is a beauty clad in terra-cotta tiles, many of them shaped like fruit. To the right of the front entrance a traditional shoeshine stand operates during the business week. The Geary is best admired from across the street, where you can see the entire building. Next door, the ❼ **Curran Theater** was built in 1922, and it and the Geary make a very compatible pair. Theaters small and large are scattered all throughout the neighborhood.

At the end of the block stands ❽ **The Clift Royal Sonesta Hotel,** which was recently remodeled under the direction of Philippe Starck and has successfully reentered the ranks of the city's most

The Dewey Monument soars over Union Square.

sophisticated hostelries. The Clift always had the Redwood Room, a gorgeous, clubby old watering hole, and those in the know long appreciated their martinis here. A velvet rope and a bouncer now maintain order on Friday and Saturday nights. On quieter weeknights, it's possible to enjoy a relaxed drink here amid early-20th-century splendor. And during the day, it's fun to pop your head in to admire the arty lobby with its oversize chairs.

Across from the Clift, ❾ **The Marker San Francisco** is a hip boutique hotel housed in a Beaux Arts building from the steamship era. You need only step into the airy ❿ **Tratto,** a modern Italian trattoria boasting communal tables and homemade limoncello, to know that this isn't your grandmother's hotel. Turn right at Taylor. Halfway up the block look for tiny Isadora Duncan Lane, a dead-end alley that rarely benefits from direct sunlight. A monkey could swing from the fire escapes on one side to the fire escapes on the other side. Named for the legendary dancer who was born within a block of here, it is a model for how all dead-end alleys ought to look.

The stately, ivy-covered redbrick fortress on the corner of Taylor and Post is home of the exclusive ⓫ **Bohemian Club.** The name was once somewhat appropriate, for when it was founded, in 1872, the club's members were writers, poets, newspaper reporters, and artists. By 1900, however, the club was dominated by businessmen and social elites—all men, of course, and all white. The club hasn't changed much (it's now about 2% nonwhite), and US presidents have attended its annual summer fetes, which are held 2 hours north of the city at a club-owned campground called the Bohemian Grove. (In 2000 George W. Bush and Dick Cheney held a pow-wow at the Grove that supposedly resulted in Cheney joining the Republican presidential ticket.) A plaque on the side of the club has a bas-relief owl on a branch, along with the club's motto, taken from Shakespeare's *A Midsummer Night's Dream:* "Weaving spiders come not here," meaning that business deals and other outside concerns are not to be discussed within the sanctuary. Kitty-corner, the **12 Owl Tree Bar** serves up stiff drinks and unpretentious warmth for bohemians of a different generation and pocketbook size.

Turn right on Post and cross Mason. On the north side of the street is **13 Farallon,** one of the city's best seafood restaurants. Step inside for a look at the outlandish underwater decor—a Jules Verne fantasy with illuminated jellyfish hanging from the ceiling.

At Powell turn left. Two local landmarks face off on this block. On the west side is humble **14 Sears Fine Food,** known the world over for its silver dollar–sized Swedish pancakes. It was opened in 1938 by Ben Sears, a retired circus clown. Opposite is the **15 Sir Francis Drake Hotel.** Cross at Sutter, backtrack to the hotel's front entrance, and be sure to smile at the Beefeater door-man on your way in. Inside, examine the magnificent staircase with its intricate cast-iron rail, and gape at the molded plaster ceiling above. Then duck downstairs if it's late afternoon, where an elevator can take you to the Starlight Room, a swanky top-floor nightclub surrounded by plate-glass windows. Back at the bottom floor, exit the Drake through the side exit onto Sutter Street, cross at the light, and turn right.

The office tower at **16 450 Sutter** is populated mostly by doctors and dentists, but the build-ing is a pure flight of fancy. It was designed by Timothy Pflueger, who also designed the magnif-icent Castro Theatre and the Paramount Theatre in Oakland. The lobby at 450 Sutter looks like a set for a never-made Cecil B. DeMille epic about the Mayan empire. It's well worth going in for a look-see. From the sidewalk the tower's jagged columns of bay windows are fine to look at too.

At Stockton turn left and you're soon facing the southern end of the Stockton Tunnel. The entry looks inviting, despite the sign that says QUIET IN TUNNEL, but it's just your usual tunnel, dank and dimly lit. Immediately within, a foul-smelling flight of steps leads up to Bush Street, which is where we're headed.

The **17 Tunnel Top** bar, a refurbished dive that's kind of hip now, welcomes you to Bush Street. If you're in a drinking mood, and it's after 4 p.m., have one of the bar's signature mojitos.

Just past the Tunnel Top, on a wall flanking narrow Burritt Alley, a plaque notes that Sam Spade's partner, Miles Archer, was done in on this spot by Brigid O'Shaughnessy. (It's always cool to see completely fictional events get historical markers.) On the other side of the street, another alley is named for Hammett.

Now turn around and walk down Bush. Elegant ⑱ **Notre Dame des Victoires,** a Catholic church, stands at No. 566. It was originally built in 1855, then rebuilt after the '06 quake. Inside the church, the grand pipe organ is worthy of landmark status, having been built in 1915 by the Johnston Organ and Piano Manufacturing Company. It is renowned for its beautiful tone, which you may hear if you attend a Saturday Vigil, with an organist accompanying a cantor, at 5:15 p.m.

At Grant turn right, stopping for a quick look at ⑲ **Café de la Presse,** a European enclave with brasserie-style cuisine and newsstand titles available in a variety of international languages. The southeast corner of Grant and Sutter is dominated by the building that once housed the White House department store and is now occupied by Banana Republic. It was designed, with Federalist overtones, by Albert Pissis and built in 1908.

Turn right onto slender Maiden Lane, a street that had its name changed in order to obscure a shameful past. Before the '06 quake, the street, then called Morton Street, was a central thoroughfare for Barbary Coast ruffians and was known for its vicious pimps, weekly murders, and seamy bordellos lining both sides of the street. It's much calmer and more respectable now. Its main architectural distinction lies within the curved brick archway of the ⑳ **Frank Lloyd Wright building** at 140 Maiden Ln. It was constructed in 1949, and its spiral ramp is often cited as a warm-up for Wright's more accomplished Guggenheim Museum in New York.

Maiden Lane ends at Union Square. Turn left, walk to the corner of Geary, and enter ㉑ **Neiman Marcus.** Immediately within, stare up at the great rotunda, with its stained glass mosaic of a ship. It's all that remains of the old City of Paris department store, which formerly stood on this corner. The rest of the building was demolished and replaced by the current modern structure in the early 1980s. Jockey your way past the perfume sprayers to take an elevator to the top floor for a closer look at the glass. If you're feeling fancy, you can join the ladies-who-lunch crowd and snag a table. Models sporting couture and jewelry for sale often strut through the dining room while you nibble popovers and sip Champagne.

Cross to the square, which was part of the original city plans of 1850 and became a more prominent address as San Francisco expanded south from Portsmouth Square; it gained its name during the Civil War. The Dewey Monument, which rises from the square's center, commemorates a major victory in the Spanish-American War. The model who posed for the sculpture, Alma de Bretteville Spreckels (see Backstory, opposite), was a work of art in herself. A parking

Backstory: Big Alma, Rebel Girl and Culture Queen

Dedicated in 1903 and soaring 85 feet high in Union Square, the Dewey Monument—constructed to honor Commodore George Dewey, a hero of the Spanish-American War—is a San Francisco icon. Likewise, the woman who modeled for the 9-foot sculpture atop the monument was a larger-than-life character and a true San Francisco success story.

Born in 1881 to dirt-poor Danish-immigrant parents living in the Sunset District, Alma de Bretteville dropped out of school at 14 to support her family, but her true passion lay in the arts. While taking art classes at what is now the San Francisco Art Institute, Alma supported herself by modeling for other artists; 6 feet tall, buxom, and happy to pose nude, Alma increased both her livelihood and her notoriety. When sculptor Robert Ingersoll Aitken hired her to model for the statue that would eventually top the Dewey Monument, her fate changed considerably: she turned the head of notorious bachelor, sugar magnate, and civic leader Adolph Spreckels, who picked Aitken's sculpture from among several submissions by competing artists. A love affair was born, and *sugar daddy*—Alma's pet name for her wealthy husband 23 years her senior—soon joined the modern lexicon.

The well-heeled society crowd did not immediately embrace this brash, outspoken beauty, and she thumbed her nose at them in return by smoking cigars in public, chugging martinis, and hanging out with drag queens. Adoring Adolph presented her with an opulent Pacific Heights mansion (see Walk 18, page 123), where they threw lavish parties that prompted rumors of skinny-dipping in the pools. The Spreckelses' hedonism was matched by their philanthropic generosity, and Alma ran hugely successful charity auctions to raise money for war efforts and Depression relief.

While on vacation in Paris in 1914, bon vivant Alma met and befriended Auguste Rodin and promptly purchased 13 of his bronze sculptures to bring back to San Francisco. She later constructed the California Palace of the Legion of Honor to house them, fueling a contentious museum rivalry with society scions the de Young sisters. (This cultural contretemps arose in part because Adolph tried to kill their father, but that's a tale for another time.) When Adolph died in 1924, he left Alma his fortune, making her the richest woman in the American West. In her final years, Alma had a hand in the construction of the San Francisco Maritime Museum (see Walk 14, Fisherman's Wharf, page 96). Her funeral, in 1968, was the largest the city had ever seen, and a fitting send-off to one of San Francisco's most influential and outrageous women.

structure—meant to double as a bomb shelter—was dug beneath the square during World War II. The square acquired its current Italian piazza styling in a dotcom-era overhaul, and it's a good spot to stop for an outdoor coffee or to see occasional midday music performances. During holidays, it's taken over by a giant tree and skating rink. The surrounding cityscape of department stores, billboards, and the awesome ㉒ **Westin St. Francis Hotel** makes this a pleasant urban space. You're seeing the St. Francis from its most flattering vantage point.

The St. Francis was built in 1904, gutted by the fire of '06, and rebuilt a year later. It's the grand dame of Union Square, but it hasn't escaped controversy over the years. In 1921 comic actor Roscoe "Fatty" Arbuckle rented a suite of rooms and threw a party that ended with the gruesome death of a young actress, Virginia Rappe. Arbuckle was tried for rape and murder, but he wasn't convicted.; the scandal nevertheless diminished his comic appeal and put an end to his career. President Gerald Ford was shot at by Sarah Jane Moore in front of the hotel in 1975. She missed, went to jail, escaped, was recaptured, and was paroled in 2007, almost exactly a year after Ford had died of natural causes. Strolling the downstairs hallways, you can delight in pictures of all manner of celebrity guests, including Shirley Temple, Douglas MacArthur, and Dwight Eisenhower. As a testament to the hotel's old-world class, they retain a coin washer—a literal money launderer, as it were—to ensure that no guest's pristine paws are sullied by grimy change.

Enter the St. Francis's main lobby, and look for the elevators. The hotel's modern high-rise annex was built in the early 1970s, with high-speed glass elevators shooting skyward along the east side of the building. For kicks, end this tour with a ride up to the top. Not all of the hotel's elevators are glass; head to the rear of the hotel past the reception desk and turn right to find the bank of glass elevators. Send yourself to floor 30 for the jaw-dropping view.

Points of Interest

❶ **Powell St. Cable Car Turnaround** Market St. and Powell St.

❷ **Flood Building** 870 Market St.; 415-982-3298, floodbuilding.com

❸ **John's Grill** 63 Ellis St.; 415-986-0069, johnsgrill.com

❹ **Tad's Steaks** 120 Powell St.; 415-982-1718, tadssteaks-sf.com

❺ **Pinecrest Diner** 401 Geary St.; 415-885-6407, pinecrestdiner.com

❻ **ACT's Geary Theater** 415 Geary St.; 415-749-2228, act-sf.org

❼ **Curran Theater** 445 Geary St.; 415-358-1220, sfcurran.com

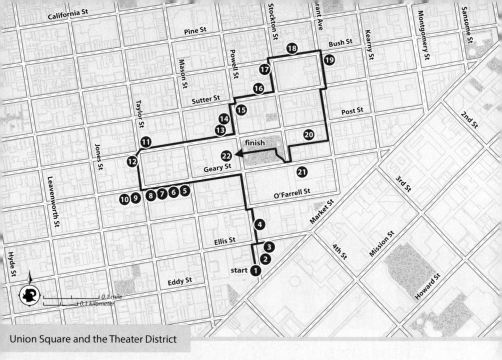

Union Square and the Theater District

8 The Clift Royal Sonesta Hotel 495 Geary St.; 415-775-4700, tinyurl.com/theclifthotel

9 The Marker San Francisco 501 Geary St.; 415-292-0100, jdvhotels.com/hotels/california /san-francisco/the-marker-san-francisco

10 Tratto 501 Geary St.; 415-292-0100, tratto-sf.com

11 The Bohemian Club 624 Taylor St.; 415-885-2440 (no website)

12 Owl Tree Bar 601 Post St.; 415-359-1600, owltreesf.com

13 Farallon 450 Post St.; 415-956-6969, farallonrestaurant.com

14 Sears Fine Food 439 Powell St.; 415-986-0700, searsfinefood.com

15 Sir Francis Drake Hotel/Starlight Room 450 Powell St.; 415-395-8595, starlightroomsf.com

16 450 Sutter Building 450 Sutter St.; 415-421-7221, 450sutter.buildingengines.com

17 Tunnel Top 601 Bush St.; 415-235-6587, tunneltop.bar

18 Notre Dame des Victoires 566 Bush St.; 415-397-0113, ndvsf.weconnect.com

19 Café de la Presse 352 Grant Ave.; 415-398-2680, cafedelapresse.com

20 Frank Lloyd Wright Building 140 Maiden Ln. (no published phone number or website)

21 Neiman Marcus Rotunda 150 Stockton St.; 415-249-2720, neimanmarcus.com

22 Westin St. Francis Hotel 335 Powell St.; 415-397-7000, westinstfrancis.com

5 Chinatown
The Far East of the West Coast

Above: *On Washington Street, this bank building used to house the Chinese Telephone Exchange.*

BOUNDARIES: Broadway, Stockton St., Bush St., Grant Ave.
DISTANCE: 1.75 miles
DIFFICULTY: Moderately easy (mild hills)
PARKING: Off-street parking is available on Vallejo St., between Powell and Stockton (1 block from the starting point for this walk).
PUBLIC TRANSIT: 30, 45 Muni buses

San Francisco's Chinatown is the oldest and second largest such district in the country, due mainly to the wave of Chinese immigrants drawn to "Gold Mountain" after the first shout of *Eureka!* ricocheted round the world. And like many Chinatowns, San Francisco's has an air of inauthenticity. Many of the buildings here reflect naive American notions of what Eastern architecture ought to look like, with shop fronts resembling pagodas painted in spectacular, often garish colors. Even the lampposts, fire hydrants, and telephone booths have a kitschy faux-Chinese look to them. The neighborhood has made appearances in numerous movies and TV shows, ranging from the 1970s sitcom *Phyllis* to the film adaptation of Amy Tan's *The Joy Luck Club*.

But there's more to the gimmicky architecture than meets the eye. In the wake of the 1906 earthquake—which did not spare the city's original Chinatown—men of overwhelming influence, including former mayor James Phelan, wanted to move the area to remote Hunters Point. Chinese businessmen preempted that campaign by rebuilding quickly with over-the-top, undeniably Chinese styles of architecture. Indeed, the abundance of clinker bricks (bricks that had literally begun to melt during the fire) in Chinatown is a by-product of this rushed pace. While these bricks would normally be thrown out, as they are hard to lay evenly, they were swiftly incorporated into reconstruction and lend a distinctive tone to many of Chinatown's brick buildings. (They later became a trend in tony Arts and Crafts–style homes, but here they were a product of necessity.)

Thanks to speedy efforts at raising "Chinese" pagodas and temples, Chinatown stayed put, and to this day it remains one of San Francisco's most vibrant and exciting neighborhoods. Its sidewalks are packed shoulder-to-shoulder with locals every day of the year, and all manner of goods literally spill out of the shops. At night, the district's commercial streets become a relatively subdued and atmospheric constellation of neon. This walk follows the main thoroughfares, Stockton Street and Grant Avenue, with frequent detours through mysterious alleys and into clamorous dim sum parlors.

Walk Description

Definitely arrive for this walk with an empty stomach, as there are all sorts of tastes and treats to enjoy. Begin under the public artwork *Language of the Birds,* the flying books just outside of City Lights Bookstore. Note that the texts reflected on the ground are in Italian, English, and Chinese. This is because we're at the crossroads of Chinatown and North Beach. Head up Broadway and turn left onto Stockton Street, the cultural heartbeat of the area. This is the district's "real" side, unadorned and untouristy, and fulfilling most of the neighborhood's day-to-day requirements. Along Stockton, household store aisles are choked with plastic buckets, Day-Glo brooms, teapots, soup bowls, meat cleavers, chopsticks, and tiny folding chairs for children. There are numerous jewelry shops, some with signs advertising gold bullion, and not quite as many hair salons. Bakeries sell moon cakes, wedding cakes, and little round balls filled with mung bean paste. Produce shops can hardly contain all that they offer: Asian pears, jujubes, lychees, longans, boiled peanuts, bok choy, water chestnuts, Chinese broccoli, yams, tangelos, and taro root. Some shops specialize in anything that has had the life dried out of it: dried shrimp, dried squid, dried oysters, countless varieties of dried mushrooms, and dried ginseng by the barrel. Roasted ducks and chickens hang in windows. Entire pigs, ghostly white, hang on meat hooks beyond side doors left wide open to the street. The shop at 1135 Stockton, between Pacific and Jackson, is a dim, damp hall that lures in its clientele with tanks filled with catatonic rockfish, tubs of live frogs that aren't hopping away, and snails packed on ice. Farther in, glass cases display the internal organs of pigs and cows, and still deeper a little shop within the larger shop stocks chickens and pigeons kept in cages.

After crossing Jackson Street, look to your left for the yellow **❶ Ming Lee Trading Inc.** sign, and enter to satisfy all your Asian snack needs. Head inside and downstairs for everything from lychee jelly cups and green-tea KitKats to crack seeds (dried fruits with the pits left in) and hot, spicy dried squid. Cash only!

Return to Stockton and keep heading south. A daytime visit to Chinatown should include a stop for dim sum, and **❷ Good Mong Kok Bakery** is an excellent place to grab some on the go. Don't be intimidated by the long lines and sometimes grumpy staff; their pork buns and shrimp *siu mai* are well worth the wait. Stroll the next few blocks, and duck into shops that intrigue you. Stockton is also the street on which you're most likely to be nudged out of an old lady's way, so watch your step. Turn right at Clay. Half a block up, the **❸ Chinese Historical Society of America** operates a small museum (Wednesday–Sunday, 11 a.m.–4 p.m.) in a former YWCA building designed by

The aisles of Ming Lee Trading Inc. are packed with tasty Asian snacks of every color and flavor.

Backstory: The Birth of the Fortune Cookie

That crunchy folded confection that charts your future destiny seems as ubiquitous as chopsticks to modern Chinese dining in America, but there's one place you won't find them: China.

Indeed, fortune cookies weren't Chinese at all originally. *New York Times* journalist Jennifer 8. Lee, who researched *The Fortune Cookie Chronicles,* made it her mission to unravel the mystery of the fortune cookie's origins. Her work led her to the research of Yasuko Nakamachi, a scholar who spent years trying to get to the bottom of the treat's lineage. Nakamachi's interest was piqued when she saw a baker outside of Kyoto making similar fortune-stuffed sweets using a centuries-old specialty grill plate. An illustration in a 19th-century text confirmed her suspicion that fortune cookies were actually Japanese in origin.

But how did they land on the menu of every Chinese food restaurant in America? Most credit the family of Makoto Hagiwara for bringing them from Japan to America's shores by way of San Francisco. Hagiwara, a landscape architect, oversaw the construction of the Japanese Tea Garden in Golden Gate Park. The garden served fortune tea cakes from Japantown's Benkyodo Bakery, which opened in 1906. Benkyodo thrived, and Chinese restaurants started buying them, too, marketing them as a pan-Asian snack for American palates.

During World War II nearly the entire Japanese population in San Francisco was rounded up and sent to internment camps. Many Chinese families took over Japanese bakeries when they were shuttered, and soon the relationship between Chinese food and cookies was cemented. Derrick Wong, the vice president of Wonton Foods, the largest fortune cookie manufacturer in the world, concedes, "The Japanese may have invented the fortune cookie, but the Chinese people really explored the potential of the fortune cookie. It's Chinese American culture." Origins aside, the manufacturing of fortune cookies was forever changed when Edward Louie of San Francisco's Lotus Fortune Cookies invented the first automatic cookie-folding machine in the 1960s; he is also credited with introducing titillating and risqué fortunes.

And the fortunes? Well, restaurants know that foreboding predictions aren't good for business, so there's a reason that most cookies highlight health, wealth, and familial optimism. See them made the old-fashioned way at the Golden Gate Fortune Cookie Company on this walk, and you can visit Benkyodo on our Japantown walk (see Walk 32, page 213).

---

renowned architect Julia Morgan. Exhibits focus on Chinese life in California from the gold rush to the present and provide a colorful depiction of life as well as good insight on the impact of the Chinese Exclusion Act of 1882. Admission at press time is $15 adults, $10 children and seniors.

Return to Stockton and turn right. The building at No. 843 is home of the ❹ **Chinese Consolidated Benevolent Association,** also known as the Chinese Six Companies. Far more than a benevolent association or social aid club, the Six Companies is a conglomeration of community groups that started in the late 19th century, at a time when Chinatown society was severely constrained by laws limiting its movements within the broader society and continually disrupted by ongoing wars between rival criminal *tongs* (gangs). For a time the Six Companies was the most powerful Chinese American political organization in the United States, and it continues to be highly influential in San Francisco's Chinese community.

Across the street, at No. 836, is Sun Yat-sen Memorial Hall; note the portrait of the hall's namesake prominently displayed above the building. (Sun Yat-sen helped establish the Republic of China and was appointed its first president in 1912.) Next door is the local Kuomintang (KMT) headquarters. The KMT, or Chinese Nationalist Party, vied with the Communist Party for control of mainland China from 1912 until 1949 and went on to dominate Taiwanese politics for most of the 20th century. The party has historically drawn wide support from San Francisco's Chinese community.

Turn left onto Sacramento and head left again under the red lanterns to walk the two-block length of Waverly Place. On the corner of Sacramento, the ❺ **Clarion Music Center** hosts performances and cultural events on everything from tea tastings to Chinese music and poetry. They also teach music lessons on a variety of modern and classic instruments, including the *erhu,* the two-stringed spike fiddle played so mournfully in some of the neighborhood's alleys. The biggest culinary draw here is ❻ **Mister Jiu's,** an acclaimed Cantonese restaurant with a California twist; its black exterior belies the light-filled Michelin-starred dining room upstairs.

In the late 19th century, Waverly Place was lined with barbershops, and because the price of a trim was 15 cents, Waverly was nicknamed 15 Cent Street. (There's still a solitary barber shop, called Li Ly's Hair Salon, that charges $6 for a cut.) Waverly is a colorful street, with many painted balconies and decorative tiles on the facades of the buildings. Signs over the doorways indicate numerous family associations, and a smattering of Buddhist temples are hidden away on some of the top floors. One, ❼ **Tin How Temple,** is open to visitors (10 a.m.–4 p.m.). It's well worth the schlep up three flights of stairs for what feels like a privileged behind-the-scenes look into this otherwise private neighborhood. The oldest Taoist temple in America, the opulent red-and-gold shrine is frequently enveloped in wafts of smoky incense. The presentation is minimal but welcoming. Volunteers deliver a prepared narration to explain the altar and the joss sticks spiraling overhead, and donations are appreciated. And while pictures aren't allowed in the temple, be sure to step out onto the balcony for a great view of the street from above.

Where Waverly meets Washington, turn left, cross the street, and head up Ross Alley, a mysterious passageway known in the 19th century as the Street of the Gamblers because so many gambling joints were located here. Down near the end of the block, beneath the nearly continuous canopy of fire escapes, slip into the ❽ **Golden Gate Fortune Cookie Company,** where you

Festive red lanterns line the many streets and alleyways of Chinatown.

can see how fortune cookies are made. The cast-iron machinery in the shop looks like it was built in the age of steam engines, and the workers who fold the still-hot cookies by hand, after first slipping the fortunes in, are quick and deft. Someone will stop and sell you a bag of fresh cookies if you like, but the staff are generally too busy to field questions. (For more information on the history of the fortune cookie, see Backstory, page 37.) At Jackson turn right and, at Grant Avenue, if you're feeling peckish, turn left for a quick detour to the ❾ **Golden Gate Bakery** for *dan tat,* a mouthwatering egg custard tart. Returning to Jackson, continue heading east to pass ❿ **Z & Y,** one of Chinatown's most esteemed restaurants. From the exterior, it doesn't look all that different from many of the other eateries in the 'hood (save for the photos of visiting dignitaries ranging from former Chinese President Hu Jintao to culinary legend Alice Waters to Barack Obama). The main draw is the spicy Sichuan and Northern Chinese delicacies.

Head back a few feet to follow the narrow Wentworth Alley to Washington Street. Across the street and to your left is Portsmouth Square. While the square's roots lie in Barbary Coast history (and are explored on the next walk, Jackson Square), today it's commonly referred to as "Chinatown's living room," and you're bound to see men with makeshift tables playing cards, chess, and checkers at all hours, seniors doing Tai Chi, and kids running amok with their families.

With the square to your back, head left to 743 Washington, where the ⓫ **East West Bank** occupies a building, constructed after the '06 quake, that is worthy of a movie set. It was once the Chinese Telephone Exchange; in order to handle the complex mix of cultures and languages in Chinatown, the operators who worked the exchange were fluent in five Chinese dialects in addition to English. The building's interior was remodeled to look more like a bank, but from the street it retains its pseudo-pagoda look.

For eight blocks Grant Avenue, Chinatown's touristy main drag, is crammed with shops selling kitschy curios. Here you'll find paper lanterns, calligraphy scrolls, silk pajamas, silk scarves, black canvas slippers, jade Buddhas, red-lacquered Buddhas, ceramic Buddhas, ceramic dragons, ceramic pigs emblazoned with floral patterns, bobble-headed cats that wave one paw, fancy kites, license plates and street signs with popular children's names on them, pink conical hats, jewelry, antiques, elephant tusks intricately carved to look like miniature Shangri-las, T-shirts that say GOT DIM SUM?, shot glasses, swords, giant vases, discount luggage, dainty parasols, life-size statues of American Indians shooting bows and arrows, and life-size statues of horses rearing on hind legs, should you need anything like any of that. Needless to say, many of the shops are worth picking through.

The friendly and informed folks at ⓬ **Red Blossom Tea Company** are purveyors of fine teas and beautiful Yixing teapots, fashioned by hand in the Sung Dynasty style of a millennium ago. They offer a tasting flight of four teas for $35, should you want to learn more about teas and the rituals surrounding them.

On the corner of Grant Avenue and Commercial Street, the ⓭ **Eastern Bakery** is Chinatown's oldest bakery. Since 1924 pineapple buns and sesame seed balls have been rubbing shoulders with apple turnovers in the pastry shelves, as the bakers have long tried to whet both Chinese and American appetites. But the real star is the homemade moon cakes, and you'd be well advised to stop in and try one. Next door, the Wok Shop is a veritable treasure trove of instruments for all your searing, stir-frying, steaming, and boiling needs.

On the next block, ⓮ **Canton Bazaar** stocks everything from chopsticks to sensual statues that are displayed behind a glass case. If you're not interested in buying anything, you can at least step in to

Step into Eastern Bakery, Chinatown's oldest, for a delicious moon cake.

admire the lovely lacquered painting, two stories tall, that hangs in the south stairwell. The intersection of Grant and California is a pivotal crossroads in Chinatown, with several landmark buildings, including the first two fake pagodas to go up after the '06 quake. The intersection is flanked by the exotic Sing Fat Building, at 717 California St., which went up in 1907, and the Sing Chong Building, at 601 Grant, which went up a year later. Also at this intersection stands **⓯ Old St. Mary's,** a quake survivor that dates all the way back to 1853. The oldest cathedral in California, the church was built by Chinese laborers using granite quarried in the old country. This old church has seen it all and was at one time nearly surrounded by houses of ill repute, which adds some weight to the sign below the clock, which quotes Ecclesiastes: SON, OBSERVE THE TIME AND FLY FROM EVIL.

The lions of Dragon Gate welcome you to Chinatown.

Cross California, turn left, and make a quick right at Quincy Street, into St. Mary's Square. The park is a hidden sanctuary amid the neighborhood's hustle and bustle. At the center of the square, a statue of Sun Yat-sen is the work of sculptor Beniamino Bufano, who met and admired the Chinese leader. Sun Yat-sen was president of China for just six weeks in 1912, but during that time he banned foot binding and played a pivotal role in overthrowing the Manchu Dynasty. He likely stood at this spot many times, as he was a frequent traveler to San Francisco.

Crossing through the park, at Pine, turn right, which gets you back to Grant. Follow it all the way to the **⓰ Dragon Gate,** at Bush Street, considered the only authentic Chinatown gate in North America. Built in 1970, with materials donated by Taiwan, the gate has a proper feng shui southern orientation and is flanked by two lions warding off evil spirits. The male lion, on the left, has his paw resting on a ball symbolizing the Chinese Empire, while the female lion, on the right, has her paw resting on a cub, representing offspring and fertility. Fashioned after ceremonial gates found in Chinese villages, the large main passage is intended for use by dignitaries, while the flanking smaller passageways are for commoners; exit in the way that you see fit.

While our walk takes us through a lot of Chinatown, the neighborhood warrants further exploration, so feel free to wander back through all the streets we haven't hit on this tour.

Backstory: Donaldina Cameron, Chinatown's Angry Angel

Where Sacramento meets Joice Alley sits the clinker-brick **1a** **Cameron House,** formerly the Presbyterian Mission House, named for missionary and social worker Donaldina Cameron. Originally from New Zealand, Cameron came to San Francisco in her early 20s to help teach sewing to young girls. Inspired by the Mission House's founder, Margaret Culbertson, Cameron was soon tackling much larger issues than embroidery. In the late 1800s, girls as young as 9 years old were bought in China and sold into slavery and prostitution in San Francisco; once in America, they rarely lived more than five years at the hands of their captors.

Upon Culbertson's death, Cameron made rescuing these girls her life's mission. Freeing the children was dangerous work—child-protection laws didn't exist, and the violent *tongs* (gangs) that ruled much of Chinatown were constantly threatening Cameron: brothel owners were found trying to dynamite the door of the Mission House open and sometimes left effigies of Cameron with a knife through her heart. Nevertheless, this hardy crusader remained undaunted. Tipped off by Chinese allies in the neighborhood, Cameron would scale ladders, climb over rooftops, and ferret out secret rooms behind trap doors where the girls were being kept, often with ax-wielding help from supporters in the Chinatown Police Squad. She was even known to spend the night in jail with girls to protect them. When the mission was rebuilt following the 1906 earthquake, Cameron designed elaborate underground rooms and tunnels to hide the girls during raids.

Cameron is credited with rescuing and educating thousands of girls over the course of nearly four decades. Despite her staunch Christian proselytizing to her wards, most historians agree that her true passion lay with saving lives. The tongs dubbed her *Fahn Quai* ("white devil"), but her girls lovingly called her *Lo Mo* ("old mother"). Today, Cameron House continues to offer a range of social services to the Chinese American community.

Points of Interest

1 **Ming Lee Trading Inc.** 759 Jackson St.; 415-217-0088 (no website)

2 **Good Mong Kok Bakery** 1039 Stockton St.; 415-397-2688, goodmongkok.com

3 **The Chinese Historical Society of America** 965 Clay St.; 415-391-1188, chsa.org

4 **Chinese Consolidated Benevolent Association** 843 Stockton St.; 415-982-6000, chinese6cos.org

Chinatown

⑤ **Clarion Music Center** 2 Waverly Pl.; 415-391-1317, clarionmusic.com

⑥ **Mister Jiu's** 28 Waverly Pl.; 415-857-9688, misterjius.com

⑦ **Tin How Temple** 125 Waverly Pl.; 415-986-2520 (no website)

⑧ **Golden Gate Fortune Cookie Company** 56 Ross Alley, 415-781-3956 (no website)

⑨ **Golden Gate Bakery** 1029 Grant Ave.; 415-781-2627, goldengatebakery.com

⑩ **Z & Y** 655 Jackson St.; 415-981-8988, zandyrestaurant.com

⑪ **East West Bank** 743 Washington St.; 415-421-5215, eastwestbank.com

⑫ **Red Blossom Tea Company** 831 Grant Ave.; 415-395-0868, redblossomtea.com

⑬ **Eastern Bakery** 720 Grant Ave.; 415-433-7973, easternbakery.com

⑭ **Canton Bazaar** 616 Grant Ave.; 415-362-5750, facebook.com/cantonbazaarsf

⑮ **Old St. Mary's Cathedral** 660 California St.; 415-288-3800, oldsaintmarys.org

⑯ **Dragon Gate** Bush St. and Grant Ave.

Backstory

⑴ₐ **Cameron House** 920 Sacramento St.; 415-781-0401, cameronhouse.org

6 Jackson Square
Time-Traveling Through the Barbary Coast

Above: *Watering holes, old and new, have always been a mainstay of Jackson Square.*

BOUNDARIES: Washington St., Kearny St., Sansome St., Broadway
DISTANCE: 0.75 mile
DIFFICULTY: Easy
PARKING: Public lot beneath Portsmouth Square
PUBLIC TRANSIT: 1, 8X Muni buses

There is little disputing that San Francisco got off to a spectacular start. By all accounts, the city was thrown up with the purposeful chaos of a carnival pulling into town in the dark of night. For decades the atmosphere in many parts of town pulsed with a stridently lawless spirit. The area between the main plaza and the wharves managed to distinguish itself as particularly rough and became known as the Barbary Coast.

The name suggested a likeness to the pirate-infested coast of North Africa, where European sailors risked being captured and enslaved on corsair galleys. The district functioned like an angler fish preying upon sin-seeking sailors. For its lure it had block after block of gambling dens, whorehouses, music halls, saloons, and boardinghouses. Serious consequences awaited those who were outsmarted here. The neighborhood was rife with swindlers and shanghaiers. For the unwary miner or shore-leave sailor, the path of least resistance generally led to a knock-out blow in the back room of a saloon.

The district began to form with the arrival of the first forty-niners and thrived until the devastating quake and fire of 1906. Ironically, the buildings in this haven of heathens were largely spared by that catastrophe. Some buildings were torn down later, but the district is now listed on the National Register of Historic Places and thus protected. Most of Pacific Street—popularly known as Terrific Street when it was the main stem of the Barbary Coast—is now a quiet row of distinguished antiques dealers and architectural firms.

Walk Description

Start in ❶ **Portsmouth Square,** which during the gold rush was the city's main plaza. City Hall stood on Kearny Street from 1852 to 1895; it occupied the former Jenny Lind Theater, so named in honor of the Swedish Nightingale, who never performed in San Francisco. Next door was a grand gambling hall called El Dorado. The legendary Bella Union, the most popular of the city's music halls, stood on Washington Street, just above Kearny.

The square itself was a barren patch of earth with crisscrossing footpaths converging in the middle. This is where important things happened in early San Francisco. In July 1846, the Stars and Stripes were raised here by Captain John B. Montgomery, formally claiming the settlement of Yerba Buena for the United States. (The town was renamed San Francisco a year later.) A plaque in the square commemorates the event. The square soon acquired the name of Montgomery's ship, the USS *Portsmouth.* Another monument, featuring a cast bronze ship, commemorates a couple of visits by Robert Louis Stevenson, author of the classic tale *Treasure Island.* Having spent a few months in San Francisco in 1879, Stevenson returned in 1888 with his new wife, Fanny. From here they embarked on the extended sea voyage that would end with the author's death in Samoa, six years later.

Now firmly part of Chinatown, Portsmouth Square looks nothing like it would have before 1906, but it is as vital as ever. It still attracts gamblers—on pretty much any day of the week, you'll spot men gathered around park benches playing fevered games of cards.

Follow Washington Street in the direction of the bay, cross Columbus Avenue, and you're entering the Jackson Square Historic District. Most of the brick structures here date to the 1850s and '60s, when this area was the city's exciting and dangerous nightlife zone.

The copper-clad Columbus Tower houses Francis Ford Coppola's Cafe Zoetrope.

The Transamerica Pyramid (which we examined in Walk 3, Financial District, page 18) stands on a historical site, that of the legendary Montgomery Block, commonly known as Monkey Block. As no-longer-extant landmarks go, this one was a doozy: built in 1853, the Montgomery Block was for a time the largest and most prestigious commercial building on the West Coast, but it's not for commerce that it is remembered. A bar on the ground floor, called the Bank Exchange, gave the city its signature drink, pisco punch. Pisco is a Peruvian or Chilean brandy that perhaps was introduced locally by Chilean immigrants during the gold rush. To make pisco punch, pineapple was infused in gum syrup and mixed with water, lemon juice, and pisco to make an innocuous-tasting beverage that packed a wallop. It was commonly observed that the drink could "make a gnat fight an elephant." The bar, alas, was done in by the Volstead Act in 1919, and the drink long ago fell out of favor. Of late, however, pisco punch has begun to reappear on drink menus around town, thanks to today's inquisitive breed of bartenders.

As the city grew, the Monkey Block's more status-conscious tenants moved down Montgomery Street, and artists, tradesmen, musicians, writers, and poets moved in. By the 1880s, the immense building was the center of the city's bohemian life. In the basement was a public bath habituated by writers such as the young Mark Twain, who worked as a reporter in town from 1864 until 1866. (Twain, having deserted the Confederate Army in 1861, spent much of the '60s in the West.) While bathing here Twain reputedly made the acquaintance of a fireman named Tom Sawyer and thought well enough of the name to use it in his best-known work. Ambrose Bierce, Jack London, and Robert Louis Stevenson all either worked in the building or had other excuses for dropping by. The building was finally demolished in 1959, and the site served as a parking lot for more than a decade before ground was broken for the Transamerica Pyramid.

Turn left onto Montgomery. This first block has numerous landmark buildings, most obvious being the Old Transamerica Building (701 Montgomery St.), a flatiron clad in white terra-cotta tiles. It was built in 1911 for A. P. Giannini, founder of the Bank of Italy, which grew to become Bank of America. It's now the San Francisco headquarters for the Church of Scientology.

Across the street, at 710 Montgomery, the Black Cat Cafe was a famous hangout for arty bohemians from 1933 until 1963. In the 1950s, drag entertainer José Sarria gained notoriety for his live operatic performances here. A few doors down, at 716–720 Montgomery, Diego Rivera and Frida Kahlo lived and worked in fellow artist Ralph Stackpole's studios on and off throughout the 1930s. Stackpole's studios were the center of the city's artistic social scene since the early 1920s, and for a time photographer Dorothea Lange subleased a photography studio upstairs.

The completely gutted building at 722 Montgomery was the office of lawyer Melvin Belli from 1959 to 1989. Belli, a flamboyant character, represented celebrity clients as diverse as Lenny Bruce, Zsa Zsa Gabor, and Jack Ruby. He also helped broker the deal that brought the Rolling Stones to the Altamont Speedway in 1969, and scenes were shot in Belli's office for the documentary *Gimme Shelter*. He even appeared once in an episode of *Star Trek*, in which he played a character named Gorgan. Married six times, he passed away in 1996 at age 88. The building that once housed his firm was allowed to deteriorate after the 1989 earthquake, and its roof eventually caved in. In October 2009, the Belli family put it up for sale, priced at $10.5 million. It currently houses both residential and commercial space, including Filson, a Seattle-based purveyor of outdoor apparel and gear since 1897.

Turn right at Jackson, and half a block down you'll reach the Hotaling Buildings (455 and 463–73 Jackson), which flank narrow Hotaling Place. Anson Parson Hotaling, who distributed liquor, among other goods, built the stately offices at 455 Jackson, then bought the second building, which he used as a warehouse for his booze. When the buildings survived the 1906 quake and fire, a jaunty little rhyme was composed by one Charles K. Field:

> If, as one says, God spanked the town
> For being overfrisky
> Why did He burn the churches down
> And save Hotaling's whisky?

The building at 415–431 Jackson St. was built in 1853 and was formerly home to Domingo Ghirardelli's chocolate company. In 1860 Ghirardelli added the structure at 407 Jackson. The older building, you'll notice, has some intriguing details, with faces watching out from the frames of the upstairs windows. The much plainer 1860 building seems to suggest Ghirardelli had his mind more on the bottom line as his business expanded.

At Sansome Street turn left and then cut back up Gold Street. Considering San Francisco owed its good fortune to the gold rush, it's interesting that Gold Street should turn out to be so inconspicuous. It's a narrow lane, one block long, much of it walled in by the back sides of brick buildings. One entrance leads to ❷ **Bix,** a spectacularly swank supper club that recreates the decadence and grandeur not of the Barbary Coast, but of the Jazz Age.

Turn right on Montgomery, then left onto Pacific Street. It's an agreeable enough street to look at, with its perfectly silent historical buildings, but there's little to suggest how terrific the

400 and 500 blocks were more than a century ago. However, saunter up the 500 block for a peek into the entry of No. 555, graced by some lovely nudes embossed in plaster. Think of this detail as an overt tribute to the neighborhood's bawdy past. The building was once the location of the Hippodrome, a dance hall. The Hippodrome was across the street during its heyday and moved to this location after the first one burned down just in time for World War II, when the district enjoyed a minor revival, thanks to the influx of military personnel embarking from the city.

At the junction of Pacific, Kearny, and Columbus, look across Columbus and you'll spot Francis Ford Coppola's ❸ **Cafe Zoetrope** (described in our next walk, North Beach) and the ❹ **Comstock Saloon,** a lovely old establishment with a questionable past. While pre-Prohibition drink recipes are mixed and served on the original mahogany bar and antique fans stir the air, this genteel establishment is a far cry from its bawdy precursors. It opened in 1907 as the Andromeda and is now the perfect place to try the aforementioned pisco punch, the original Barbary Coast cocktail.

Head up Kearny toward Broadway. These are the declining remnants of modern sleazeville, with Kearny a lusterless adjunct of the Broadway striptease strip. Missing from this scene is the Lusty Lady, a rare worker-owned strip joint that shuttered in 2013. In the 1990s, the strippers here unionized and went on strike, and in 2003 they bought their bosses out. But waning revenue and rising rent forced them to close their peep-show doors a decade later.

At Broadway turn left. Based on the signs above the shops here, it's obvious that this is a very sexy street. Broadway looks great at night, when the neon creates a reassuring tent of light that obliterates the darkness overhead. At the corner of Broadway and Columbus, the ❺ **Condor Club** is once again a strip joint, after dallying in the food industry for the past two decades. In the 1960s it was the Taj Mahal of San Francisco's burlesque scene, defined by the topless—*and* bottomless—act of the late Carol Doda (1937–2015). A plaque on the Columbus Street side of the building makes hay of two landmark dates: June 16, 1964, when Doda first unveiled the marvel that was her silicone-augmented bosom (which had reputedly ballooned from size 34B to 44DD); and September 3, 1969, when she first shimmied out of her skivvies on stage. Fondly remembered by old-time San Franciscans is the Condor's sign, which featured a larger-than-life caricature of a bikini-clad Doda with blinking red lights for nipples.

The Condor, incidentally, was the site of a grisly death that made local headlines because of its salacious nature. One night after hours, in November 1983, a dancer and a bouncer were making love on top of a piano, which was supported by a hydraulic pole that was used to raise and lower it during performances. One thing led to another, the hydraulics were activated, and the paramours were crushed between the piano and the ceiling. The dancer survived; the bouncer did not. But they both lived on in tragic infamy.

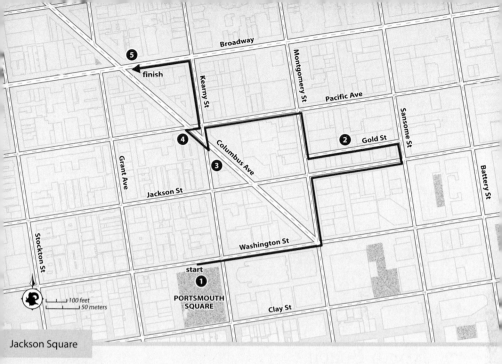

Jackson Square

Points of Interest

1 **Portsmouth Square** Kearny and Clay Sts.; 415-831-2700, sfrecpark.org/destination/portsmouth-square

2 **Bix** 56 Gold St.; 415-433-6300, bixrestaurant.com

3 **Cafe Zoetrope** 916 Kearny St.; 415-291-1700, cafezoetrope.com

4 **Comstock Saloon** 155 Columbus Ave.; 415-617-0071, comstocksaloon.com

5 **Condor Club** 560 Broadway; 415-781-8222, condorsf.com

7 North Beach
A Village of Aging Beatniks and Italian *Famiglie*

Above: *Grant Avenue has everything from secondhand-record stores to handmade-shoe shops.*

BOUNDARIES: Washington St., Powell St., Filbert St., Grant Ave.
DISTANCE: 1 mile
DIFFICULTY: Easy
PARKING: Underground lot beneath Portsmouth Square, at Washington and Kearny Sts., 1 block
   from the starting point
PUBLIC TRANSIT: 1, 10, 30X, 41 Muni buses

More village than neighborhood, this was once Barbary Coast oceanfront property, as the name implies. Having weathered waves of bawdy pirates, homesick Italians, authority-challenging bohemians, and onslaughts of tourists and tech workers, North Beach continues to both evolve and retain its character. North Beach no longer swarms with the goatee-and-beret crowd, and the Italian language is less commonly heard than it once was, yet the neighborhood continues to benefit from its heritage as an enclave of beatniks and Italian immigrants. The chief links to the past are cafés and historic bars, which retain a somewhat earthy, European charm that no doubt appealed to the poets and painters of the Eisenhower years. Italian American families still own most of the businesses, many of them after several generations.

The off-kilter, diagonal slice of Columbus Avenue, the main drag, and the closeness of Russian and Telegraph Hills, which rise above North Beach, make this quarter feel more intimate and self-contained than other parts of San Francisco. It's somewhat touristy, especially on weekends. Drop in on a weekday afternoon, or in time for lunch, and you'll get a more local sense of the area. Return at night to take the next walk, North Beach Bars.

Walk Description

Start at the foot of Columbus Avenue, where the Financial District abruptly ends and North Beach gradually cranks up. Columbus Avenue mainlines into the neighborhood. The first sign of North Beach character is ❶ **Caffè Macaroni,** a cramped little Neapolitan trattoria at No. 59, where the waiters are notorious for joking in Italian and occasionally belting out an operatic lyric or two. It's a bit early in the walk to stop and eat, but at least have a look at the menu and make a note to drop by for dinner sometime. This is a great local eatery.

On the next block, on the opposite side of the street, 124 Columbus Ave. is the former home to the renowned basement-level ❷ **Purple Onion.** This place was the stuff of comedy and music legend: Phyllis Diller and the Kingston Trio got their starts here. Jim Nabors sang here in his pre–Gomer Pyle days, and the owner, Bud Steinhoff, was in the habit of smashing glass when Nabors reached for high notes. A young Maya Angelou sang folk songs here, and in the 1970s Robin Williams worked the stage for tips. In recent years, the space has rotated between stints as a bar, comedy club, and other ventures, but it hasn't been able to yet find solid footing.

On the triangle formed by intersecting Columbus and Kearny stands the green-copper-clad Columbus Tower, formerly known as the Sentinel Building, and one of the city's most photographed sites. Like most spots in North Beach, the Beaux Arts flatiron has a colorful history. It was originally built for corrupt political boss Abe Reuf, but his move-in date was delayed by his incarceration at San Quentin. The expansive basement once held the popular restaurant Caesar's Grill, until it was shuttered for serving booze during Prohibition, although Neptune's Grotto sprung up in its place shortly thereafter. The Kingston Trio later purchased the building and established a recording studio where they and other musicians, including the Grateful Dead, played. Today it's the headquarters for the Coppola family's filmmaking company, American Zoetrope. Francis

Ford Coppola bought the building in 1972, the year *The Godfather* was released. Coppola was already a fixture in the neighborhood, frequenting local bars and cafés; he keeps an office on the top floor, beneath the building's graceful cupola. (Incidentally, a *coppola,* in Italian, is a type of cap once popular among the common folk of Sicily.) ❸ **Cafe Zoetrope,** on the ground floor, is a fine spot for sharing a pizza and a bottle of wine.

A block up, Jack Kerouac Alley is named for the author of *On the Road* and other tomes that captured the restlessness of the Beat Generation. It's a perfect alley for Kerouac, who liked to drink at Vesuvio, the bar that overlooks the alley. He also associated with poet Lawrence Ferlinghetti, whose ❹ **City Lights** bookstore is just across the alley. Ferlinghetti opened the shop in 1953. He made headlines in 1956 when he published a pocket edition of Allen Ginsberg's *Howl* and the poem was banned for containing obscenities. Ferlinghetti won a high-profile court battle, and the book was put back on the shelves. City Lights is a fantastic bookstore, so step inside and head upstairs to the intimate Poetry Room, where volumes of verse—Beat and otherwise—fill the shelves. Ferlinghetti's office is just off this little reading room, so you might even run into him. Outside the bookstore, look up and admire the "books" flying above your head and illuminated by solar power. Titled *Language of the Birds,* by artists Brian Goggin and Dorka Keehn, the image is especially magical at night. As the books take flight over a pedestrian alley that links Chinatown and North Beach, note that the words imprinted on both the books and the ground beneath are in English, Italian, and Chinese, taken from original texts.

At Broadway, on the northwest corner, take a look at the *Jazz Mural*, by Bill Weber and Tony Klaas. Clarinetist Benny Goodman (who was not a local figure) presides over a group of San Francisco characters, including Joshua Abraham "Emperor" Norton, Herb Caen, and some Italian fishermen.

Turn right on Broadway. A block down, on the north side, step into the ❺ **Beat Museum** to look at Beat memorabilia and a collection of old editions by Kerouac, Ginsberg, Burroughs, and other Holy Goofs. There is a bathtub filled with banned books for your perusal. While there is no charge to enter the bookstore, admission to the museum is $8 and gains you entry into a quirky little museum that is clearly a labor of love. Within its two small floors, you can view films, admire first-edition books, and see period furniture and clothing worn by legendary beatniks.

Backtrack to head left, up narrow Romolo Place for a look at North Beach's back-alley side and turn left on Vallejo Street. At Grant, make a caffeine stop at ❻ **Caffè Trieste,** a historic coffeehouse that has been run by the Giotta family since 1956. Papa Gianni first opened the café and imported the espresso he loved from his native Italy, claiming to be the first to bring it to the United States. He also aspired to sing opera, and he and his family would sing cantos in the small café on Saturday afternoons (they still host concerts every Saturday). Trieste has a comfortable, timeworn feel to it, and literary types have always dropped in to kick-start their muses (Francis Ford Coppola worked on his *Godfather* screenplay at one of the tables). The walls are covered with old photos. It's part family album, part celebrity schmoozefest—well worth studying over a cappuccino.

On the opposite corner of Grant and Vallejo, duck into **❼ Al's Attire** for a peek at custom-made suits, shoes, and shirts that exude vintage flair and charm. Owner Al Ribaya has been making the magic happen for decades; wander around the hat blocks and fabric bolts and you may soon find yourself sporting a pair of bespoke shoes for your next walk. Tom Waits and Carlos Santana have both been clients.

Half a block up, at Vallejo and Columbus Streets, the **❽ National Shrine of St. Francis of Assisi** was built in 1860. It's the second-oldest Catholic church in the city after Mission Dolores. Kitty-corner from the church, at 373 Columbus St., **❾ Molinari Delicatessen** is a classic deli with hanging salamis, shelves of olives and table wines, and the tantalizing scent of dry cheese. Established in 1896, Molinari was beloved by neighborhood great Joe DiMaggio, who specifically requested in his will that Molinari cold cuts be served at his wake. Drop in for a whiff or to grab a sandwich, if you have visions of a picnic at the park later on. (This tour ends at a park.)

The illuminated books of Brian Goggin and Dorka Keehn's *Language of the Birds* fly over Columbus Avenue, complemented by Bill Weber and Tony Klaas's iconic *Jazz Mural* in the background.

Old-world delis such as Molinari's keep North Beach's Italian heritage alive.

Follow Columbus to Green Street and turn left. At No. 649, the Green Street Mortuary is notable for providing a marching band that leads funeral corteges through Chinatown. The marching
band, led by Lisa Pollard, aka the Saxlady, includes many local jazz musicians and even some
members of the San Francisco Symphony. If they happen to be marching out as you pass by, quit
this tour and follow the band, man.

Across the street, take note of ⑩ **Club Fugazi,** the attractive theater at No. 678. It's home to
the zany *Beach Blanket Babylon,* the world's longest-running musical revue, which has ruled the
stage here since 1975. Featuring performers in outlandish hats and gaudy costumes, the show
is a frequently updated satirical mashup of current politics and pop culture that *The New York
Times* has called "No less a part of San Francisco than the Golden Gate Bridge and Coit Tower." In
the 1950s and '60s, the Beats put on poetry readings in the club, and Thelonius Monk recorded
an album here in 1959.

Turn right on Powell Street and right again on Union Street. Cross Columbus and turn right.
This block is one of the street's busiest (and most touristy), alive with cafés and restaurants. Turn
left on Green Street and proceed to two blocks to ⑪ **Caffè BaoNecci,** a family-run establishment

that typifies North Beach's old-world feel. The original owners, Danilo and Danila DiPiramo, retired, and rather than close the shop they sold it to another couple, Walter and Stefania Gambaccini, in 2005. (The place is still known to neighborhood old-timers as Danilo Bakery despite the name change.) The Gambaccinis, from Altopascio, Italy, have broadened the menu to include panini, pizza, and pasta, which still relies heavily on the bakery's century-old oven.

Turn left onto Grant Avenue, which locals will contest plays host to the "real" North Beach. Off the main drag, the narrow street is packed with shops selling clothing, rare maps, secondhand records, and antiques, along with grocers, restaurants, cafés, and bars. Study the window displays as you walk by, and duck in wherever your curiosity is piqued. At Filbert turn left and walk down toward Washington Square. On the corner of Stockton, poke your head into **⑫ Liguria**, an admirably nondescript shop that sells just one thing: focaccia. Indeed, three generations of the Soracco family have been making focaccia in their century-old oven since 1911, so they clearly know what they're doing. In the age of one-stop shopping, this place constitutes the ultimate anachronism, but it manages to get by on the strength of a single quality product. If you've been assembling the fixings for a picnic along this tour, be sure to add a warm half-sheet of focaccia to your sack of victuals. They close at 2 p.m., but don't be surprised if they've already sold out before then. This is truly the gold standard of focaccia, and an authentic glimpse into the North Beach of yore.

Also overlooking the park is **⑬ Saints Peter and Paul Church.** (A bit unsettlingly, the church's address is 666 Filbert St.) Built in 1924, it's very popular for weddings. Lawrence Ferlinghetti dubbed it the "marzipan church," and indeed its facade has a cakelike aspect. In 1954 Joe DiMaggio and Marilyn Monroe, unable to wed in the church because they were both previously divorced, snapped their wedding photos on the front steps after getting officially hitched at City Hall. DiMaggio's funeral was held here as well in 1999.

Washington Square itself is an odd-shaped square, as diagonal Columbus Avenue slices off a chunk of it, leaving a small triangular remainder on the west side of the street. Still, the square is a nice patch of green with some trees and statues, and you'll invariably find dogs chasing Frisbees. Most interesting is the statue of Benjamin Franklin, erected in 1897 by a dentist named Henry D. Cogswell. Cogswell, an ardent prohibitionist, wasn't so much intent on honoring Franklin as he was on luring the town's heavy drinkers away from the bottle. Around the statue's base are water taps with labels indicating the waters' sources—one indicates the water is from Vichy, France. (The spouts have been out of order for decades now.) Also in the square is a firemen's statue, put here by fire chaser Lillie Hitchcock Coit. (For more on her, see Walk 9, Telegraph Hill, page 62.) Pick a bench or a spot on the grass, and settle in for a while. Or join the groups that are often doing Tai Chi in front of the church.

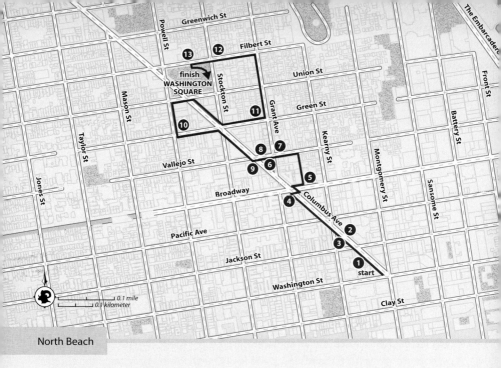

Points of Interest

1. **Caffè Macaroni** 59 Columbus Ave.; 415-956-9737, caffemacaroni.com

2. **Purple Onion (former)** 140 Columbus Ave. (no published phone number or website)

3. **Cafe Zoetrope** 916 Kearny St.; 415-291-1700, cafezoetrope.com

4. **City Lights** 261 Columbus Ave.; 415-362-8193, citylights.com

5. **Beat Museum** 540 Broadway; 415-399-9626, kerouac.com

6. **Caffè Trieste** 601 Vallejo St.; 415-392-6739, coffee.caffetrieste.com

7. **Al's Attire** 1300 Grant Ave.; 415-693-9900, alsattire.com

8. **National Shrine of St. Francis of Assisi** 610 Vallejo St.; 415-986-4557, shrinesf.org

9. **Molinari Delicatessen** 373 Columbus Ave.; 415-421-2337, molinaridelisf.com

10. **Club Fugazi** 678 Beach Blanket Babylon Blvd.; 415-421-4222, beachblanketbabylon.com

11. **Caffè BaoNecci** 516 Green St.; 415-989-1806, caffebaonecci.com

12. **Liguria** 1700 Stockton St.; 415-421-3786 (no website)

13. **Saints Peter and Paul Church** 666 Filbert St.; 415-421-0809, salesiansspp.org

8 North Beach Bars
In Search of the 90-Proof Muse

Above: *Beat Generation landmark Vesuvio specializes in stiff drinks and tattered memorabilia.*

BOUNDARIES: Union St., Columbus Ave., Grant Ave., Jack Kerouac Alley
DISTANCE: About 0.75 mile
DIFFICULTY: Easy (and getting easier)
PARKING: Driving is a bad idea if you plan to imbibe, but there's a parking lot on Vallejo between
   Columbus and Mason.
PUBLIC TRANSIT: 30 and 41 Muni buses

North Beach is one of San Francisco's best neighborhoods for barhopping, simply because the district is awash in a variety of fine watering holes within a small, walkable area. The offerings range from rowdy local taverns to historic beatnik dives to urban hipster lounges, and the crowds tend to be a diverse mix of local denizens, sozzled poets, and chatty tourists. While it would be irresponsible to drink in every bar on this tour, your throat is liable to be a bit dry at some point during your walk, and you'll be following in the steps of raucous pirates, boundary-pushing writers, and community-minded Italians by bellying up to the bar for a drink and conversation.

The best time to hit the bars in North Beach is the latter half of the week, when things are on the upswing. The weekends can be crowded when the bridge-and-tunnel crowd invades the neighborhood, but they also offer more occasion for live music to spill onto the street. Late afternoon or early evening can be quite nice, if you're inclined toward enjoying a drink or two before a meal.

Walk Description

❶ **Mario's Bohemian Cigar Store,** on the corner of Columbus Avenue and Union Street, is always a good place to start for its central location and its early hours. But mostly because Mario's represents what so many are seeking when they come to North Beach: authenticity, family legacy, deep Italian roots, and unpretentious warmth. Mario's is a friendly joint with a limited menu, and the toasted-focaccia sandwiches are excellent. Their bread comes from nearby Liguria Bakery, who has been perfecting the craft since 1911. A retired cop from Trieste, Italy, Mario Crismani opened the place in 1972, and his son took it over when he died. You'll spot photos of Mario and his family above the bar. Signore Mario also served as president of the city's bocce association. The bar once really did sell cigars, and it was originally a hangout for older Italian gents. These days, the crowd is younger and more mixed, and of course there's no smoking. Other than that, the place hasn't changed a bit.

After departing Mario's, saunter east on down Union Street to Stockton Street and turn right. Midway up the block is a classy little joint called ❷ **Tony Nik's.** The sign above the door, one of the oldest in North Beach, is a throwback to when food needed to be served with alcohol. Tony Nik's flung open its doors immediately following the repeal of Prohibition in 1933, and the retro vibe is the real deal. Wood paneling, a starburst clock, and bartenders you can trust to mix excellent old-school cocktails ensure that Don Draper would feel comfortable tossing a few back here. There's a small lounge in the rear with intimate tables, and the best time to come is for happy hour (4–7 p.m.).

At Green Street, hook left, and in less than a block you'll reach ❸ **Gino and Carlo,** one of North Beach's enduring neighborhood bars. This place is purely local in the best possible way: it's nothing fancy but always lively, and newcomers will feel welcome. It has some history too. Long ago, hard-drinking *Chronicle* columnist Charles McCabe—known as the Fearless Spectator—regularly penned his daily column from a table here. And Janis Joplin reputedly frequented the bar in the 1960s. In an interview with *Hoodline,* beloved bartender and co-owner Frank Colla (who retired in 2015) fondly recalls when Francis Ford Coppola brought the whole crew from *Apocalypse Now*

Devil's Acre has the booze-based cure for what ails you, as well as a speakeasy-style basement bar.

in to quench their thirst. The drinks are relatively cheap, there's a pool table and pinball machine, and there's usually a game playing on TV.

At Grant Avenue, turn right and head for the ❹ **Saloon,** just past Vallejo Street. It's the oldest bar in San Francisco, having opened its doors in 1861. Originally called Wagner's Beer Hall, it's a true survivor—it has endured the demise of the Barbary Coast, the 1906 quake, the Prohibition era, and the 1960s. The Saloon, bless it, is no model of gentrification. It's dusty, sagging, and peeling. The faded painted ladies over the bar lack Victorian propriety. But the overall vibe is good and welcoming. At night, the Saloon features live blues bands—good ones, usually.

Head up narrow Fresno Street and then right on Romolo Place. ❺ **15 Romolo** is the address and name of a sultry little hideaway that opened in the late 1990s. Formerly a Basque restaurant, it's a stylish watering hole without pretense. The barkeeps are keeping up with the current renaissance in mixology, and the drink list regularly introduces original concoctions and seasonal cocktails along with updated classics. They also serve upscale pub food and a cocktail brunch.

Romolo Place leads to Broadway; turn right and make your way back to Columbus. Immediately upon turning, the apothecary-themed ❻ **Devil's Acre** beckons with aproned "pharmacists" who mix drinks designed by an in-house herbalist. The moniker comes from the nickname of a particularly tawdry stretch of Barbary Coast bars and brothels, and the proprietors have gone heavy on the vintage medicinal theme, creating an atmospheric bar with top-notch cocktails. But the real treat lies in the candlelit basement gin mill, Remedie, found by descending stairs at the back of the bar.

We hope you've still got your sea legs beneath you, because we've saved three of the biggest heavy hitters for last. Turn left on the squib of a street called William Saroyan Place (named after the author) to make your way to **7** **Specs' Twelve Adler Museum,** one of North Beach's most storied watering holes. Specs' is a little grotto that oozes atmosphere without trying too much. The place is a dark and dusty museum of the best possible sort, filled with the lurid and the arcane, much of which has been sent from bar loyalists on their travels. The crowd is a jovial mix of juiced philosophers and loosened-tie types, and Specs himself (*né* Richard Simmons and nicknamed because of his Coke-bottle glasses) saw it as a place for people to swap stories about their lives.

Just beyond William Saroyan Place is **8** **Tosca Cafe,** a North Beach staple with Italian arias on the jukebox, red-leather booths, and brandy-laced house cappuccinos (that don't actually have any coffee in them). Rumors about the place abound: Did Bono really jump on the bar at 4 a.m. and sing along with a Pavarotti record? Did Dennis Quaid really apprehend a purse snatcher here? Did Sean Penn really once blow a hole through the wall to stop Kid Rock from playing music? Jeanette Etheredge presided over the bar's most colorful period, and her lips are mostly sealed. But despite the patron's list being a who's who of creative giants, Tosca remains a welcoming, dignified place. When Etheredge handed over the keys in 2013, the new owners promised to honor the history and style of the place. Take a seat and see if they've succeeded. On the opposite side of Columbus Avenue, two Beat landmarks, **9** **Vesuvio Cafe** and City Lights bookstore, flank narrow Jack Kerouac Alley. They don't serve drinks at City Lights, so make your way to Vesuvio Cafe, where faux stained glass, Beat Generation memorabilia, and art covers every inch of the walls. Opened in 1948, the place has its own native eccentricity and a place in North Beach history. When in town, writers such as Kerouac and poet Dylan Thomas drank and told fish stories here. Owner Henri Lenoir traded in on the beatnik craze by marketing a kit that included a beret, sandals, black turtleneck sweater, and false goatee. Vesuvio still has the beatnik spirit. Sit downstairs to soak in the bar's history or at an upstairs window to watch Columbus Avenue flow by.

Farther down on Columbus, the **10** **Comstock Saloon** and **11** **Cafe Zoetrope** are both mentioned in our Jackson Square and North Beach walks (see the previous two walks, respectively). Try a Barbary Coast cocktail at the former and a great Coppola wine at the latter.

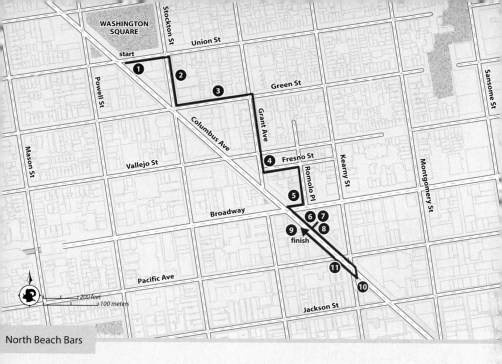

North Beach Bars

Points of Interest

1. **Mario's Bohemian Cigar Store** 566 Columbus Ave.; 415-362-0536 (no website)

2. **Tony Nik's** 1534 Stockton St.; 415-693-0990, tonyniks.com

3. **Gino and Carlo** 548 Green St.; 415-421-0896, ginoandcarlo.com

4. **Saloon** 1232 Grant Ave.; 415-989-7666, facebook.com/saloonsf

5. **15 Romolo** 15 Romolo Place; 415-398-1359, 15romolo.com

6. **Devil's Acre/Remedie** 256 Columbus Ave.; 415-766-4363, thedevilsacre.com

7. **Specs' Twelve Adler Museum** 12 William Saroyan Place; 415-421-4112 (no website)

8. **Tosca Cafe** 242 Columbus Ave.; 415-986-9651, toscacafesf.com

9. **Vesuvio Cafe** 255 Columbus Ave.; 415-362-3370, vesuvio.com

10. **Comstock Saloon** 155 Columbus Ave.; 415-617-0071, comstocksaloon.com

11. **Cafe Zoetrope** 916 Kearny St.; 415-291-1700, cafezoetrope.com

9 Telegraph Hill
Scaling the Stairways to Bohemian Bliss

Above: Stairway climbs past well-tended gardens ensure epic city views.

BOUNDARIES: Stockton St., Greenwich St., Sansome St., Vallejo St.
DISTANCE: 1.5 miles
DIFFICULTY: Strenuous
PARKING: Off-street parking is available on Vallejo St., between Stockton and Powell Sts., opposite the police station. Curbside parking is very difficult to find and limited to 2 hours Monday–Saturday.
PUBLIC TRANSIT: 30, 41, 45 Muni buses

On most days Telegraph Hill feels like San Francisco's Shangri-la, its wooden stairways zigzagging up hills too steep for paved streets. Walkers are naturally drawn to the steps, which weave through dense gardens and past Victorian houses both humble and refined. This little refuge tells us the rest of San Francisco hasn't taken full advantage of its spectacularly impractical topography. Telegraph Hill wasn't always so pretty a spot, however. Its east face was once a rock quarry overlooking a fleet of rotting ships. By the early 20th century, the hillside had become a de facto dumping ground. Beginning in the 1950s, the hill's bohemian inhabitants transformed their hidden quarter, mostly through tasteful and imaginative landscaping.

The neighborhood is fairly luxe now, thanks to escalating real estate values, but it continues to offer the city's best walking. A good time to walk this one is on a lightly overcast morning, when details are drawn out from the shadows beneath the trees.

Walk Description

The hill slopes up from North Beach, so we'll start at Washington Square, on the corner of Filbert and Stockton. You'll likely notice the long lines snaking down the street for ❶ **Mama's on Washington,** one of the city's most sought-after brunch spots thanks to its fluffy omelets and fresh-baked pastries. Mama's also sells to-go items if you need something to fuel you up the hill. Owner Frances "Mama" Sanchez died in 2000, but her family is keeping the delicious tradition alive and well.

Head north one block over to Greenwich. Just before you reach Greenwich, the Swiss chalet at 1736 Stockton is the ❷ **Maybeck Building,** said to be the sole Arts and Crafts–style building in North Beach. Berkeley-based Bernard Maybeck, one of California's most influential architects, designed it in 1907; it was originally the Telegraph Hill Neighborhood House, which offered services to immigrant families. Enter into a shady courtyard, which is a pleasant composition with a brick patio surrounded by varying inner faces of the building.

At Greenwich Street, turn right and head up (and up and up). At Grant, turn right and half a block down, at Gerte Alley, you'll get an attractive preview of ❸ **Coit Tower.** It's a more-than-adequate excuse for breaking up the upward trek. Back on Greenwich head up the steps through Pimentell Garden, named for Samantha Pimentell, who tended the flora here for 25 years. The steps lead to Telegraph Hill Boulevard, on which cars spiral up to the summit. Rather than follow the road, look on the other side for the stone steps that lead to the top.

Pioneer Park, on the leveled summit of Telegraph Hill, is where you'll find Coit Tower and a statue of Christopher Columbus, which was a gift from Columbus's hometown of Genoa, Italy. The explorer, who for better or worse got so many things rolling in the Americas, never laid eyes on San Francisco Bay, but this bronze likeness appears to be admiring the view of it. You should do the same. The vantage here is as wide as it gets, ranging from the Golden Gate to the west and on past Treasure Island to the east. In the early days of San Francisco, the arrival of ships entering the Golden Gate was observed from this lookout, and through semaphore signals, the news, along with the type of ship, was "telegraphed" to the bustling downtown clustered on Yerba

Buena Cove. Touts would sail or row out to meet the ships as they slowly proceeded into the bay. The city's economy revolved around shipping, and the bulk of the population would rush to the docks to greet each ship as it tied in.

Coit Tower, visible from just about anywhere to the east of Nob and Russian Hills, is one of the city's more puzzling architectural monuments. A fluted column topped by an arched observatory, it was originally derided by locals, who saw it as a sore thumb. San Franciscans are notoriously negative when it comes to new structures invading their skyline, but the city eventually came around to accepting this one. It looks particularly attractive at night, when it's illuminated by lamps beaming up from the ground. It bears the name of Lillie Hitchcock Coit, who funded the project through an endowment specified in her will. Coit (1843–1929) was raised in San Francisco and became a big fan of a company of volunteer firefighters called Knickerbocker Engine Company No. 5. In those days, multiple companies would respond to fire alarms, and it was a competition to see which company arrived at a scene first to put out the fire. Some citizens, such as young Lillie, cheered on their favorite companies much as sports fans cheer on their favorite teams. Coit's passion for Knickerbocker No. 5 far surpassed the norm, however, and by the age of 20 she had become an honorary member of the company. She considered it a point of honor to appear at

Coit Tower rises above its already-lofty hilltop perch.

every fire along with her beloved crew of smoke eaters. Consequently, many have speculated that Coit Tower was designed to resemble a firehose nozzle, but architect Henry T. Howard always maintained this was not his intention.

You can enter Coit Tower free of charge and circle the lobby to inspect the beautiful Works Progress Administration murals, which were added a year after the tower's completion in 1933. These frescoes sparked a huge controversy, as some have socialist undertones and depict laborers struggling to keep up with the demands of industry. Some of the more overt details in the original works were censored before the murals were unveiled. The fresco technique is one that requires a lot of training; the plaster absorbs the paint so that it becomes part of the wall. When the frescoes were being constructed, more than 30 artists were working at once, grinding minerals for pigment and using careful application techniques. Access to the observation deck and second-floor murals costs $8 for nonresidents. On a clear day, the view from the deck is

Backstory: An Explosive Disagreement Among Neighbors

For many years, rock was blasted out of Telegraph Hill's eastern side by a company called Gray Brothers. Using dynamite, the company regularly shook the foundations of the workingmen's cottages above, and in some instances the blasts actually toppled homes into the quarry. Property on the hill, though very central, was affordable to dock hands because the grades were too steep to attract the wealthy. Gray Brothers intended to continue quarrying until Telegraph Hill was completely flattened, along the way buying out neighbors upset by the disturbance of daily blasts. Once the hill was flattened, real estate values would naturally increase, and the company could then sell the land for top dollar.

Gray Brothers used dirty tactics such as timing its blasts with Fourth of July fireworks, a fact not lost on local newspapers that described the fury this brought on, with residents "swarming to the verge of the cliff between Vallejo and Sansome Streets, with stones and brickbats and even pistols in their hands." Indeed, Telegraph Hill residents fought back, getting a court injunction to stop the blasting, and when Gray Brothers defied the court, the neighbors rolled rocks down on the company to slow their progress. Unrelenting cheats and notorious bribers, Gray Brothers was sued more than 50 times by everyone from grocery suppliers to explosives manufacturers. Eventually karma caught up with the brothers, and one of them was killed by a company employee over unpaid wages, putting a stop to rock quarrying on Telegraph Hill. Despite the cold-blooded murder, the perpetrator was let off for reasons of temporary insanity, and no one seemed to argue that justice wasn't served.

astounding and highly recommended for a 360-degree view of bridges, Alcatraz Island, and the hills of San Francisco.

Exit the tower, descend the front steps, turn right, and look for the street sign for Greenwich Street. This leads not to a paved road but to some brick steps. Follow these down through dense greenery all the way to Montgomery Street. Turn left at the bottom of the stairs, and you'll reach ❹ **Julius' Castle,** one of the hill's kookier structures. This turreted fortress was the dreamchild of restaurateur Julius Roz, who opened the establishment in 1922. It closed in 2009 after operating for nearly nine decades and welcoming such high-profile diners as Ginger Rogers, Cary Grant, and Robert Redford. Neighborhood resident Paul Scott purchased the building in 2012 and has received permission to reopen it as a restaurant (it still hasn't yet as of press time), so with any luck the castle will reign supreme over the hill once again.

From the castle, walk along the east (lower) side of Montgomery past two buildings, and find steps cutting back and then down Greenwich Street, a pretty darn peaceful hideaway. These gardens here are the main attraction for the neighborhood's flock of parrots, who you'll often hear squawking in the canopy overhead. At 231 Greenwich you'll see some wooden steps to the right. Head up a little ways for an up-close look at some rusticated shacks that reflect the old neighborhood's bohemian past, and then return to the Greenwich Steps and head down to the bottom. At Sansome Street, turn right and walk one block to Filbert Street.

From the bottom of Filbert, it should be instantly obvious that you have your work cut out for you. A concrete-and-metal stairway ascends a sheer cliff carved out by rock quarrying in the 19th century. Flowers cling to the cliffside, thanks to adventurous gardeners who rappelled down to plant seedlings.

From the top of the cliff rustic wooden steps lead into the ❺ **Grace Marchant Gardens,** which are the most elaborate and lovingly tended gardens on the hill. Grace Marchant, a retired Hollywood stuntwoman, resided at the corner of Filbert and Napier Lane, where in 1950 she began planting the gardens that now flourish here. Her daughter, Valletta, took on a similar mission on Greenwich Street. Today, the gardens are tended by neighborhood volunteers. The land itself belongs to the city.

A wood-plank walkway leads down narrow Napier Lane, where we ought to make a short detour, for this is surely the sweetest cul de sac in all San Francisco. Little more than a footpath, it accesses a row of small houses shaded by trees. Farther up Filbert, Darrell Place is a similarly narrow, though paved, lane.

Peekaboo views of the Transamerica Pyramid greet hardy stairway climbers.

At the top of the block, the Art Deco ❻ **Malloch Building** at 1360 Montgomery appeared in the 1947 film noir classic *Dark Passage,* starring Humphrey Bogart and Lauren Bacall; the building housed Bacall's apartment in the film, where she allowed the fugitive Bogart to hide out. Scenes in the neighborhood reveal that the steps weren't nearly so beautiful then as they are today. The silver nautical motifs on the building's side make it instantly recognizable, and its streamlined Moderne style is reflected by curves both inside and out. In impeccable shape, it even retains its original elevator with a backlit glass brick shaft.

Turn left onto Montgomery and left again half a block later, onto historic Alta Street. On the south side of the block, the redbrick house with upstairs

Backstory: Parrots Gone Wild

The parrots you're likely to see on Telegraph Hill are cherry-headed conures, which first appeared here in the late 1970s or early 1980s with green bodies and bright red heads. Research seems to suggest that a romantic duo (parrots are monogamous for life) likely escaped from a pet shop. Or perhaps they were released; conures are known for being quite vocal about their unhappiness at being caged, and incessant squawking isn't so good for business. Once free, they went in search of fruits, flowers, and leaves and made their way to the lush gardens of Telegraph Hill. The colorful birds now number in the hundreds among multiple flocks and fly all over the city. Mark Bittner, author of *The Wild Parrots of Telegraph Hill* and subject of the documentary film of the same name, squatted in a former artist's shack on Greenwich Street for many years, studying and getting to know the birds. The book and film are highly recommended for anyone desiring a fascinating perspective on Telegraph Hill. And thanks to the imported-bird ban instituted in 1992, no more parrots are hatching escape routes from their cages. Today's San Francisco parrots are free at last.

galleries at 31 Alta was a speakeasy during Prohibition. On the north side, the house at 60–64 Alta is known as the Duck House for the ducks painted beneath the eaves. Author Armistead Maupin lived in one of the building's apartments in the early 1970s; actor Rock Hudson, a friend of Maupin's, used to visit him here.

Alta dead-ends, so backtrack to Montgomery, turn left, and turn left again onto Union Street, which leads to a nub called Calhoun Terrace. Here some of the city's oldest houses rub shoulders with modern masterpieces. The ❼ **Kahn House,** at 66 Calhoun, is the work of Richard Neutra, the architect often credited with introducing the International style of modern architecture to California. His cliffhanger doesn't look at all out of place here, and its expansive windows fully exploit the view of the bay. For the best vantage point, walk a little ways down the Union Street steps and look up at Neutra's building. Loop around to the upper side of Calhoun. The house at 9 Calhoun was built in 1854—very early days for this city—and it has been lovingly restored.

Return to Montgomery Street, and head left to meander back down to North Beach. Half a block past Union, Montgomery dead-ends, and the steps leading down afford a perfect perspective of the Transamerica Pyramid and the Financial District skyline. Continue descending and make a right turn to climb our final set of stairs, the lushly planted Vallejo Street steps. Be sure to keep turning around for beautiful views of the bridge through the swaths of roses and bougainvillea that grace the staircase. It's a straight shot to ❽ **Caffè Trieste** in North Beach (see Walk 7, page 50), where an espresso or beer surely has your name on it.

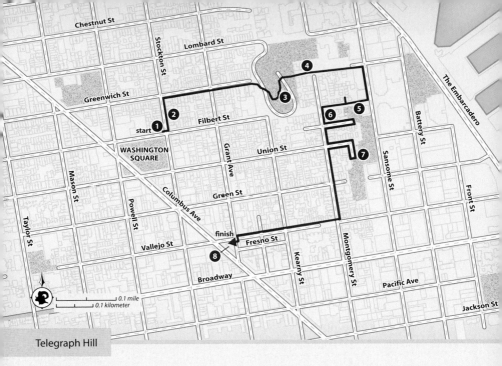

Telegraph Hill

Points of Interest

1. **Mama's on Washington Square** 1701 Stockton St.; 415-362-6421, mamas-sf.com

2. **Maybeck Building** 1736 Stockton St. (no published phone number or website)

3. **Coit Tower** 1 Telegraph Hill Blvd.; 415-362-0808, tinyurl.com/coittower

4. **Julius' Castle** 1541 Montgomery St. (no published phone number or website)

5. **Grace Marchant Gardens** Filbert St. and Napier Ln.; gracemarchantgarden.com (no published phone number)

6. **Malloch Building** 1360 Montgomery St. (no published phone number or website)

7. **Kahn House** 66 Calhoun Terrace (private residence)

8. **Caffè Trieste** 601 Vallejo St.; 415-392-6739, coffee.caffetrieste.com

10 Nob Hill
Sky-High Luxury and Haute Hotels

BOUNDARIES: Washington St., Mason St., California St., Jones St.
DISTANCE: About 1.75 miles
DIFFICULTY: Mildly strenuous
PARKING: St. Mary's garage, California St. and Grant Ave.
PUBLIC TRANSIT: Powell–Mason cable car

The tycoons and their opulent mansions are long gone, but Nob Hill still has a prestigious feel to it. Indeed, most agree that the name Nob Hill comes from a shortening of *nabob,* or rich and important person, and the air really does seem more rarefied here. In the 1870s, soon after the advent of cable cars simplified getting up the hill from downtown, the silver kings and railroad magnates moved in. Three decades later, the 1906 earthquake turned their privileged perch into an ash heap. High-class hotels, a lovely park, and awe-inspiring Grace Cathedral now stand where San Francisco's robber barons once lived. Add to the mix a handful of unexpected curiosities, and you've got yourself a sweet little tour with impeccable views. Our walk ends with a dip down toward Polk Gulch and a no-frills, quintessentially San Francisco seafood experience.

Walk Description

Because Nob Hill began with the development of cable cars, we'll start our tour at the ❶ **Cable Car Museum,** at the corner of Washington and Mason Streets. If you're a perfectionist, you can take the Powell–Mason cable car and get off directly in front of the museum. This is more than a historic site—it's the powerhouse that makes all the cable cars move. Inside, take a look at the system of wheels that turns the cables like spindles in a cassette tape. These cables run under the tracks of the entire system. Each individual car moves by gripping onto a cable, which pulls it up or down a street. Exhibits here demonstrate how the system works and also include some historic cars and photos.

Head up Mason Street for two blocks to reach the summit of Nob Hill. At the corner of Sacramento Street, just about everything we've climbed these heights to inspect comes into view. At 1000 Mason St. are the stately ❷ **Brocklebank Apartments,** which were featured in the 1958 Hitchcock film *Vertigo.* James Stewart, waiting behind the wheel of his car, began stalking Kim Novak when she emerged from this building.

Across the street, the imposing ❸ **Fairmont** hotel is one of many eye-catching buildings on Nob Hill. It's on the site of silver king James Fair's mansion, which was torn down by Fair's daughter before the quake of '06. The hotel she built on the site was nearly completed when the quake and fire turned it into a burned-out hull. Architect Julia Morgan drew the plans to restore the hotel, which finally opened a year to the day after the quake. Note the statue of famed crooner Tony Bennett outside, a gift from the city in 2016 to commemorate his 90th birthday. A frequent guest at the hotel, Bennett first performed his iconic "I Left My Heart in San Francisco" here in 1961, and devoted fans can book a night in the Tony Bennett Suite, complete with his artwork, for a hefty chunk of change. Enter the Fairmont's grand lobby, have a seat in a plush chair, pretend you're waiting for someone, and admire the marble columns and stately stairs. Then poke around a bit. Peer into the swank Venetian Room restaurant, study the charming dated murals of circus performers in the otherwise-dowdy Cirque Bar (designed by Timothy Pflueger), and stroll the rooftop garden with its lovely fountain, comfortable chairs, and excellent skyline view. In 2010 the hotel started raising bees and cultivating their own honey; you can see their hives and boxes in an enclosed culinary garden near the rooftop garden. For the hotel's biggest surprise, you'll have to head down to the basement. Here you'll find the ❹ **Tonga Room and Hurricane Bar,** a tiki bar (since 1945) that spared no expense when it came to the decor. The walls are fake lava rock, thatched roofs cover the tables, drinks are served in plastic coconut shells, and every 30 minutes a simulated monsoon strikes in the lagoon while a band plays on the floating schooner. In 2011 Anthony Bourdain called it "the greatest place in the history of the world." We suggest that you return for happy hour, order a mai tai, and judge for yourself.

Back outside, keep your ears peeled for the sound of the California Street cable car. It's the oldest of the surviving lines, having begun service April 10, 1878.

Continue on Mason to California Street. At the southeast corner of the Mason–California intersection stands the ❺ **InterContinental Mark Hopkins Hotel.** Mark Hopkins was among the Big Four railroad barons, and his mansion—which photos reveal to have been the hill's most extravagant—stood on this site. The mansion was a quake casualty, but the stone retaining wall survives. Note the way this building and the Brocklebank Apartments, a block away, complement each other. The main attraction at the Mark Hopkins is the ❻ **Top of the Mark,** a snazzy bar with 360-degree views, a martini menu that's several pages long, and jazz combos several nights a week.

The distinguished brownstone mansion across the street from the Fairmont belonged to James Flood, the shrewd saloon keeper who made his fortune on the Comstock Lode. Walk along California Street to get a good look at it. The 1906 quake and fire failed to bring the mansion down, but significant restoration was required; Willis Polk designed the additions. The Pacific Union Club, one of the city's most exclusive private clubs, has owned the house since 1906.

Make a left onto California Street. Beguiling ❼ **Huntington Park** shares the block with the Flood mansion and has a decidedly European flair. It's a good spot to claim a park bench and admire Grace Cathedral, across the street. The park's *Tortoise Fountain* and *Dancing Sprites* bronze sculptures are also worth looking at for half a minute or so.

Rather than head directly to Grace Cathedral, cross California Street. The Huntington Hotel, another of San Francisco's finest, stands on the southeast corner. From here, your eye may naturally drift over to the ❽ **Masonic Memorial Temple,** on the southwest corner. Don't fight that impulse. The building isn't exactly beautiful, but it is adorned by some impressive art, most notably the immense 45-by-48-foot "endomosaic" window in the lobby. Artist Emile Norman invented the endomosaic style, pressing crushed glass, sea shells, soil, and other materials between sheets of translucent plastic. The art is illuminated from behind by sunlight, giving it the vibrancy of a projected Kodachrome slide. After two years of working on it, Norman completed his endomosaic in 1957. It depicts Masonic history in California with typically mysterious symbols and a stark 1950s style. During business hours you can go inside for a closer look.

Now cross California Street and head back to the entrance of ➒ **Grace Cathedral** that faces Huntington Park. Before entering, pause to inspect the bronze doors, which are lovely copies of Lorenzo Ghiberti's *Doors of Paradise* in Florence, Italy. Tuck in your shirt and go inside. (The cathedral requests a $10 donation.) The immensely lofty cathedral was erected on the charred grounds of the mansion of Charles Crocker, a Big Four magnate. The cathedral was designed by Lewis P. Hobart, who studied at the École des Beaux-Arts in Paris. It was built not of stone but of formed concrete. Construction began not long after the '06 quake and was completed in 1964. Once you step inside, you will note the large labyrinth on the floor. By all means enjoy a walking meditation in the middle of your walking tour. The progressive church offers monthly candlelit labyrinth walks and weekly yoga on the labyrinth. There is another labyrinth outside. If you've got your smartphone and headphones on you, the amazingly thorough GraceGuide app provides a bounty of history on the church's past and present, complete with meditative music. Before departing, be sure to admire the elegant and awe-inspiring 25-foot-wide rose window, above the main entrance.

From here, emerge onto Taylor Street, return to Sacramento Street, and turn left for a look at some relatively modest but still eye-pleasing residential architecture. The bougainvillea-clad apartments at 1230 and 1242 Sacramento have an elegant, Belle Époque Parisian style. On the corner of Jones, at 1298 Sacramento St., the ➓ **Chambord Apartments** are well loved for their extravagant rounded balconies that call to mind Antoni Gaudí's ebullient style. Designed by architect James Dunn, the Chambord was one of the city's first luxury apartment buildings and is now a San Francisco Landmark.

Continuing down Sacramento, turn left when you reach Hyde Street. At the corner of California and Hyde, the ⑪ **Hyde Out** is the archetypal neighborhood dive bar: two floors of cheap drinks, dated jukebox tunes, and friendly locals. Heading down California, turn right at Polk Street, and halfway down the block you'll come to our final destination, the ⑫ **Swan Oyster Depot**. The doors have been open since 1912, when four Danish brothers set up shop and delivered seafood up and down the streets of San Francisco using a horse-drawn carriage. Under the purview of the Sancimino Family since 1946, the eatery still has just 18 seats available, and the lines invariably snake out the door for hours, but *Bon Appétit* magazine and hundreds of sated diners all agree that it's worth the wait for the freshest seafood in San Francisco, served with a heaping side of Old World charm. This section of Polk Street is called Polk Gulch, and it was the city's gay center in the 1950s and beyond, long before the Castro District became popular.

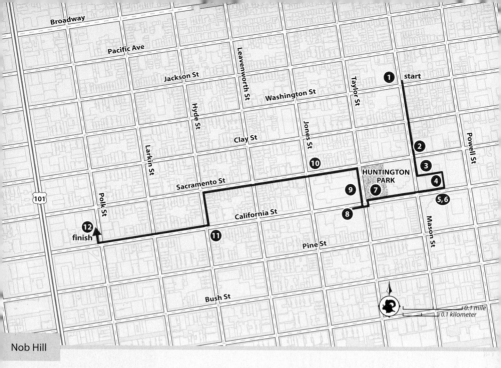

Nob Hill

Points of Interest

1 **Cable Car Museum** 1201 Mason St.; 415-474-1887, cablecarmuseum.org

2 **Brocklebank Apartments** 1000 Mason St.; 415-421-2200 (no website)

3 **The Fairmont** 950 Mason St.; 415-772-5000, fairmont.com/san-francisco

4 **Tonga Room and Hurricane Bar** 950 Mason St.; 415-772-5278, tongaroom.com

5 **InterContinental Mark Hopkins Hotel** 999 California St.; 415-392-3434, intercontinentalmarkhopkins.com

6 **Top of the Mark** 999 California St.; 415-616-6916, topofthemark.com

7 **Huntington Park** California and Taylor Sts.; 415-831-2700, sfrecpark.org/destination /collis-p-huntington-park

8 **Masonic Memorial Temple** 1111 California St.; 415-776-7457, sfmasonic.com

9 **Grace Cathedral** 1100 California St.; 415-749-6300, gracecathedral.org

10 **Chambord Apartments** 1298 Sacramento St. (no published phone number or website)

11 **Hyde Out** 1068 Hyde St.; 415-441-1914 (no website)

12 **Swan Oyster Depot** 1517 Polk St.; 415-673-1101, swanoysterdepot.us

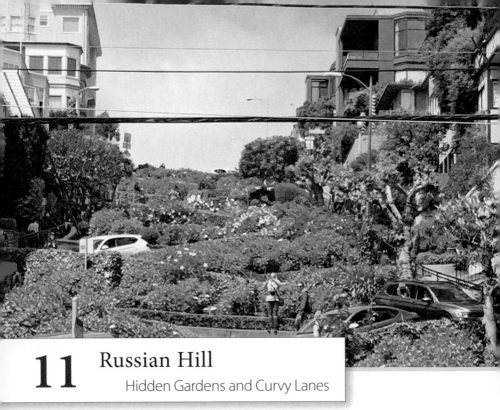

11 Russian Hill

Hidden Gardens and Curvy Lanes

Above: *The impeccably landscaped curves of Lombard Street never fail to draw a crowd.*

BOUNDARIES: Hyde St., Lombard St., Mason St., Vallejo St.
DISTANCE: 1.5 miles
DIFFICULTY: Strenuous (steep hills)
PARKING: Street parking is nearly impossible to find and is limited to 2 hours.
PUBLIC TRANSIT: The Hyde St. cable car stops at the starting point of this tour. The 41 and 45 Union
    buses stop at Hyde St. just a few blocks away.

Russian Hill is more hilly than it is Russian. The name comes from a small graveyard that once graced the top of the hill. Wooden crosses with dedications in Cyrillic lay over bodies assumed to be those of Russian sailors or fur trappers. Kids who played nearby dubbed the area Russian Hill. The cemetery was removed in the 1850s, but the name stuck, and the Russian government even installed a commemorative plaque.

This was once a bohemian enclave, and it retains much of its quirkiness—in large part due to the neighborhood's uncompromising topography. Russian Hill is not at all conducive to the grid system in which downtown San Francisco's streets are laid out, so some streets simply dead-end, giving way to narrow footpaths, secret gardens, and hidden stairwells. This did not stop San Franciscans from building their houses here, and today it seems the more inaccessible the house, the more desirable the property. Gardeners have made the most of the neighborhood's secluded pedestrian zones, and walkers are likely to marvel that such tranquility is to be found so near the dense heart of the city.

Walk Description

Begin at the corner of Hyde and Francisco Streets, where the ❶ **Norwegian Seamen's Church** commands a beautiful view of the bay. Originally conceived as a way for sailors to worship while in foreign ports, it also serves as a social and cultural meeting point. Services are conducted in Norwegian (and, once a month, there is a service in Swedish as well). If they're open, pop in for a fresh-baked waffle and cup of coffee. They have a small gift shop, where you can fill up on specialty Scandinavian packaged goods, baked pastries, and other sundries. Should you long to practice your Norwegian, this is certainly the place to do it. (Open Tuesday–Saturday, noon– 5 p.m.; Sunday,10 a.m.–2 p.m.)

Continue up Hyde Street to join the masses at the top of the curvy block of Lombard Street— commonly billed, with sideshow hyperbole, as the crookedest street in the world. Russian Hill's best-known landmark is a tidy, picture-perfect example of urban landscaping. Gardeners tend to yawn at the choice of planting, which looks like the work of a fussy old granny. Meanwhile, some locals argue that this isn't even the curviest street in the city, citing the sinuosity index. (The other candidate—Vermont Street between McKinley and 22nd Streets at the foot of Potrero Hill—has five full turns and two half turns crammed into a single city block, versus Lombard's eight turns, but they're steeper. The decision goes to Vermont Street, but Lombard is certainly more beautifully planted, and Potrero Hill residents are happy to keep the secret to themselves.) As you walk the curvy steps down, marvel over these facts: the hill has a 27-percent grade, the street originally ran straight down it, and the curves were introduced in 1922 to slow down cars and beautify the street. The postcards began to appear soon after that.

After negotiating that last curve, turn left onto Leavenworth Street and look for sweet little ❷ **Fay Park** on your right, replete with terraced gardens, ornamental trees, and gazebos. Donated by Mary Fay Berrigan upon the death of her husband, the Fay family first built a home on the site in 1869 (the current home is closed to the public). The carefully manicured garden was designed by lauded landscape architect Thomas Church, and there is a light fixture in the park that once served as a street lamp in Copenhagen, Denmark.

Turn right on Chestnut Street. The ❸ **San Francisco Art Institute** beckons. It's architecturally interesting, exhibiting the hallmarks of Spanish Revival, such as a tower and a courtyard, while being built almost entirely of formed concrete. But the real attraction here is the Diego Rivera Gallery, featuring a fresco by the master himself. Rivera painted it in 1931 and called it *The Making of a Fresco Showing a Building of a City*. You'll notice that Rivera painted himself into the scene. The gallery can be reached by walking through the courtyard and heading left. The institute's photography department, founded by Ansel Adams in 1945, was the first college program devoted to fine-art photography. Photographers Dorothea Lange, Imogen Cunningham, and Minor White all taught here, as did painters Clyfford Still and Robert Stackpole. Former students include painter Richard Diebenkorn, sculptor Sargent Johnson, photographer Annie Leibovitz, graffiti artist Barry McGee, and musicians Jerry Garcia and Courtney Love.

Continue down Chestnut Street to Columbus Avenue, the Main Street of North Beach. From the corner, you'll spot the marquee of ❹ **Bimbo's 365 Club,** one of the swankiest live music clubs in San Francisco. The name comes from the shortened *bambino,* which was the Italian nickname for club manager Agostino Giuntoli, and the 365 Market Street address, which was its first location in 1931. It was here that a young Rita Hayworth (then Margarita Cansino) danced in the club's chorus line. During its early speakeasy days, the club had a one-way mirror installed to evade police officers who might be searching for bootleg alcohol. At its present location since 1951, Bimbo's 365 has lured guests for decades with Dolphina, the miniature woman who swims for hours in a fishbowl behind the bar, clad only in her birthday suit. Angled mirrors and a periscope allowed burlesque dancers in a hidden room on a rotating platform to appear only 6 inches tall. Dolphina used to perform nightly, although now it's just on special occasions. But really any night is a special occasion at this neighborhood mainstay that still attracts top-name performers, mermaid or no.

From this corner follow Taylor Street uphill for several blocks. Stay on the right side of the street. After crossing Union Street, be on the lookout for a wooden staircase heading skywards from the sidewalk. This is not a private entrance—it is ❺ **Macondray Lane,** an actual city street (you'll spot the street sign) that inspired author Armistead Maupin's Barbary Lane in *Tales of the City*. Climb on up and stroll the deeply shaded footpath—which switches from wood steps to rough-cut stone to brick—and you'll see why this is one of the least urban streets in the city. It's lined on one side with nondescript Victorian houses, and local gardeners have turned some of the terraced spaces here into jungles of bamboo, tree ferns, and ponds. Ina Coolbrith, a poet and literary socialite, hosted her legendary salon at 15 Macondray Lane during the early 20th century. She later had a park named for her; we'll visit it a bit later.

Follow Macondray past Jones Street to Leavenworth and turn right. Head left on Union and cross the street at Hyde to reach the original ❻ **Swensen's** ice cream parlor, established in 1948 by Earle Swensen, who learned the craft of making ice cream while working on a Navy ship during World War II. (While he developed more than 150 flavors, he always claimed vanilla was his favorite.) Swensen sold the franchising rights in the 1970s, but he kept sole ownership of the flagship San Francisco store and operated it until shortly before his death in 1994 at age 83. Longtime residents remember Earle himself handing out cones to trick-or-treaters on Halloween. Surely you've earned a scoop or two with all this walking! Either way, this commercial stretch of Hyde has all sorts of wine bars, taco bars, coffee shops, pizza joints, and sushi spots to fill most any culinary craving.

Heading left on Hyde Street, make a slight right detour on Russell to see the small shingled home at 29 Russell St. This is the former ❼ **home of Neal and Carolyn Cassady**, where Jack Kerouac

Pedestrian-only Macondray Lane wends past secret gardens and Victorian homes.

famously holed up in the attic for six months to work on *On the Road*. Neal Cassady was the real-life inspiration for Dean Moriarty, best friend of the novel's protagonist, Sal Paradise. A lover to both men and a muse of the Beat Generation, Carolyn Cassady took an iconic photo of Kerouac and Cassady with their arms around each other, leaning against the building across the street.

Return to Hyde and turn left at Green Street. The block after you cross Leavenworth is historic, with 12 buildings listed on the National Register. The charming Swiss chalet at 1088 Green was originally a firehouse—Engine House No. 31, built in 1907. Nearly every house on the south side of the street predates the 1906 earthquake and fire. The obvious standout is number 1067, the Feusier Octagon House. Built in 1857–59, this was one of many eight-sided homes built in San Francisco (another can be seen on the Marina and Cow Hollow Walk; see Walk 15, page 104). Orson S. Fowler, a phrenologist, developed the idea of octagon houses, saying they let in more light and offered improved ventilation. The mansard roof and dormers were added in the 1880s. The house at 1055 Green was built around 1866. It was originally an unassuming Italianate house, but in 1915 it was completely remodeled by Julia Morgan, who turned it into a Beaux Arts villa with stucco siding and a beautiful cast-iron balcony. Turn right at Jones Street. Two ramps to your left, link Jones to a short block of Vallejo Street, adding to the secluded feel of this charmed cul-de-sac. The ramps, designed by Willis Polk in 1914, were commissioned not by the city but by a wealthy resident of the block. Polk also designed the lovely shingle-sided Craftsman house at 1015–19 Vallejo St. For a good vantage of it step into the lawn at the end of the street. From this point, you'll also get a fine view of North Beach far below.

Continue down the Vallejo Street steps to Taylor Street, noting that photographer Dorothea Lange lived in an apartment at No. 1637 for several years during the late 1920s and early '30s. Cross Taylor and enter Ina Coolbrith Park, which, like the steps you've just descended, stands in for what would have been Vallejo Street if the hill hadn't been so steep. A plaque on a rock to the left of the park's entrance tells the story of Coolbrith, who was named California's first poet laureate but is largely forgotten by today's literati (she is better remembered in Oakland, where she served as the city's first librarian). Meander down the steps, admiring the varying view as you lose altitude. At the bottom, you'll find yourself just a couple of blocks from the heart of North Beach—and at the end of this tour.

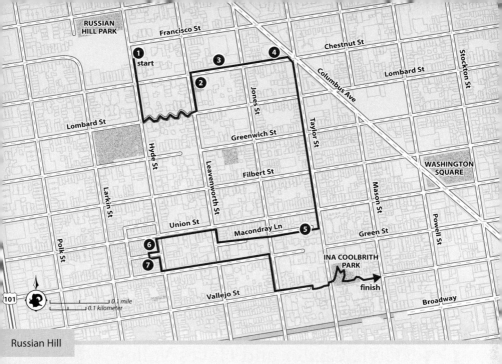

Points of Interest

1. **Norwegian Seamen's Church** 2454 Hyde St.; 415-775-6566, sjomannskirken.no

2. **Fay Park** 2366 Leavenworth St.; 415-831-2700, sfrecpark.org/destination/fay-park

3. **San Francisco Art Institute** 800 Chestnut St.; 415-771-7020, sfai.edu

4. **Bimbo's 365 Club** 1025 Columbus Ave.; 415-474-0365, bimbos365club.com

5. **Macondray Lane** Taylor St. and Macondray Ln.

6. **Swensen's** 1999 Hyde St.; 415-775-6818, swensensicecream.com

7. **Neal and Carolyn Cassady Home (former)** 29 Russell St. (private residence)

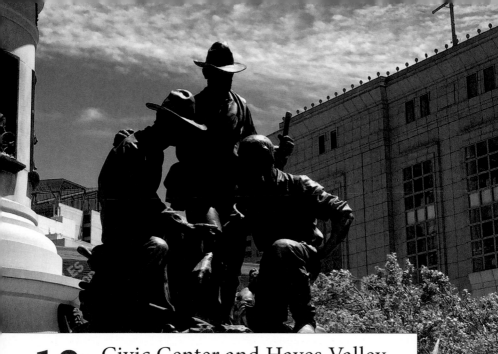

12 Civic Center and Hayes Valley
Cathedrals of Culture and Urban Newcomers

Above: *This trio of miners is part of the Pioneer Monument, sculptor Frank Happersberger's tribute to San Francisco's gold rush past.*

BOUNDARIES: Market St., Leavenworth St., McAllister St., Van Ness Ave.
DISTANCE: 1.5 miles
DIFFICULTY: Easy
PARKING: There is an underground parking lot beneath Civic Center Plaza.
PUBLIC TRANSIT: Civic Center BART station; F streetcars; 5, 6, 9, 21, 31, and 71 Muni buses

San Francisco's Civic Center is one of the most elegant and cohesively planned such complexes in the United States. Monumental Beaux Arts structures went up after the 1906 earthquake, making the area impressive but cold on the surface. Some of the buildings house offices of government, while others are pillars of high culture that contribute much-needed warmth to the neighborhood. The opera, the symphony, the Main Library, and the Asian Art Museum all cluster around City Hall, which itself is one of the country's finest government buildings. The area is always busy, especially on weekdays when local, state, and federal workers file in and out of the buildings. On Wednesday and Sunday the farmers' market, going strong since 1981, adds even more life and diversity to the area, making these days ideal for a trek through the neighborhood. Adding to the cultural heavyweights, the newly minted SF Jazz Center, the reborn Nourse Theater, and neighboring Hayes Valley, rife with boutiques and eateries, bring a contemporary twist to the classic arts scene.

Walk Description

Start at ❶ **United Nations Plaza,** at the corner of Market and Leavenworth. Designed by Lawrence Halprin in the mid-1970s and named in commemoration of the 1945 signing of the United Nations Charter near here (see Herbst Theater, page 83), the plaza is a somewhat awkward open space that on most days merely serves as a shortcut from Market Street to the library and City Hall. The lively and upbeat Heart of the City Farmers' Market changes that on Wednesday and Sunday, when vendors from Northern California farms set up stalls overflowing with produce, nuts, seafood, baked goods, and flowers. An arts collaboration with the Exploratorium museum has also breathed life into the walkway, as rotating exhibits provide a distraction from the seagulls and drifters who congregate around the plaza's fountain. From anywhere in the plaza, you can turn around and see Rigo's *Truth* mural (2002) emblazoned on the top floors of a Market Street building.

Pass through the plaza and cross Hyde Street. Head west, up Fulton Street, which separates the Main Library (to the left) and the ❷ **Asian Art Museum** (to the right). In the middle of the street stands the intriguing Pioneer Monument, commissioned by millionaire James Lick, who made his fortune by playing the real estate game in the gold rush city. Lick hired sculptor Frank Happersberger to create a tribute to the argonauts of that era. Thus, we have this large monument with bronze miners panning for gold beneath the bronze figure of the Roman goddess Minerva, standing on what appears to be a huge granite fire plug.

The Asian Art Museum, home to one of the most comprehensive Asian art collections in the world, occupies the former Main Library, a Beaux Arts structure built in 1917. When the library moved into its current home across the street, the old library building was completely gutted and remodeled to accommodate the immense holdings of the Asian Art Museum, which had outgrown its space in Golden Gate Park. The core of the collection was donated to the museum by Avery Brundage, the Chicago developer who also served as president of the International Olympic Committee for two decades. Brundage's huge bequest was the impetus for the founding of the museum and still composes nearly half the collection. Religious, military, and artistic objects span the entire region, from the Philippines to Iran, and some date back 6,000 years. The architecture is luxurious inside and out, and the collection and second-floor tearoom exhibit are well worth the $15 general admission price.

Retrace your steps and cross Fulton Street to the ❸ **Main Library,** which opened in 1995 to mostly positive reviews. Enter the building on the Larkin Street side, head down the stairs, and take an elevator to the fifth floor. From here, you can look down the building's central atrium, or climb to the top floor via Alice Aycock's Seussian spiral staircase, which ascends toward a fetching geometric glass ceiling. The library has many reading and research rooms that are worth perusing, including special collections with materials relating to the varied ethnic and cultural groups of San Francisco. The top floor is occupied by the excellent San Francisco History Center, which always has an informative exhibit of photos, newspaper clippings, and other items from its collection. Other thoughtful and interesting exhibits, some culled from the History Center collection, are in the Jewett Gallery, on the basement level of the library.

The gleaming dome of City Hall

Cross Larkin and walk through the middle of Civic Center Plaza toward the front entrance of ❹ **City Hall.** The plaza is home to two playground structures, as well as a fair number of homeless sunbathers. Sometimes you'll catch a large group of office workers participating in an organized exercise routine.

On the left side of City Hall, a statue of Abraham Lincoln appears ready to converse with anyone walking by. Head up the steps and enter City Hall, which is open to anyone not brandishing a firearm. The building has had a tumultuous past. Its predecessor, which once stood where the Asian Art Museum is now, took two decades to build, and soon after its completion it crumbled to the ground in the initial temblor of 1906, shoddy construction having apparently resulted in a flimsy structure. All that remains is the head of the *Goddess of Progress* statue that stood atop the old City Hall dome (you'll see her in the south-wing exhibit). The current Beaux Arts City Hall, completed in 1915 and designed by the firm of Bakewell and Brown, has much to admire. The dome, lovingly restored during Mayor Willie Brown's tenure, is taller than the US Capitol dome in Washington, DC. Wander the main floor to gaze up at the magnificent rotunda and at the staircase spilling down like the train of a bridal gown.

Tragedy came to City Hall in 1978, when then-Mayor George Moscone and Harvey Milk, the first openly gay SF supervisor (city councilor), were shot to death in their offices by former supervisor Dan White. White's lawyers persuaded a jury that he was mentally unstable owing in part to a junk food diet (the now-infamous "Twinkie defense"), and on the night that he was convicted of manslaughter rather

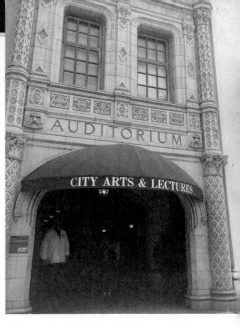

A former high school auditorium, the Spanish Revival–style Nourse Theater now hosts arts programming.

than murder, outraged citizens rioted in front of City Hall—an event remembered as White Night. On a lighter note, Marilyn Monroe and Joe DiMaggio were married in a civil ceremony here in 1954. Fifty years later, so were some 4,000 same-sex couples in a remarkable display of civil disobedience. Newly elected mayor Gavin Newsom defied state law by permitting the weddings, and he even presided over some of them. Gay brides and grooms lined out the doors of city hall for weeks with an armada of media trucks clogging up traffic, creating a street-party atmosphere. Newsom was soon stopped and the state revoked the unions, only to reverse its stance a few years later.

After looking around City Hall, exit through the back on the Van Ness Avenue side. Two nearly identical landmark buildings share the block across the street. On the right (north) side is the ❺ **War Memorial Veterans Building,** also designed by Bakewell and Brown and completed in 1932. Inside, the Herbst Theater is an intimate performance hall that gained renown in June 1945 when the United Nations Charter was signed in a ceremony on its stage. Off the front lobby, the ❻ **San Francisco Arts Commission Gallery** is a never-dull exhibition space for contemporary artists. Admission is free, so definitely take a look.

From Veterans Hall, mosey on over to the ❼ **War Memorial Opera House.** The two buildings, which commemorate the soldiers who fought in World War I, were built at the same time; Arthur

Linden Street is rife with vibrant street art, such as this mural by Sam Flores.

Brown Jr. (of Bakewell and Brown) designed the Opera House, and G. Albert Lansburgh designed its elegant interior. The San Francisco Opera was founded in 1923, and the opening night of each opera season is a big event among opera aficionados and socialites. The San Francisco Ballet also performs here, and on Christmas Eve in 1944 it hosted the American premiere of *The Nutcracker*, a still-beloved holiday tradition.

At Grove Street, turn left to admire **8 Louise M. Davies Symphony Hall,** a modern structure that looks its best on performance nights, when its curved glass facade is ablaze with warm light. The hall was built in 1980 and has housed the city's lauded symphony ever since. Turn left on Gough Street to enter the lively Hayes Valley art gallery and restaurant corridor. One of the mainstays of the neighborhood, **9 Absinthe Brasserie and Bar** is on the corner of Hayes and Gough Streets. It's a stylish re-creation of a Belle Époque brasserie where you can slurp raw oysters or eat traditional French fare.

Turn right at Hayes Street to meander a stylish block of art galleries, high-end boutiques, and trendy watering holes. It's hard to believe that in the 1980s this was considered one of the seediest parts of the city. After the 1989 Loma Prieta earthquake, the elevated freeway that used to shadow Hayes Valley was damaged and eventually removed amid the rallying cry of local activists, and the neighborhood has been gentrifying ever since. At Octavia, turn left and enjoy ❿ **Patricia's Green,** a beautiful open space featuring rotating art exhibits and playground structures. The park is named for Patricia Walkup, who spent decades working to curb crime in the community and was one of the most vocal champions in keeping the freeway from being rebuilt. If it's sunny out, there's no better patio to alight onto than that of the charming ⓫ **Biergarten,** across the street from Patricia's Green. You can also grab a snack from one of the many shipping containers–turned–snack shacks that overlook the green space.

To continue our walk, head east on narrow Linden Street, admiring the arty bars, cafés, and colorful murals that line the path. Turn right on Gough and left on Fell to make your way to the glass-enclosed ⓬ **SF Jazz Center,** at the corner of Franklin Street. Christened in 2013, the $64 million building was designed by Mark Cavagnero and is billed as the first freestanding building dedicated to jazz performances and education in the country. Custom-designed acoustics and decades-long planning hope to ensure that this jewel box brings jazz back to the forefront of San Francisco's musical scene.

Charles Gadeken's soaring LED sculpture, *Squared,* in Patricia's Green

As you continue left on Franklin, the Spanish Revival–style ⓭ **Nourse Theater** takes up the block where Hayes meets Franklin. Originally built as an auditorium for the High School of Commerce, its storied walls have since seen everything from Allen Ginsberg and Lawrence Ferlinghetti reading poetry to Jim Morrison performing with an experimental-theater company to a historic courtroom case on asbestos. After decades of gathering dust as a storage facility for the public school system, City Arts & Lectures, a venerable live-conversation and arts-programming series, sank considerable cash into restoring the theater to its formal glory, staying true to its architectural highlights and details. The Nourse opened its doors again in 2013. On the other side of Franklin and Hayes, ⓮ **The Grove** is a fun casual eatery that's family owned and operated.

Outdoor eateries like the sun-drenched Biergarten lure hungry theatergoers to Hayes Valley.

Continuing past the Nourse awning on Hayes Street, turn left on Van Ness Avenue, and then head right on Grove Street. Keep your eyes peeled for the tiny ⑮ **Please Touch Community Garden,** which occupies a once-abandoned lot between Van Ness and Polk Street. Artist GK Callahan partnered with the Lighthouse for the Blind and Visually Impaired to create a community space accessible to all, including a scented corner for those with visual impairments. It's currently open to the public only on Wednesdays, but you can peek through the fence to watch the greenery grow.

As you cross Polk Street, the ⑯ **Bill Graham Civic Auditorium** faces Civic Center Plaza. Named for the legendary rock and roll impresario Bill Graham, who based his operations in San Francisco, the auditorium is frequently the sight of performances by major rock artists. On the sidewalk in front of the building, you'll stroll over a Walk of Fame embedded with plaques honoring local music figures.

Points of Interest

① **United Nations Plaza** Market and Hyde Sts.; 415-831-5500, sfrecpark.org/reservablefacility/united-nations-plaza

② **Asian Art Museum** 200 Larkin St.; 415-581-3500, asianart.org

③ **Main Library** 100 Larkin St.; 415-557-4400, sfpl.org

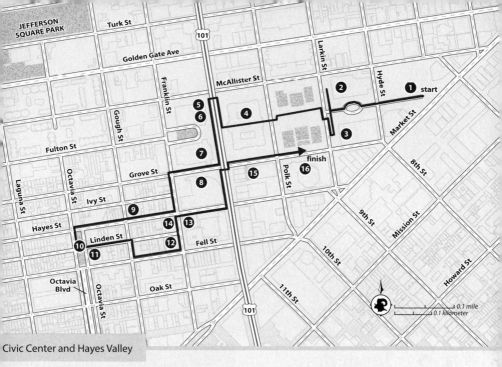

Civic Center and Hayes Valley

④ **City Hall** 1 Dr. Carlton B. Goodlett Plaza; 415- 554-4000, sfgov.org/cityhall

⑤ **War Memorial Veterans Building/Herbst Theater** 401 Van Ness Ave.; 415-621-6600, sfwmpac.org

⑥ **San Francisco Arts Commission Gallery** 401 Van Ness Ave.; 415-554-6080, sfartscommission.org

⑦ **War Memorial Opera House** 301 Van Ness Ave.; 415-861-5600, sfballet.org/visit/opera-house

⑧ **Louise M. Davies Symphony Hall** 201 Van Ness Ave.; 415-864-6000, sfsymphony.org

⑨ **Absinthe Brasserie and Bar** 398 Hayes St.; 415-551-1590, absinthe.com

⑩ **Patricia's Green** Fell St. and Octavia Blvd.; 415-274-0291, sfrecpark.org/destination /patricias-green-in-hayes-valley

⑪ **Biergarten** 424 Octavia Blvd.; 415-252-9289, biergartensf.com

⑫ **SF Jazz Center** 201 Franklin St.; 866-920-5299, sfjazz.org

⑬ **Nourse Theater** 275 Hayes St.; 415-392-4400, cityarts.net/nourse

⑭ **The Grove** 301 Hayes St.; 415-624-3953, thegrovesf.com

⑮ **Please Touch Community Garden** 165 Grove St.; 707-975-6409, pleasetouchgarden.org

⑯ **Bill Graham Civic Auditorium** 99 Grove St.; 415-624-8900, billgrahamcivic.com

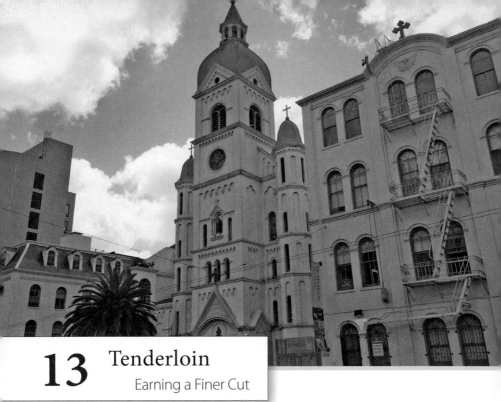

13   Tenderloin
Earning a Finer Cut

Above: St. Boniface Catholic Church is a refuge for Tenderloin denizens and visitors alike.

BOUNDARIES: Market St., Taylor St., Post St., Polk St.
DISTANCE: 2 miles
DIFFICULTY: Easy
PARKING: Street parking is metered and not necessarily safe. There's a lot next to Original Joe's (corner of Taylor and Turk) and another at 550 O'Farrell St.
PUBLIC TRANSIT: Civic Center BART station; all Market St. buses and streetcars

Squeezed between Union Square and Civic Center, the Tenderloin has long been a marginalized part of town: block after block of skid rows lined mostly with residential hotels, rescue missions, and dive bars. The name dates back to the 1800s, when beat cops could afford better cuts of steak working rough districts thanks to the bribes passed by business owners who wanted increased police protection. Day and night, the sidewalks are crowded with sidewalk sleepers and the mentally ill, as well as a retinue of hustlers and drug dealers—all in all, an uncomfortable reminder that the American Dream doesn't quite pan out for everybody. But beneath the grime is a real sense of community. Many of the people aren't actually homeless but rather live in tiny SRO (single room occupancy) units and treat the sidewalks like their living room. And while drug use is up, gunshots are down.

It's admittedly not a very pretty or even pleasant place, but the Tenderloin is an incredibly interesting part of town that has intriguing history, good Vietnamese restaurants, inviting drinking establishments, and buildings that intimate compelling stories—stories perhaps in the Dashiell Hammett vein, for it was here that the great crime writer penned his best works. The gay community has had a presence here for decades. Immigrants and families have settled and started small businesses here, and a growing number of techies favor the neighborhood's urban edge. We'd like to introduce you to the rich history of the area, as well as some of the people making a real difference in people's lives here. There is inspiration and hope amid the grit, along with art and stories to buoy your spirit.

Walk Description

We'll start from United Nations Plaza on Market Street and head up Leavenworth into the 'Loin. On the corner of Golden Gate Avenue and Leavenworth, duck into King Carl's Emporium, the pirate-supply storefront for ❶ **826 Valencia Tenderloin Center,** a nonprofit dedicated to helping kids with their writing skills via academic tutoring, writing workshops, and more. A much-needed resource given that the Tenderloin is home to the city's largest concentration of children, 826 makes learning (and avoiding scurvy) good fun. Across the street you'll spot ❷ **St. Boniface Catholic Church,** built in 1906. Its German Romanesque style is a reflection of the immigrant parishioners of that time. Today St. Boniface, while still quite beautiful, is better known for opening its doors each weekday morning as a daytime refuge for the homeless, hundreds of whom snooze in the pews from 6:30 a.m. to 2 p.m. Daily Masses, funerals, and even weddings take place in the church to the accompaniment of a quiet chorus of snores. Known in the neighborhood as a place of "sacred sleep," The Gubbio Project, which coordinates the effort, emphasizes that "it also sends a message to those attending Mass that the community includes the tired, the poor, those with mental health issues, and those who are wet, cold, and dirty." It is a moving experience to witness, and you are welcome to observe; Gubbio Project volunteers are in the back of the church and gratefully receive donations of clean socks and toiletries. Sunday Mass always livens the place up, and when the weather is nice, parishioners sell homemade tamales in the church's courtyard.

Past St. Boniface, still heading east on Golden Gate Avenue, ropes along the sidewalk lead around the corner to ❸ **St. Anthony's Dining Room,** where hot meals have been ladled out to the needy since 1950. When they first opened their doors, they served 400 meals daily; today, they provide 2,400 meals each and every day to the hungry. The St. Anthony Foundation (SAF) also provides clothing, housing, and medical care in a determined effort to "put ourselves out of business," as foundation literature puts it.

On the corner of Jones, stop to admire artist Mona Caron's ❹ *Windows into the Tenderloin,* a mural honoring the neighborhood and its history as it depicts the street's past, present, and utopian green future. In it, you'll see buildings demolished long ago drifting into the sky like ghostly balloons and hundreds of painted figures based on local residents. Don't be deterred by people sitting on the sidewalk in front of the mural—they don't mind if you want a closer view, as the art is a celebration of their community.

Turn left on Jones and right on Turk to reach ❺ **Aunt Charlie's Lounge,** the district's oldest gay bar, which is short on space but long on personality. You'll note that this stretch of Turk is also signposted VICKI MAR LANE, a pun honoring Miss Vicki Marlane ("The Lady with the Liquid Spine"), a pioneering drag queen who was a fixture at Aunt Charlie's. The beloved Marlane—acknowledged

A divey gay bar and drag venue, Aunt Charlie's Lounge has been a Tenderloin fixture since 1987.

as one of the oldest working drag entertainers in the United States before her death in 2011, at age 76—was a mentor to other performers and transgender youth, as well as the subject of an award-winning documentary by filmmaker Michelle Lawler. Aunt Charlie's continues to host its Hot Boxxx Girls drag revue every Friday and Saturday night, and you can glimpse a large portrait of Marlane toward the end of the bar. Leaving Aunt Charlie's, turn left on Taylor and go two blocks to reach **❻ Glide Memorial United Methodist Church.** This congregation calls itself "radically inclusive," and indeed the church has been at the rallying point of counterculture movements since the 1960s. Under the direction of the legendary Rev. Cecil Williams, Glide became the largest provider of social services in the city, providing food, healthcare, spiritual guidance, after-school care, and sanctuary. Not to be missed are their jubilant Sunday celebrations featuring the Glide Ensemble and Change Band, bursting with music, dancing, and inspiration designed to lift even the darkest of spirits.

Turn left on Ellis Street, left again on Jones, and right on Eddy Street to stand outside the historic **❼ Cadillac Hotel.** Built in 1907, the Cadillac was a tony hotel catering to wealthy clientele at its inception, but this is not what gives us reason to pause. In 1924, Billy Newman leased the hotel ballroom and converted it into a boxing ring. And not just any boxing ring: many of boxing's greatest legends graced Newman's Gym, including George Foreman, Sonny Liston, and a young Cassius Clay; Miles Davis was also known to drop by and spar when he was in town. And in 1961, Jerry Garcia lived here long before he formed the Grateful Dead. In 2015, the small but mighty **❽ Tenderloin Museum** took up shop next door on the corner of Leavenworth and Eddy. Dedicated to helping visitors understand the rich history of this maligned neighborhood, $10 buys you access to thorough educational, photographic, and artistic displays that celebrate the Tenderloin's past and present. They also offer walking tours led by Tenderloin residents for an additional fee.

Turn right on Leavenworth and make a left on Ellis to find the red gates that lead you unexpectedly to **❾ Tenderloin National Forest,** a somewhat tongue-in-cheek designation for a rather sweet green space amid the urban blight. Formerly known as Cohen Alley, the space was a literal dumping ground until a group of artists from the nonprofit Luggage Store Gallery took matters into their hands. The first redwood tree was planted in 2001, and the park now boasts a wood-burning oven, a mural by artist Rigo, and dozens of mature trees and plants.

After your time in the forest, retrace your steps to Leavenworth and turn right on Eddy Street. In a few paces, you'll pass the easy-to-miss **❿ Onsen Bathhouse and Restaurant.** A sign of a changing neighborhood, Onsen is a repurposed auto body shop–turned–Japanese bathhouse and tearoom. Tiny, serene, and artful, it's a lovely place to take a break from the undeniable grit of the Tenderloin. Turn left on Hyde and walk a block to reach Turk–Hyde Mini Park, a rare public space in the Tenderloin, filling a lot where an apartment building once stood. Also on the

Turk–Hyde corner, a vacant parking lot is a poor substitute for the legendary Blackhawk nightclub, which once occupied the site. On this spot, in April 1961, Miles Davis's quintet recorded the celebrated live album *In Person Friday and Saturday Nights at the Blackhawk, San Francisco*. (It's still available in a four-disc box set.)

Turn right on Turk, and at the corner of Larkin pause to look up and read the latest quotable quote on the marquee above ⑪ **Kahn and Keville** tire shop, a witty fixture since the 1950s. Herb Caen, legendary San Francisco columnist, once referred to it as the "world's biggest fortune cookie," and it was originally the work of co-owner Hugh Keville, a World War I vet who kept inspirational quotes in a notebook to lift his spirits. (An example from 2014: "We would like to welcome Twitter to the neighborhood, but we have too many characters.") The shop has changed hands since Keville's passing, but each owner has continued with the tradition, much to locals' delight. Turn right on Larkin and then left on Eddy Street, and you'll soon spot the ⑫ **Phoenix Hotel.** It's a classic mid-20th-century motel, with parking, two levels of rooms, and a kidney-shaped pool—but over the past two decades it's become much more than that. It's become the de rigueur crash pad for rock stars and younger movie stars to alight when they're in San Francisco. Nirvana, Pearl Jam, Norah Jones, Debbie Harry, David Bowie, The Red Hot Chili Peppers, and countless others have parted the sheets here. The sleek attached bar and restaurant, Chambers, is an homage to vinyl and the hipsters who still collect it.

Directly across the street from the Phoenix, the somewhat drab apartment building at 620 Eddy was the home of author Dashiell Hammett, who lived here with his wife and two daughters from 1921 until 1926. Hammett was largely unknown at the time, but he published many of his Continental Op stories, about an unnamed gumshoe, while living here. (We'll see Hammett's next home in just a few blocks.)

Rather than heading any farther up Eddy, turn right on Larkin Street and pass through the portals to Little Saigon, a two-block concentration of Southeast Asian restaurants and shops that, for many, is the Tenderloin's only allure. ⑬ **Saigon Sandwich** (you need to backtrack half a block) is highly regarded for its banh mi sandwiches, and people flock to ⑭ **Pho 2000** for its namesake dish. That said, plenty of other intriguing holes-in-the-wall serve inexpensive noodles and sandwiches.

Turn left on Ellis Street. If you weren't in the mood for Vietnamese, you can belly up to a plate of ribs, a beer, and a down-home welcome at ⑮ **Rusty's Southern.** In addition to serving award-winning cuisine, Rusty's is committed to giving back to the neighborhood, collaborating with its neighbor, City Hope, a nonprofit that helps provide housing for those transitioning from jail or recovering from addiction. Turning right on Polk Street, we enter Polk Gulch, world renowned for the gay scene that formed here during the 1970s. (Polk Gulch was the decidedly less-refined

A dragon marks the entrance to Little Saigon, home to numerous Vietnamese restaurants and shops.

flip side of the Castro District.) At Olive Alley, a huge whale mural comes into view. It tattoos the side of the ⑯ **Mitchell Brothers O'Farrell Theatre,** a true neighborhood landmark that opened in 1969. Here, Artie and Jim Mitchell screened the low-budget porn films they made, including such X-rated classics as *Behind the Green Door,* starring the late Marilyn Chambers. The Mitchell Brothers' empire grew to include 11 theaters throughout California. In 1991 Jim shot and killed Artie, copped a manslaughter conviction, and served six years in jail. The theater subsequently became a strip club with the slogan "Where the Wild Girls Are." A couple of doors down, the ⑰ **Great American Music Hall** is a former bordello that's surprisingly posh inside. It's an excellent live-music venue that books touring acts several nights a week.

Continue on Polk and turn right at Geary Street. You might be tempted to stop for a pint of Fullers or a dram of Laphroaig at ⑱ **Edinburgh Castle,** but the huge old pub is worth a visit not just for its selection of spirits but also its cultural contribution to the neighborhood and the city at large. Manager Alan Black, a man with an admirable fondness for working-class literature, has turned the pub's upstairs room into a theater where plays, live music, and readings are performed; Black and his partners also run a publishing house. Irvine Welsh, author of *Trainspotting,* has made several appearances at the pub, where he has read from his work and been guest of honor at a stage adaptation of *Trainspotting* (the novel was also made into an acclaimed movie in 1996). Welsh took a liking to San Francisco and moved to the city from his native Scotland in 2003 (he now lives in Chicago).

Continue on Geary, noting some of the historic old dives, such as the ❿ **Ha-Ra Club,** which opened way back in 1947. The next couple of blocks of Geary are transitional. At Hyde Street, turn left and then pause at the corner of Post. The apartment building at ⓴ **891 Post** was home to Dashiell Hammett at least from late 1927 through the end of 1928. He may have lived here even longer, as a plaque on the side of the building suggests. It is very likely that Hammett wrote *Red Harvest* and *Dain Curse* while living here, and he probably drafted *The Maltese Falcon* in the apartment as well. Literary sleuths like Don Herron, reading *Falcon* very closely, have deduced that Sam Spade's apartment must have been in this building.

At the other end of this block, ㉑ **Kayo Books** sells old paperback mysteries and pulp fiction from the 1950s and '60s—it's a fun little shop and a true homage to the neighborhood's history and culture. It's open by appointment only, but if you knock and they're there, they'll happily let you in to browse.

Make a right at Leavenworth Street, then turn left on Geary for a look at the fantastic ㉒ **Alcazar Theatre.** Built for the Shriners in 1917 and designed by T. Patterson Ross (himself a Shriner), the theater is meant to evoke Byzantine grandeur with intricate archways clad in ornate tiles. You'll notice some familiar motifs: above a second-story window on the far right, look for a Shriner fez.

From here, head on down Geary to Union Square, or return to Leavenworth to make your way back to UN Plaza.

Points of Interest

❶ **826 Valencia Tenderloin Center** 180 Golden Gate Ave.; 415-642-5905, 826valencia.org

❷ **St. Boniface Catholic Church/The Gubbio Project** 133 Golden Gate Ave.; 415-863-7515, stbonifacesf.org, thegubbioproject.org

❸ **St. Anthony's Dining Room** 121 Golden Gate Ave.; 415-241-2600, stanthonysf.org

❹ *Windows into the Tenderloin* Mural Jones St. and Golden Gate Ave.; monacaron.com/murals /windows-tenderloin

❺ **Aunt Charlie's Lounge** 133 Turk St.; 415-441-2922, auntcharlieslounge.com

❻ **Glide Memorial United Methodist Church** 330 Ellis St.; 415-674-6000, glide.org

❼ **Cadillac Hotel** 380 Eddy St.; 415-673-7223, cadillachotel.org

8 **Tenderloin Museum** 398 Eddy St.; 415-351-1912, tenderloinmuseum.org

9 **Tenderloin National Forest** Cohen Alley and Ellis St.; 415-255-5971, luggagestoregallery.org/tnf

10 **Onsen Bathhouse and Restaurant** 466 Eddy St.; 415-441-4987, onsensf.com

11 **Kahn and Keville** 500 Turk St.; 415-673-0200, kk1912.com

12 **Phoenix Hotel/Chambers** 601 Eddy St.; 415-776-1380, phoenixsf.com

13 **Saigon Sandwich** 560 Larkin St.; 415-474-5698, facebook.com/saigonsandwich

14 **Pho 2000** 637 Larkin St.; 415-474-1188, pho2000sf.com

15 **Rusty's Southern** 750 Ellis St.; 415-638-6974, rustyssf.com

16 **Mitchell Brothers O'Farrell Theatre** 895 O'Farrell St.; 415-441-1930, ofarrell.com

17 **Great American Music Hall** 859 O'Farrell St.; 415-885-0750, slimspresents.com

18 **Edinburgh Castle** 950 Geary St.; 415-885-4074, tinyurl.com/thecastlesf

19 **Ha-Ra Club** 875 Geary St.; 415-673-3148, harasf.com

20 **891 Post** 891 Post St.; 415-673-1608, tinyurl.com/891postsf

21 **Kayo Books** 814 Post St.; 415-749-0554, kayobooks.com

22 **Alcazar Theatre** 650 Geary St.; 415-441-6655, goldstar.com/venues/san-francisco-ca/alcazar-theatre

14 Fisherman's Wharf

From Crab Traps to Tourist Traps:
Maritime History Along the Waterfront

Above: *Can you smell the salt air and hear the seagulls? You're in the right place.*

BOUNDARIES: Beach St., Jefferson St., Grant Ave., Aquatic Park
DISTANCE: 3 miles
DIFFICULTY: Easy
PARKING: Off-street parking is available at Anchorage Square, corner of Leavenworth and Beach
   Sts. Most street parking is metered 7 days a week. On side streets south of Bay St. you might find
   unmetered street parking, limited to 2 hours for nonresidents (on Sunday you can park for an
   unlimited time in these zones).
PUBLIC TRANSIT: Powell–Mason cable car; F streetcar; 47 Muni bus

Most San Franciscans roll their eyes at the thought of walking through Fisherman's Wharf, but this
is because they equate it with mass-produced T-shirts, overpriced waffle cones, and tacky tourist
schlock. And while all of this does exist along the quay, you'll also find a rich history of Italian and

Chinese immigrants, a still-vibrant fishing trade, fascinating museums, and some unexpected surprises lurking beneath the surface. From penny arcades to submarines to barking seals—not to mention the gorgeous views of the Golden Gate Bridge and Alcatraz—the area is not without merit if you're willing to look for the worthwhile sights. Further, to understand San Francisco is to understand how Fisherman's Wharf came to be in the first place. So while street hawkers pitching soup in a bread bowl and wax museums lend an air of inauthenticity, there's actually quite a bit of genuine San Francisco hiding in plain sight here.

Walk Description

Start at ❶ **Longshoremen's Hall,** a homely but historical structure at the corner of Mason and Beach Streets. It houses the headquarters of the International Longshoremen's and Warehouse-men's Union. Bodies outlined on the sidewalk suggest that this corner was a crime scene, but these figures are tributes to the striking longshoremen who were shot by police in the general strike of 1934. The riot and shootings took place not here but at the corner of Mission and Steuart Streets, where the Coast Seamen's Union kept its offices. A significant historic event did take place in this building in January 1966, when the Trips Festival was held here. The three-day event, organized by Ken Kesey (who penned *One Flew over the Cuckoo's Nest*), rock promoter Bill Graham, and others, ushered in the hippie era. Entertainment was provided by the Grateful Dead, Big Brother and the Holding Company, light shows, and a "stroboscopic trampolinist" who hopped up and down while a strobe light flickered on him. The real point of the festival was to drop acid, and some 6,000 people showed up to do just that. Take a look through the plate-glass windows and imagine the place full of wigged-out flower children.

Turn right onto Beach Street, take a left on Stockton Street, and cross the Embarcadero to enter ❷ **Pier 39.** This open-air shopping center is about as touristy as it gets, with businesses obviously preying upon impulsive shoppers. One attraction that is heads above, however, is the Smithsonian affiliate ❸ **Aquarium of the Bay,** which features a walk-through fish tunnel and touch pools. If you're not checking out marine life, then head straight to the San Francisco Carousel, a handcrafted classic, made in Italy. Horses and chariots rotate around a mechanical organ in the center, while hand-painted San Francisco scenes decorate the top. Rides cost $5. (Interestingly, when Pier 39 first opened, there was a diving pool where the carousel sits, and sometimes it was filled with Jell-O for various games.) When you reach the end of the pier, turn left to pay a visit to ❹ **K Dock,** where a small colony of raucous California sea lions overtook a row of boat docks in 1990. The colony quickly grew, and now as many as 1,000 barking sea lions compete for space on the docks on a winter's day. In summer, most of them migrate to warmer waters to breed, but a few usually haul out here year-round. They're rightly the biggest attraction on Pier 39.

Exiting the pier, turn right onto the Embarcadero (which feeds into Jefferson Street), and walk two blocks until you see and smell ⑤ **Boudin Bakery.** The modern building is nothing much to look at, but the company has been providing the city with sourdough bread since 1849, and some of its "mother dough" is said to have been carried over from the first batch, surviving in the fog-cooled air.

Creepy or cool? Musée Mécanique's vintage automaton, Laffin' Sal

Veer right onto Pier 45, and allow yourself to be drawn into the magical penny arcade ⑥ **Musée Mécanique,** the undeniable hidden gem of Fisherman's Wharf. For some, it's the only excuse to venture into this part of town. It's the private collection of the late Edward Galland Zelinsky, consisting of mechanical amusements and games, mostly from the early 20th century. Risqué mutoscope moving pictures (mostly of women showing their ankles), player pianos, and old-fashioned black-and-white photo booths will easily suck the quarters out of your pockets. Save a few coins for the real showstoppers—automated displays of carnivals and circuses, toothpick Ferris wheels, and even a Chinese opium den with a dragon that peeps out from behind a curtain. Be sure to pump some quarters into Laffin' Sal to keep her howling. Her belly laughs are infectious or terrifying, depending on your sensibilities. Some of the one-of-a-kind machines here are fine works of folk art.

Exit through the back doors onto the waterfront, where the sight of a submarine and a Liberty-class ship from World War II will tell you you're on the right track. The submarine is the ⑦ **USS *Pampanito*,** which patrolled the Pacific during the latter half of the war. For 20 smackers, you can board the sub to see how uncomfortable life beneath the waves must have been, and to puzzle over the state-of-the art technology of a bygone era. The Liberty ship is the ⑧ **SS *Jeremiah O'Brien*,** a cargo-carrying vessel that delivered supplies to Normandy on D-Day. Fully outfitted and in working order, it was used to shoot scenes from *Titanic,* among others. For an additional $20, you can climb aboard—we suggest heading straight for the engine

Many wharf mainstays like The Grotto began as tiny seafood stalls intended to help Italian fishermen cover their operating expenses.

room for an astonishing view of the ship's awesome 2,700-horsepower, triple-expansion steam engine. (Liberty ships were America's answer to Hitler's U-boats, and the goal was to build them as quickly as possible. Unbelievably, a ship as big as the *Jeremiah O'Brien* could go from start to launch in 60 days with the help of female riveters.)

When you're done exploring, head back on Taylor Street toward Jefferson Street. On the way you'll pass the oldest seafood restaurants in the district. Fishermen's Grotto No. 9 was the postcard establishment of the local tourism industry about half a century ago. In 1935, Sicilian immigrant Mike Geraldi transformed his humble fish stand into one of the city's largest restaurants. It stayed in the Geraldi family for three generations and was sold in 2016 to new owner Chris Henry, who frequented the establishment as a kid. Renovations, in frequent consultation from the Geraldi family, confirm that Henry is committed to honoring the family's tradition and also to breathing new life into the restaurant, now known simply as **⑨ The Grotto.** Inside you'll find a swanky midcentury bar and an elegant dining room over the water. Most of the seafood restaurants on the wharf are named for Italian families, reflecting the traditional preeminence of Italian fishermen in the local seafood industry. The families of fishermen often ran little seafood stalls to augment their income, and these eventually became restaurants. Most of the restaurants still operate sidewalk stalls, selling boiled crab and clam chowder served up in hollowed-out loaves of sourdough bread. These are your best bet if you're hungry.

Between The Grotto and Alioto's Restaurant (in business since 1925), look for a "blink and you'll miss it" set of glass doors. Head through them to the inner lagoon, where the real working fishing boats of the wharf are docked (as opposed to the vessels catering to tourists, which line Jefferson Street). Head right to make your way to the simple wooden ❿ **Fishermen's and Seamen's Memorial Chapel.** The charming chapel is dedicated to all who have lost their lives at sea and has a beautiful stained glass window, a gift from the Women's Propeller Club. A full Roman Catholic Mass is conducted in Latin (the chapel is the only place in the Bay Area that still does so), and the first Saturday in October, the church hosts the Blessing of the Fleet, a seafaring tradition since medieval times. Returning to the lagoon, follow it back out to Jefferson Street, and turn right.

Just after Jones Street, you'll see a tiny alley marked AL SCOMA WAY. If you're a seafood lover, follow this path to reach family-owned-and-operated ⓫ **Scoma's,** the only harbor restaurant with its own fishing boats and pier for the ultimate fresh catch since 1965. Linen tablecloths and suited waiters hark back to the days of yore, and this is one of the best places to try the cioppino (seafood stew) for which the wharf is famous. These bragging rights don't come cheap, so be prepared to drop some coin.

Returning to Jefferson Street, you'll find the ⓬ **Alioto-Lazio Fish Company,** just past Leavenworth, notable not only for its live crab (the only spot on the wharf that sells them this way) but

The vintage schooners of the Hyde Street Pier invite exploration.

for being owned and operated by three generations of women—a rarity in the male-dominated fishing world. Known around the wharf as "the girls," the owners have earned respect and accolades for their grit, expertise, and strict attention to quality. Even if you don't have room in your backpack for a live crab (they pack and ship too), they offer "crab shots" if you just want a small taste fresh off the boat. Across the street is ⑬ **The Cannery,** an old Del Monte canning plant that was converted into a shopping center in 1968. The old brick plant was built in 1907 for the Fruit Packers Association, which processed fruit and produce grown in the Central Valley and was at one time the largest such facility in the world. A courtyard that separates The Cannery from the brick Haslett Warehouse is a nice space where a few restaurants and a bar have tables on the patio and musicians perform around lunchtime. The olive trees in the courtyard are purported to be well over 100 years old. Beach Street lines the other side of The Cannery, and as the name implies this area was once completely under water. Beneath your feet lurk old pirate ships, silt, and a variety of other gold rush treasures.

In the Haslett Warehouse, at the corner of Jefferson and Hyde Streets, the ⑭ **San Francisco Maritime National Historical Park Visitor Center** is a gateway to the shipping history that pervades so much of this tour. There's a beautiful antique lighthouse glass up front, affording a rare up-close look. The bulk of the space here is dedicated to excellent exhibits of art and archival material that tell the story of the seafarers and explorers who passed through the Golden Gate. Entry is free. Across Jefferson, the entry to ⑮ **Hyde Street Pier** is obvious, thanks to a large sign spanning the pier. You'll also quickly spot the fleet of 19th-century ships tied up here. These include the *Balclutha,* a square-rigger that regularly traveled the route around Cape Horn from San Francisco to Europe; the *Alma,* a graceful flat-bottomed scow that transported grain to communities around San Francisco Bay; and the *C. A. Thayer,* a three-masted schooner that carried lumber up and down the Pacific Coast. There are many more vessels and items of interest here, and visitors are free to casually explore them. The pier itself was a ferry launch for Route 101 automobile traffic until the Golden Gate Bridge was completed in 1937. Current admission is $10.

Hyde Street Pier flanks one side of Aquatic Park, which slopes down to a narrow crescent of sand. A sidewalk leads from the pier round the beach, where you'll spot hearty swimmers braving the icy cold waters of the bay.

Rather than round the beach, though, cut straight out on Hyde Street. (We'll make our way back to the water in a few minutes.) The ⑯ **Buena Vista Cafe,** at the corner of Hyde and Beach, overlooks the park. It's one of San Francisco's classic saloons, having opened in 1916 in an old boardinghouse. The place stakes its reputation on having introduced Irish coffee to the United States in 1952, and there's usually a row of glasses lined up on the bar awaiting hot coffee, a jigger of Irish whiskey, and a dollop of whipped cream. On a clammy San Francisco day, it's just what the doctor ordered.

Turn right on Beach Street, and you'll soon reach **⑰ Ghirardelli Square,** to which the Ghirardelli Chocolate Company moved from its former location in Jackson Square (see Walk 6, page 44). The redbrick Chocolate Building was completed in 1899, and as the company grew, founder Domingo Ghirardelli's sons added the Cocoa Building (1900), the Clock Tower (1911), and the Power House (1915). The huge sign atop the complex is one of San Francisco's most recognizable landmarks. The company moved its operations to the East Bay in the early 1960s, and the complex reopened as a shopping center in 1964.

At the corner of Beach and Polk Streets, overlooking Aquatic Park, is the **⑱ San Francisco National Maritime Museum**. Appropriately housed in the Art Deco Sala Burton Building, shaped like a steamship and replete with portholes, it was a public bathhouse and a casino before being repurposed as a museum. If you do nothing else, head to the lobby to see Hilaire Hiler's whimsical floor-to-ceiling mural depicting a trippy underwater scene. Exhibits rotate both up- and downstairs, but you'll note that the abstract mosaic work by Sargent Johnson on the veranda is unfinished. Originally hired by the Depression-era Works Progress Administration to work on a Federal Arts Project in 1939, Johnson became disillusioned when he realized that an exclusive private restaurant would bear the fruits of his labor and that it wouldn't be available to the masses. As a matter of principle he quit, and the mosaic remains unfinished to this day. If the museum is closed, you can still admire Johnson's green slate carvings around the front entrance.

From the Maritime Museum, make your way back toward the beach and turn left onto the walkway, which will lead to the eyelash-shaped **⑲ Municipal Pier,** which gets you out into the bay without a boat.

Points of Interest

① **Longshoremen's Hall** 400 North Point St.; 415-776-8100

② **Pier 39** Beach St. and Embarcadero; 415-750-5500, pier39.com

③ **Aquarium of the Bay** Beach St. and Embarcadero; 415-623-5300, aquariumofthebay.org

④ **K Dock Sea Lions** Western dock near Beach St. and Embarcadero at Pier 39

⑤ **Boudin Bakery** 160 Jefferson St.; 415-928-1849, boudinbakery.com

⑥ **Musée Mécanique** Pier 45, Shed A, Fisherman's Wharf and Embarcadero; 415-346-2000, museemecaniquesf.com

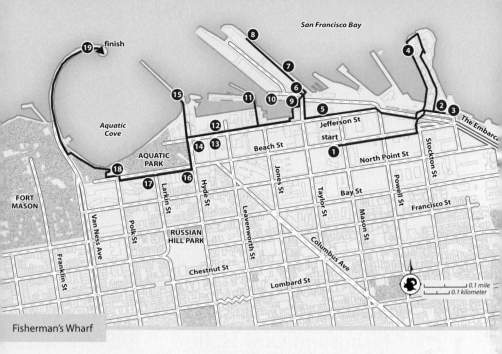

Fisherman's Wharf

15   Marina and Cow Hollow
Lifestyles of the Young and Beautiful

Above: *A placid lagoon surrounds the faux ruins of the Palace of Fine Arts.*

BOUNDARIES: Van Ness Ave., Baker St., Green St., and San Francisco Bay
DISTANCE: 3.5 miles
DIFFICULTY: Moderate (some stairs)
PARKING: Off-street parking in Fisherman's Wharf is your best bet.
PUBLIC TRANSIT: Powell–Hyde cable car; 30, 47 Muni buses

The Marina might be summed up as the new-money counterpart to old-money Pacific Heights (see Walk 18, page 123). Both are upper-class enclaves, but while Pacific Heights rises above the city with a Victorian regalness, the Marina thrusts its chest out into the bay with a 20th-century brashness. Cow Hollow, being neither up the hill nor along the bay, more or less slides into the Marina, and the two neighborhoods feel like two parts of a whole.

Single professionals have been drawn to the area since the yuppies of the 1980s claimed the neighborhood. You'll encounter young urban professionals throughout the city, but those in

Marina and Cow Hollow still seem to be of their own special stripe. The districts are remarkably mainstream, at least by San Francisco standards. The city's countercultural leanings are little felt here, but the waterfront is postcard perfect. On this walk we'll set out to appreciate the Marina's location with a brisk hike along the bayfront before looping back down the commercial Main Streets of both neighborhoods.

Walk Description

Start at Aquatic Park, just beyond the end of Van Ness, where a paved footpath follows the curve of a rare bayside beachfront. Follow the path toward (but not onto) the eyelash-shaped pier; then go left on McDowell Road and follow the ramp up to Fort Mason. (The FORT MASON BAY TRAIL sign tells you that you're on the right track.) Toward the top of the hill, make a left on Battery and then unmarked Bunker Road to walk behind the youth hostel, and look for the dirt path on your left that leads to the 1863 Black Point Battery and Civil War–era cannon in the grass. So far, the cannon has never been fired in hostility—let's hope it stays that way. This promontory became a defensive battery way back in 1797, when the Spanish established Battery San Jose here.

Follow the trail past the cannon, and then look for concrete stairs leading up on your right. At the top of the steps, a concrete path leads into the residential part of Fort Mason. The fine Victorian houses along the east side of Franklin Street were originally built for civilians. Although the military always owned the land, as the city grew quickly in the 1850s developers went ahead and built homes here, in what was then known as Black Point. It was a gamble worth taking, for the front-row views of the bay from the bluffs here are spectacular. Eventually, these homes housed military officers. The large building on the left, at the corner of Franklin Street and MacArthur Avenue, is the Fort Mason Officers' Club.

Nothing against officers, but head in the opposite direction, crossing in front of the chapel. You'll soon reach the visitor center, where you can grab maps and literature for future visits to the Golden Gate National Recreation Area (GGNRA), of which Fort Mason is a part. Past the visitor center, look for the blacktop path that wends through the green of the Great Meadow. In one corner, before a grassy amphitheater, a statue of the late congressman Phillip Burton appears to be orating. Burton chaired a subcommittee on national parks and increased the amount of protected parkland in the United States during the late 1970s.

Turn right and follow the path across the Great Meadow staying right until you see a large green placard and a set of stairs leading down to the lower half of Fort Mason. Three piers and five whitewashed wooden warehouses, built circa 1915, remain from what used to be the US's largest

The 10,000-year clock inside The Interval at Long Now assures ample time to belly up to the bar.

embarkation port on the Pacific, from the Spanish-American War on through to World War II. During the 1960s, as the military began shutting the fort down, Congressman Burton set his sights on creating a national park, the GGNRA, to include these scenic bluffs and historic buildings. The sheds today house an assortment of cultural, nonprofit, and culinary institutions, including the renowned Magic Theatre, which has premiered works by Sam Shepard and David Mamet, among others. Also here is ❶ Greens, one of the most critically acclaimed vegetarian restaurants in the country. Founded by the Zen Center of San Francisco, Greens opened in 1979. If it's mealtime, you can grab a healthy sack lunch and find a spot on the piers for a picnic. Also while here, take a look inside the San Francisco Museum of Modern Art's Artists' Gallery, where works by contemporary artists are exhibited and sold. Then duck into the ❷ Readers Bookstore, where the Friends of the San Francisco Public Library sell the library's cast-off and donated books and movies at bargain prices; the adjacent Goody Café serves coffee and baked goods. One of the newest and coolest members on the scene at Fort Mason is ❸ The Interval at Long Now, a self-described bar, café, museum, and home to the Long Now Foundation, whose mission is "to creatively foster long-term thinking and responsibility in the framework of the next 10,000 years." Even if you aren't parched, take a peek inside to check out their 10,000-year clock, the bottle reserve hanging from the ceiling, and the "ambient painting" by Brian Eno that hangs behind the bar. You may want to return for one of their salon lectures on topics that range from climate change to robots.

From Fort Mason, an asphalt path rounds a small yacht harbor before meeting the sidewalks of the Marina Green, a long, gusty lawn along the bayshore that's perfect for kite flying. As the flatness of the terrain here makes apparent, much of the Marina is landfill, created shortly before and directly after the 1906 quake. Some of the fill is said to be rubble from buildings toppled during the quake—ironic considering that buildings on landfill are particularly vulnerable during earthquakes. Liquefaction occurs as the earth beneath the streets is shaken, turning the ground beneath foundations into jelly. This was cruelly borne out during the 1989 Loma Prieta earthquake, which inflicted more damage on the Marina than on any other part of the city.

The Marina Green is a long, uneventful stretch, so just enjoy the view and the exercise. You'll likely be passed by joggers, scooters, skaters, cyclists, soccer players, Frisbee tossers, in-line skaters, and dog walkers. The sailing craft moored in the harbor here belong to members of the exclusive St. Francis Yacht Club, founded in 1927, and the Golden Gate Yacht Club, founded 12 years later. The landfill and the harbor here were completed in time for the 1915 Panama-Pacific International Exposition, which ostensibly celebrated the opening of the Panama Canal. Of course, the fair also demonstrated the reemergence of San Francisco, just nine years after the city was laid to waste, and it promoted the new patch of real estate that would soon become the Marina District. Strange and exotic buildings covered much of the fairgrounds, only to be torn down immediately afterward. The Mediterranean-style housing you see here now mostly went up in the 1920s.

The Marina Green sidles along Marina Boulevard for several blocks. At Baker Street, turn right and then right again onto Yacht Road. Follow the road all the way to the end to reach the ❹ **Wave Organ,** an unusual example of environmental art, sponsored by the Exploratorium. Built by artist Peter Richards and mason George Gonzales in 1986, the Wave Organ is constructed of PVC pipe and busted headstones salvaged from a dismantled graveyard. The idea is to appreciate the sounds created by the tides passing through the pipes. Press an ear against the listening tubes that poke up out of the cobblestones—each one sounds different. The rumbling tones have a profound hush, like an amplified seashell. There's even a stereo booth, with various sounds coming at you from several tubes. The Wave Organ sounds best during high tide, which sometimes occurs at an unaccommodating time of day. (Check the website saltwatertides.com to see a tidal timetable for the day of your walk.) At lower tides, the sound emanating from the tubes resembles the chugging and wheezing of an old toilet. Still, it's unusual enough to warrant an out-of-the-way side trip, and it's a beautiful setting regardless of the sound.

Return to Marina Boulevard and turn left on Baker Street. A block up, the stately pillars of Bernard Maybeck's ❺ **Palace of Fine Arts** reflect off a duck pond. The palace, designed to look like a gutted classical ruin, is the only architectural showpiece spared after the Panama-Pacific International

Exposition. When it was up for demolition, Phoebe Hearst, philanthropist and mother of William Randolph Hearst, swept in to save it,. The original, made of plaster and chicken wire, wasn't designed to last, but it was faithfully rebuilt of durable concrete in the 1960s and then made seismically sound in 2009. The lagoon plays host to swans, migrating ducks, and turtles, while the grounds are the scene of weddings, prom photos, and innumerable selfies.

Stay on Baker until you reach Chestnut Street, where a left turn eventually leads into a fashionable shopping strip. Among the expensive clothiers and training centers are a handful of spots to grab a cup of coffee or a bite to eat, as well as the old Presidio Theater, which still shows first-run films. **6 Tacolicious,** an immensely popular locally sourced take on tacos, started as a takeout stand in the ferry building. After acquiring a cult following, they opened their first store here on Chestnut. While it has moved locations, the crowds have followed, multiple Bay Area outposts have sprung up, and a cookbook has been published. Across the street, cozy **7 Books Inc.** is an outpost of the West's oldest independent bookseller, having provided the written word to the masses since 1851. This location opened in 1998, and an exceptionally friendly staff, notable author events, and a wide-ranging supply of titles have made it a neighborhood draw. A few blocks up, **8 Lucca Delicatessen** has all the hallmarks of a great Italian deli, with the aroma of salamis and cheeses luring you in. There's a park ahead, if you want to grab a sandwich to go.

At Fillmore Street turn right. After crossing busy Lombard Street, you enter Cow Hollow. As the name suggests, this was once home to dairy farms and vegetable gardens. A block down, the **9 Balboa Cafe** welcomes you to the neighborhood. It's a great old bar and grill, open since 1913, with an interior that would look right at home in an Edward Hopper painting. The etched numbers over the door read 1914, but we haven't made a typo: the original owners were superstitious about the number 13 and so chose to date themselves a year older. Over lunch you can enjoy the place for its historical atmosphere, but be warned that at night the neighborhood's noisy singles scene engulfs it. On the yuppie-socialite map during the 1980s and still a hot spot today, Balboa Cafe is now part of former mayor Gavin Newsom's PlumpJack wine ventures.

Turn left on Filbert. At the corner of Webster Street, **10 Vedanta Temple** is one of the most exotic-looking places of worship in San Francisco and is the first Hindu temple in the Western Hemisphere. The Victorian pile is a purple flight of fancy with Moorish arches and turrets. It was built in 1905 by Swami Trigunatitananda, the Hindu monk who founded the Vedanta Society of Northern California. The swami explicitly specified the creation of the five domes, each of which represents a different religion or emulates a temple (including the Taj Mahal) to create an overall sense of universality. And truly his vision of unity seems very San Francisco in its vibrant eclecticism. Turn right on Webster Street to admire it from all sides.

A block farther down Webster make a left on Union Street, the main drag. Nearly everything on Union speaks to a privileged lifestyle, where you can wax, peel, brush, and contour away any blemishes when not whiling away the hours shopping for expensive activewear. The pinnacle of this indulgent lifestyle would be ⑪ **Le Marcel,** a specialty bakery for dogs, featuring homemade hypoallergenic birthday cakes and bonbons for the mutt in your life. If the thought of this drives you to drink, ⑫ **Perry's,** at No. 1944, can come to the rescue. The bar has the feel of an old New York tavern, and indeed it moved here from the Upper East Side in 1969. Most of the time it's a casual neighborhood joint where you can watch a few innings of baseball over a beer and a burger. Late at night, though, Perry's becomes more of a singles-mingle meat market.

Turn right on Gough for a look at the ⑬ **Colonial Dames Octagon House** at No. 2645. Built in 1861, the house was actually constructed across the street but it had fallen into disrepair from neglect when the Colonial Dames of America purchased it and moved it for restoration. At first not much was known about the house or its earliest occupants, but in 1953 an electrician was doing renovation work and stumbled upon a tin canister hidden by the original owners under the stairs. William and Harriet McElroy had stashed a time capsule that included newspaper clippings, an ambrotype photo of the family, and letters that solved the mystery. See the Russian Hill tour (Walk 11, page 74) for background on unusual eight-sided houses such as this one. Next to it is wooded Allyne Park, surrounded by an unpainted picket fence—a good spot to get off your feet after a long walk. Van Ness Avenue is just two blocks away.

Cow Hollow's peaceful Allyne Park affords plentiful shade and benches for resting tired feet.

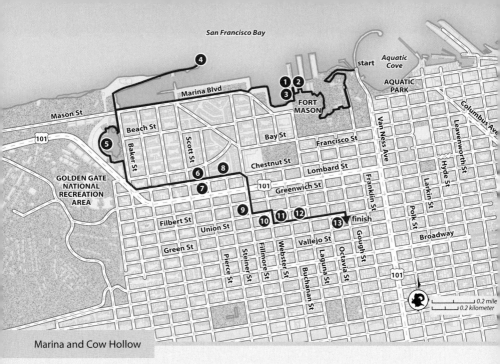

Marina and Cow Hollow

Points of Interest

1 **Greens** Fort Mason Center, Landmark Building A, 2 Marina Blvd.; 415-771-6222, greensrestaurant.com

2 **Readers Bookstore** Fort Mason Center, Landmark Building C, 2 Marina Blvd; 415-771-1076

3 **The Interval at Long Now** Fort Mason Center, Landmark Building A, 2 Marina Blvd.; 415-496-9187, theinterval.org

4 **Wave Organ** 83 Marina Green Dr.; 415-528-4444, exploratorium.edu/visit/wave-organ

5 **Palace of Fine Arts** 3301 Lyon St.; 415-563-6504, palaceoffinearts.org

6 **Tacolicious** 2250 Chestnut St.; 415-649-6077, tacolicious.com

7 **Books Inc.** 2251 Chestnut St.; 415-931-3633, booksinc.net/sfmarina

8 **Lucca Delicatessen** 2120 Chestnut St.; 415-921-7873, luccadeli.com

9 **Balboa Cafe** 3199 Fillmore St.; 415-921-3944, balboacafe.com

10 **Vedanta Temple** 2963 Webster St.; 415-922-2323, sfvedanta.org

11 **Le Marcel** 2066 Union St.; 415-440-2498, lemarceldogbakery.com

12 **Perry's** 1944 Union St.; 415-922-9022, perryssf.com

13 **Colonial Dames Octagon House** 2645 Gough St.; 415-441-7512, nscda-ca.org/octagon-house

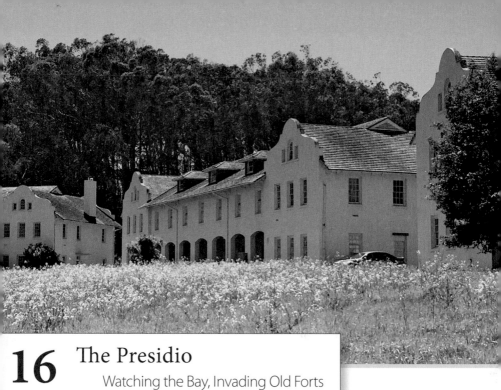

16 The Presidio
Watching the Bay, Invading Old Forts

Above: The Mission Revival structures of Fort Winfield Scott reflect the Presidio's Spanish heritage.

BOUNDARIES: Crissy Field, Golden Gate Bridge, Letterman Complex
DISTANCE: 6 miles
DIFFICULTY: Moderate (but long)
PARKING: Free parking available in several lots along Crissy Field
PUBLIC TRANSIT: The 30 Muni bus terminates on Broderick St., a block outside the park,
near Crissy Field.

The Presidio, along with Mission Dolores, was just about all there was to San Francisco during the city's Spanish period. It was Spain's military outpost, linked to the mission by a trail that later became Divisadero Street. Its location overlooking the Golden Gate was suitable for guarding the entrance to San Francisco Bay.

The Presidio's 1,000 acres remained a military outpost under the Mexican government. Later, under US rule, the Presidio was an Army base until 1994, when it was turned over to the National

Park Service. As a park, it has a lot to offer. Its historic buildings include one of the city's very oldest structures, as well as many buildings from the Civil War period. Some rows of military housing built in the Colonial Revival style resemble a Norman Rockwell vision of small-town American life, with wide porches and plenty of red brick and white trim. San Francisco's most recognizable architectural feature, the Golden Gate Bridge, touches down on the park's northern tip.

Meanwhile, postmilitary tenants of the park include George Lucas, whose film production companies are based here, and numerous nonprofit organizations. But it's the land and the location that make the Presidio special, for during its two centuries as a military base the area was spared the rapid development that went on outside its walls. Thus, an extraordinary swath of nature has been preserved for the leisurely enjoyment of the modern civilian. It is a huge and varied parkland, with cliffside trails overlooking the Pacific Ocean and a long, low-lying bayshore that draws walkers and bicyclers in great numbers.

This tour is lengthy—more than 5 miles—but doesn't even cover half the park. Regard it as an introduction to the key sights, and come back to explore the park further on your own.

Walk Description

Start at Crissy Field, where San Franciscans come to appreciate their bay, and walk in the direction of the Golden Gate Bridge. The level, grassy strip to the left was an airfield, formed by the army in 1919. These were fairly early days in the development of flight, and many landmark voyages took off or landed here, including test runs at transcontinental flights. (Then, it took three days to make it from here to New York, with numerous pit stops along the way—not unlike a cross-country trip by Greyhound bus today.) In 1924, the first round-the-world journey by air made a heroic stop at Crissy Field before concluding at its starting point in Seattle. Two of the four aircraft that began the journey made it to the finish; the other two crashed. Needless to say, it was a dangerous endeavor for the times. The runway is said to be usable still, but only kites and Frisbees take off here these days.

Along the cinder path you'll see marshlands that are being restored to their pre-Army state. The marshes are home to great blue herons, great egrets, and double-crested cormorants, and attract plenty of migrating surf scoters, Caspian terns, and Western grebes. It's busier than an international airport.

Just beyond Crissy Field is the ❶ **Warming Hut,** a welcoming gift shop, bookstore, and snack stand housed in a historic 1909 building that serves up hot beverages and sandwiches made with local and organic ingredients. Along the waterfront here, you're sure to find stacks of carefully balanced rocks; local artists host an annual instructional gathering each April, but you can find folks testing their hand at this gravity-defying art form nearly every day.

Continue along the bayfront to ❷ **Fort Point,** with the Golden Gate Bridge arching dramatically overhead. Along the way, take note of steps heading uphill to the left (we'll walk up there in a bit). Also check out the seawall, from which Kim Novak took her dip into the bay in Hitchcock's *Vertigo.* (She was fully clothed, and James Stewart leapt in after her, took her to his apartment, and managed to get her into a bathrobe without violating the strict film code.) On some days you'll see surfers riding the waves just off the point. Fort Point itself, a huge brick-and-granite fortress, was built in 1853 to protect the entrance to the bay. Construction continued through the Civil War, when it was thought that a Confederate attack might arrive by sea. Many other buildings rose in the Presidio during that time, as San Francisco's importance became clear to the vulnerable Union. From Fort Point the perspective of the Golden Gate Bridge—from underneath it—will knock your socks off. The graceful immensity of the bridge fully registers here.

Backtrack toward the Warming Hut and follow those steps we passed earlier. Toward the top, bear right on the trail that leads to Battery East. Built in 1876, this armed lookout is one of many built in the latter half of the 19th century along the bluffs overlooking the Pacific. When you reach the juncture with the Presidio Promenade, bear right and then right again on the unpaved path to continue on the trail, which passes beneath the bridge toll plaza and by a few more historic batteries before reaching the coastal Golden Gate Overlook, just beyond Battery Godfrey. Quite a few trails crisscross here, but if you follow the Coastal Trail, you'll be fine. From the overlook, head inland through the parking lot to cross Lincoln following Langdon Court. Head down the slight incline to your left to reach the playing field of Fort Winfield Scott. This complex, built in 1910, has many Mission Revival structures that are fairly consistent with California architecture from the time (as opposed to the Colonial Revival structures, which are anomalous in the region). The iconic Presidio style of white buildings with red roofs began here.

Chilly bay waters surround Fort Baker.

Turn right to follow the pedestrian path bordering the playing field, and look for the unmarked paved pedestrian path that crosses the field next to two twin trees. Follow the path to make your way through Fort Winfield Scott, and look for Ruckman Avenue to your left. Follow Ruckman Avenue past some housing as it turns into Rod Avenue and dips beneath the CA 1 overpass to reach wide Lincoln Boulevard. Cross Lincoln and turn left; then take the first right onto unmarked Cowles Avenue.

Turn left on McDowell Avenue for a quick detour to the charming and folksy **❸ Presidio Pet Cemetery,** where you can pay respects to well-loved critters named Skippy; Knucklehead; and Peep, Pet Pigeon of Johnnie Burke. It's by turns touching, humorous, and overblown. After your visit, return uphill on McDowell Avenue and turn left on a trail marked PRESIDIO PROMENADE to Lincoln Boulevard, which sweeps past the military cemetery on its way to the Main Post and Parade Ground. Just past the military cemetery, you'll reach the **❹ Korean War Memorial,** on your left. Established in 2016, this beautifully planted and informative tribute honors those who served in the so-called forgotten war.

Turn right on Sheridan Avenue to take a shortcut to the southern end of the Parade Ground. The grounds have been converted into a parking lot, which adds convenience but detracts from the beauty of the surrounding buildings. Along Montgomery Street, you will note the historic Colonial Revival structures, uniform in design, that were once barracks housing for enlisted men. Where Sheridan meets Anza Avenue, you will find the historic **❺ Powder Magazine,** which dates back to the Civil War and now houses an indoor Andy Goldsworthy sculpture, *Tree Fall* (see Backstory, opposite), instead of gunpowder and munitions. Note the 4-foot-thick walls, important in the case of an accidental explosion so that neighboring buildings wouldn't be damaged and the debris would shoot through the roof.

Turn right on Anza Avenue to reach Moraga Avenue and the **❻ Presidio Officers' Club,** which still has some adobe walls from the original commandant's headquarters, built in 1776. Other parts of the building were added throughout the 19th and 20th centuries, but go inside and enter the Mesa Lounge (to the left immediately after you enter), where a cutaway reveals some of the old adobe. Note the deep recesses in the walls for the windows—it's a thick old structure. The club is home to the haute-Mexican restaurant Arguello, which pays culinary homage to the Spanish explorers who first established the club. Regardless of your appetite, the building is open to the public and now serves as a cultural center and museum. Be sure to check out the small Andy Goldsworthy work *Earth Wall* in the courtyard.

Turn right on Graham Street along the east side of the Parade Ground. The **❼ Walt Disney Family Museum,** which chronicles Disney's life and career from *Steamboat Willie* to Tomorrowland with drawings, home movies, and innovative machinery, will be to your left across the esplanade. Continue to Lincoln Boulevard and the **❽ Presidio Transit Center and Cafe**, which has the best grab-and-go food, wine, coffee, and pastries of any bus stop we've ever seen. Follow Lincoln to Letterman Drive and the Letterman Digital Arts Center, where many branches of George Lucas's multimedia empire, including Industrial Light and Magic (Lucas's Oscar-winning special

Backstory: Making a Muse of San Francisco

British artist Andy Goldsworthy, who makes his home in Scotland, has installed five pieces of art in San Francisco, making it the largest public collection of his work on view in North America. A renowned sculptor and environmentalist known for his site-specific art, his work has been captured in two visually evocative documentaries: *Rivers and Tides* (2001) and *Leaning into the Wind* (2017), both of which explore his fascination with the interplay of man and nature.

Known for his large-scale sculptures, often temporal, from found natural objects, Goldsworthy completed his first San Francisco installation in 2005. Titled *Drawn Earth*, it explores the city's seismic topography in a cracked line wending its way toward the de Young Museum.

Most of his San Francisco work, however, is concentrated in the Presidio. In 2008 he told the *The New York Times*, "I love the fact that the Presidio is a complex landscape, both geologically and socially." Fans of his work will want to make their way to the following installations:

> *Spire,* created in 2008, found on the Bay Area Ridge Trail, north of the Presidio Golf Course Clubhouse
>
> *Wood Line,* created in 2011, located on Lovers' Lane
>
> *Tree Fall,* created in 2013, inside the Powder Magazine, 95 Anza Ave.
>
> *Earth Ball,* created in 2014, inside the Presidio Officers' Club, 50 Moraga Ave.

In a 2017 interview with *SF Weekly*, Goldsworthy said, "The *Wood Line* in the Presidio is the most socially active sculpture I've ever made. Just the way people walk it, visit it. I don't see people as audience but as participants in the work. And people are as much a part of the Presidio as the trees, the sand, the soil, and the sky—they're bound up in that. That's why I'm particularly attracted to a place like that. There's a certain flow of human energy in that place."

effects company), are based. Following Letterman Drive, walk around Building B, where (to borrow a familiar Star Wars patois) a fountain presided over by a statue of Yoda is. After admiring the ❾ **Yoda Fountain,** walk through the buildings into the complex's carefully landscaped parklike grounds. Nearing the end of our long walk, you've certainly earned a beer at ❿ **Sessions,** if you feel so inclined. They fancy themselves a "New American Public House," and everything here is sustainably harvested and locally grown. They boast more than 100 craft beers and an extensive cocktail menu as well. An artificial stream trickles down to a lagoon. Walk through or around the gardens, depending on how enchanted you are, and head out via Gorgas Avenue. Turn left on Girard Avenue and then make the first right on an umarked street to cross between buildings to make your way to Halleck Street. Turn right to follow Halleck Street, up and over Doyle Drive, and cross over to Crissy Field. From here it's just about 100 yards back to where you started.

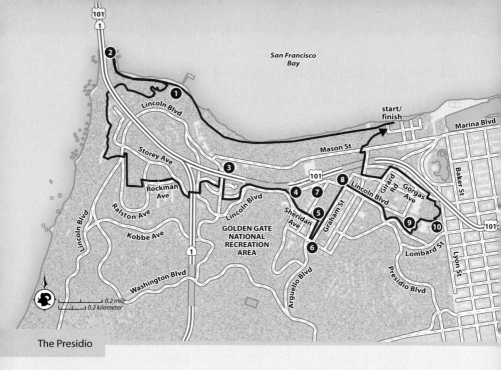

The Presidio

Points of Interest

1. **Warming Hut** 983 Marine Dr.; 415-561-3042, parksconservancy.org/visit/eat/warming-hut.html

2. **Fort Point** Long Ave. and Marine Dr.; 415-504-2334, nps.gov/fopo

3. **Presidio Pet Cemetery** 667 McDowell Ave.; 415-561-4323, presidio.gov/places/pet-cemetery

4. **Korean War Memorial** Lincoln Blvd. and Sheridan Ave.; 415-561-4323, kwmf.org

5. **Powder Magazine/*Tree Fall* sculpture** 95 Anza Ave.; 415-561-2767, presidio.gov/places/andy-goldsworthys-tree-fall

6. **Presidio Officers' Club/Arguello/*Earth Wall*** 50 Moraga Ave.; 415-561-3650, arguellosf.com

7. **Walt Disney Family Museum** 104 Montgomery St.; 415-345-6800, waltdisney.org

8. **Presidio Transit Center and Cafe** 215 Lincoln Blvd.; presidio.gov/places/presidio-transit-center

9. **Yoda Fountain** Building B courtyard, 1 Letterman Dr.

10. **Sessions** 1 Letterman Dr.; 415-655-9413, sessionssf.com

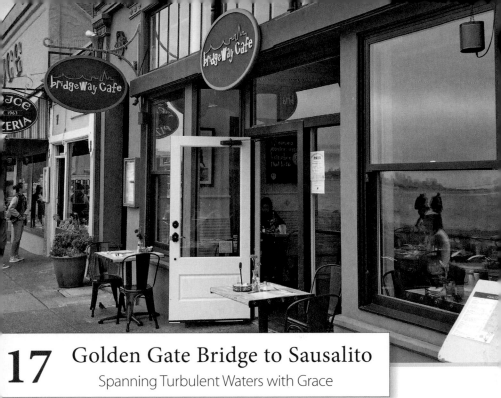

17 Golden Gate Bridge to Sausalito
Spanning Turbulent Waters with Grace

Above: The jaunty seaside shops of Sausalito beckon artists and tourists alike.

BOUNDARIES: From Fort Winfield Scott in the Presidio to the Sausalito Ferry Landing
DISTANCE: About 4 miles
DIFFICULTY: Easy; be careful walking the shoulder of the road into Sausalito
PARKING: Public transit is recommended for this walk. However, there are spaces on Lincoln Blvd. opposite the softball field near Fort Winfield Scott.
PUBLIC TRANSIT: 28 Muni bus; Golden Gate Transit buses following Marin County–San Francisco routes; San Francisco–Sausalito ferry, which docks at Pier 39 at Fisherman's Wharf

Gracing postcards, T-shirts, and countless movie sets, the Golden Gate Bridge is an undeniably elegant civil engineering feat recognized the world over. The silhouette of taut cable swags is an emblem of the city. Named for the Golden Gate Strait rather than the hue it wears, the bridge is actually painted international orange. The Navy had wanted the bridge to be black with yellow stripes for maximum visibility, but designer Irving Morrow made a passionate plea for the winning color (mixed specially for the bridge), commending its visual accent to the surrounding hills and ever-present fog.

The bridge stands apart from the city—buffered by the parklands of the Presidio on the south end and the Marin Headlands on the north end—and its structure and natural setting complement each other. Very subtly, however, the bridge gets the upper hand over its environs. The bridge is obviously not as old as the hills that receive either of its ends, but the hills nevertheless appear to be there for the bridge. And the fog, which has always poured into San Francisco Bay through the Golden Gate Strait, seems to serve the purpose of dramatically enhancing the bridge, concealing and unveiling its two towers and continually adjusting the natural light reflected on the bridge during the day.

Ultimately, of course, the bridge serves us, making it possible for human traffic to travel to and from Marin County and beyond. Most thoughtfully, the bridge has a walkway on its eastern side, enabling walkers to cross the Golden Gate on foot to admire the views and ponder all that this bridge stands for.

This walk starts in San Francisco and ends at the ferry terminal in Sausalito, so plan accordingly. The ferry ride from Sausalito to Fisherman's Wharf is a perfect way to finish your outing, but if you've parked in the Presidio, you'll need to continue from the ferry terminal by bus or other means of transit back to the parking area near the Golden Gate Bridge. The entire length of the bridge itself, including approaches, is 1.7 miles. This walk is more than twice that distance, so be ready for some exercise.

Walk Description

Start near the corner of Lincoln Boulevard and Merchant Road, where two parking lots provide access to cliff-hugging coastal trails. Rather than head down Merchant Road toward the bridge toll plaza, walk toward the sea cliffs to inspect a collection of old military batteries, such as Battery Boutelle, which hasn't been in use since World War I. From here the Golden Gate—the narrow mouth of the bay and the widening funnel of the sea cliffs that embraces the Pacific—comes fully into view. Because pedestrian traffic on the bridge is restricted to the walkway on the bay (east) side, this rugged strait on the ocean side is often overlooked. To fully appreciate this perspective, walk over to these army battlements and follow the unpaved trail that leads from here to the bridge. Signs point the way, although the looming bridge is hard to miss. To the northwest is Point Bonita, punctuated by its lighthouse in the Marin Headlands. To the southwest, the Cliff House marks Point Lobos on San Francisco's coast. Very likely a container ship is passing between these points on its way to Far East ports and another nearly identical ship is issuing forth beneath the bridge, as part of the continual movement of cargo in and out of San Francisco Bay. Here and

Stretched out in all her glory, the Golden Gate Bridge links San Francisco with suburban Marin County.

there the trail affords flattering vantage points of the bridge, including a much-photographed angle from which the distant north tower appears to fit snugly within the south tower.

The path soon dips beneath the bridge's south viaduct for an up-close look at its trussed and riveted underside, a treat for anyone interested in engineering; check out the interesting display on ongoing seismic retrofitting just before you head under. Earthquake engineers are gradually replacing the older supports but doing so in a way that preserves the aesthetics. The viaduct here extends over two concrete pylons flanking the top of Fort Point. An artful arch braces the two pylons, and hidden in the works you may notice the bridge cables slicing downward to their southern anchorage. All that concrete beneath the south viaduct houses the cable anchorage. Much thought went into the design of this structure to protect picturesque Fort Point, which dates back to the Civil War. (The fort saw no action, but during the war San Francisco Bay was considered vulnerable to Confederate attack.) Look up to marvel at the sheer enormity of what went into creating the Golden Gate Bridge—the mind-boggling quantity of materials and the ingenuity behind it all.

After passing beneath the bridge, be sure to peer down at the daredevil surfers riding the waves beneath Fort Point; then follow the trail that curves up to ❶ **Strauss Plaza,** where you'll soon be in the company of hundreds of tourists who have come from around the world to see the bridge and snap a few photos.

Before making your way onto the bridge, look for the statue of Joseph Strauss, the chief engineer who guided the bridge's planning and construction. Strauss submitted his first plans for a bridge to span the Golden Gate in 1917. After several major revisions, and arguments with the War Department over the advisability of building a bridge above the mouth of an important harbor, Strauss settled on an all-suspension design and then oversaw its construction from January 1933 to May 1937. He didn't work alone, of course: he hired structural engineer Charles Ellis and other advisors to help solve challenges posed by the span's length and the depth of the channel, as well as strong currents, stiff winds, and the possibility of earthquakes. He also brought on architects John Eberson and Irving F. Morrow, who contributed the bridge's elegant Art Deco style. Strauss commendably went to greater-than-usual lengths to protect the safety of the workers building the bridge. Some 19 workers were saved by netting Strauss insisted on installing beneath the building sites; still, 11 men died during construction of the bridge. Strauss himself died, while recovering from exhaustion, just 12 months after the bridge opened.

Also in the plaza adjacent to a perennially full parking lot and restrooms, you'll find an excellent ❷ welcome center run by the National Park Service, which provides historical information as well as an impressive selection of souvenir gifts a cut above your typical touristy junk. If you need to grab a bite before proceeding, the Art Deco ❸ Round House Café serves classic fare such as hot dogs and clam chowder in a sourdough bread bowl. Originally opened in 1938 as a roadside diner to complement the new bridge it was reimagined as a family restaurant in 2015. Before you leave the plaza, look for the cross-cut section of cable, some 36 inches in diameter. It's a persuasive demonstration of the bridge's unseen power. Don't bother to count the thick wires bound together within the cable—there are 27,572 of them.

Continue onto the bridge. As you walk, stay alert for cyclists. The mixed traffic of commuting cyclists, weaving families, and camera-toting tourists can get a bit ugly, so keep your wits about you. Looking down, you'll notice you are still above land for a while, and below the bridge you can see the roof of Fort Point. Once you've cleared Fort Point, you've reached the bridge's suspension span, and you will see the cable rise at an oblique angle toward the south tower.

Pause at the south tower to inspect the bronze plaques acknowledging the bosses of the men who hoisted the cables and poured the concrete and risked their lives for this bridge. The tower is 746 feet tall, as is the north tower. Standing next to it, you will notice the tower is a sound barrier that offers respite from the bridge's constant thrum of traffic. Look up to appreciate the design of the tower: each segment is slightly narrower than the one beneath it, each braced by horizontal trusses that are masked by decorative plates embellished with a repeating chevron motif. Corbels beneath the trusses further contribute to the textured design of the towers. Of course the towers are hardly aesthetic in purpose. They support the bridge's two cables, each weighing some 160 tons, and the cables in turn support the suspension span. The bridge is literally being held up from above, its weight distributed along the entire length of its cables.

The main span between the two towers is 4,200 feet long. Pause again at the point midway between the two towers, and look down. The water beneath the bridge is where the Pacific Ocean and San Francisco Bay meet. The water here is never calm—it chops and eddies and looks somewhat menacing. You might spot a sea lion swimming with evident playfulness barely below the water's surface, and a few pelicans may coast on loping wings beneath the bridge. Sailboats, cruising vessels, tankers, and tugs frequently travel through the Gate's narrow channel, all reflecting the bay's never-ending enterprise and sport. Nevertheless, death lurks in those waters. By now, you may have noticed the California Highway Patrol officers on bikes, who stop to chat with anyone who looks lonely or desperate. ("Hey, how's your day going?" is the usual opener.) You have probably spotted the phones for crisis counseling. The sad truth is that the bridge has an undeniably fatal attraction for some and is one of the world's leading spots for suicides—so much so that local media largely does not cover the events, as they don't want to inspire more jumpers. But increased patrols of officers trained in crisis management have helped, and a stainless-steel mesh net is being built as both a savior and a deterrent.

Continue beyond the end of the bridge, where the path will lead you to the parking lot of the Golden Gate Bridge Vista Point. From here, follow the bike and pedestrian lane that leads away from the bridge toward Sausalito. The pedestrian path will end as you join Alexander Avenue. It's downhill the entire way, but there's no sidewalk: stick to the shoulder, and maneuver carefully around parked cars. Alexander will become Second Street. Make a right on Richardson, which becomes Bridgeway, to make your way through the center of town. While the street names are confusing, if you follow the coastline, you'll find it easily.

The affluent and picturesque, albeit touristy, town of Sausalito, formerly a fishing village, attracts hordes of day-trippers every day. Walking the waterfront, you can pick up tasty meats, cheeses, or sandwiches at the old-school Italian delicatessen ❹ **Venice Gourmet** and then eat them by the fountain in tiny ❺ **Viña del Mar Park,** near the ❻ **Ferry Landing.** The park, named for Sausalito's sister city in Chile, features two elephants from the 1915 Panama-Pacific International Exposition. Originally made out of papier-mâché, Jumbo and Pee Wee were later remodeled in cement for preservation. For a more formal affair, head to ❼ **Poggio Trattoria,** an untouristy spot near the Ferry Landing, for pastas, wood-roasted meats, and panini flavored with herbs from their kitchen garden. An ice cream at ❽ **Lappert's** is always a good idea before heading back on the ferry (check goldengateferry.org and blueandgoldfleet.com for current schedules).

Getting out on the water is the perfect complement to a bridge walk. The air is fresh, and the continual surge of the water beneath the boat gives you a palpable sense of the powerful immensity of the bay and the graceful bridge that spans the Golden Gate.

Golden Gate Bridge to Sausalito

Points of Interest

1 **Strauss Plaza** Coastal and Battery E Trails; 415-415-921-5858, goldengatebridge.org

2 **Golden Gate Bridge Welcome Center**   Coastal and Battery E Trails; 415-426-5220, goldengatebridgestore.org

3 **Round House Café**   Coastal and Battery E Trails; 415-426-5228, presidio.gov/places /round-house-cafe

4 **Venice Gourmet** 625 Bridgeway, Sausalito; 415-332-3544, venicegourmet.com

5 **Viña del Mar Park** Bridgeway at El Portal, Sausalito; 415-289-4152, tinyurl.com/vinadelmarsausalito

6 **Sausalito Ferry Landing** Anchor St. and Humboldt Ave., Sausalito; 415-455-2000, goldengateferry.org

7 **Poggio Trattoria** 777 Bridgeway, Sausalito; 415-332-7771, poggiotrattoria.com

8 **Lappert's Ice Cream** 689 Bridgeway, Sausalito; lapperts.com (no published phone number)

18 Pacific Heights
Victorian Splendor

Above: The Atherton House epitomizes Pacific Heights grandeur. It's also rumored to be haunted.

BOUNDARIES: California St., Franklin St., Broadway, Fillmore St.
DISTANCE: 2 miles
DIFFICULTY: Moderately strenuous
PARKING: Off-street parking at 1700 California St., just off Van Ness Ave.
PUBLIC TRANSIT: California St. cable car; 1, 47, 49 Muni buses

San Francisco's elite moved up to Pacific Heights' lofty, rarefied environs back in the 1870s and have never left. (Well, the original people have died, but their latter-day ilk remain.) The advent of cable cars made these previously unattainable photogenic perches available, and soon the area was an affluent bedroom community. It seems Nob Hill wasn't big enough for all of the incredibly wealthy citizens of the Victorian city, and the well-to-do staked their claim to hilltop lots here to complement their vast estates down in San Mateo County. The grandest mansions in the Heights were once (and in some cases are still) homes of magnates, tycoons, industrialists, and dignitaries who also have office towers, parks, and streets named for them; contemporary millionaires from the entertainment industry have joined the club relatively recently. Thus, this tour is largely an appreciation of jaw-dropping architectural phenomena. Interestingly, the neighborhood is densely packed, with front and side yards as rare as in any other part of the city, and many streets are dominated by luxury apartment buildings. On a weekday morning, sightseers will share the sidewalk with dog walkers and stroller-pushing nannies.

Walk Description

Start at the corner of Van Ness Avenue and California Street, historically a key intersection for the neighborhood. Here the California Street cable car line terminates, but in the 1870s this line and several others continued up from the downtown area to the top of Pacific Heights, making the area accessible to residents in pre-automobile days. The lines ran up and down most of the east–west streets of the neighborhood. Initially Van Ness Avenue was a residential street where some of the city's very wealthiest built their mansions. At 125 feet wide, Van Ness is the city's broadest thoroughfare. Ironically, during the 1906 conflagration the street's lavish mansions were systematically dynamited to create the firebreak that stopped the flames from climbing farther west. Van Ness was rebuilt as a retail strip, and by the middle of the 20th century it was lined with steakhouses and flashy auto showrooms.

Head one block west on California Street, and you'll begin to see what remains of the neighborhood's Victorian grandeur. The ❶ **Coleman Mansion** at 1701 Franklin St. was built by Edward Coleman, a forty-niner who, unlike most, actually struck it rich during the gold rush. It stands on a large corner lot, which is typical for Pacific Heights—the biggest houses stand on corners, the smaller ones midblock. Up near the eaves, the house is banded by a whimsical ornamental trim, with a recurring motif of laurels and torches; the Franklin Street side has a comely stained glass window. With 11 bedrooms and a parklike yard, the house sold for a cool $7 million in 2018.

Turn right (north) on Franklin. Another stately corner mansion stands at the intersection of Franklin and Clay. Now occupied by the ❷ **Golden Gate Spiritualist Church,** this white weddingcake house was built for the Crocker family in 1900. The church meetings that go on inside are much more interesting. Founded in 1924 by Rev. Florence S. Becker, the congregation practices the Spiritualist rite of communing with the dead. Among the church's beliefs is that "the existence and personal identity of the individual continue after the change called death." Services are conducted by mediums. A little farther on the same side of Franklin Street, the large Victorian at No. 1945 was owned for many years by actor Nicolas Cage.

The elite chose Pacific Heights as their nesting point for its grand vistas of the sea and the hills beyond.

On the next block of Franklin Street, at No. 2007, the ❸ **Haas-Lilienthal House** cuts an impressive figure. Built in 1886 for William Haas, the austere house is one of the city's finest Victorians and reflects the elegance that once typified the neighborhood. Haas's daughter, Alice Haas Lilienthal, lived in the house until 1972, and it was turned over to the Foundation for San Francisco's Architectural Heritage a year later. One of the only Pacific Heights homes open to the public, it offers guided tours on Wednesdays, Saturdays, and Sundays ($10).

Turn left at Jackson Street and left again at Octavia Street. This curved, cobbled block was designed to slow traffic as it passed the immense ❹ **Spreckels Mansion,** at the top end of the block. Adolph Spreckels, son of sugar magnate Claus Spreckels, built the grand edifice in 1925 and gifted it to his wife, Alma de Bretteville (see Backstory, page 31). To acquire the view he desired, Spreckels purchased several occupied adjacent lots. Evidently Alma hated to see the homes destroyed, so she and Adolph paid to have eight of the period Victorians moved and reassembled elsewhere. Today, romance novelist Danielle Steele lives in it, and has incurred wrath from neighbors for planting privacy hedges that hide the limestone Beaux Arts exterior. The house's exterior was used to portray the nightclub Chez Joey in the 1957 film *Pal Joey*, starring Frank Sinatra, Kim Novak, and Rita Hayworth.

Across from the Spreckels place, ❺ **Lafayette Park** is an expanse of rolling green lawns, tennis courts, a children's playground, and picnic tables with great views. The park's leveled peak was the sight of Samuel Holladay's mansion during the latter half of the 19th century. Holladay was a prominent citizen—he was a judge who also served on the city council—but there was no record of his ever having purchased the land here. The city regarded him as a well-to-do squatter and tried to evict him, but Holladay knew the ins and outs of the law well enough to evade the city's efforts. He lived here until his death in 1915, and the city demolished the house in 1930. Turn right at Washington, and you'll quickly reach the gates of the ❻ **Phelan Mansion,** at No. 2150. It was the home of James Phelan, who served as the city's mayor from 1897 to 1902 and in the US Senate from 1915 to 1921. The Renaissance Revival structure is awkward, with an unusual glassed-in mezzanine over the front entry. The former mayor's greatest architectural legacy is the Phelan Building, on Market Street (see Walk 1, Lower Market Street, page 2).

Turn right at Laguna Street. A block up, the corner house at 2090 Jackson is the ❼ **Whittier Mansion.** Just before the United States entered World War II, this honey-toned sandstone house was purchased by the Nazi government, which intended to use it as a consulate. Those plans were obviously waylaid by the war. Featured on many "Haunted San Francisco" tours, the mansion is rumored to be full of paranormal activity, and visitors have claimed to see shadowy figures or feel icy drafts of air.

Continue on Laguna and turn left at Broadway. A block and a half up, the huge house at No. 2120 is one of two Flood mansions on the street. This one, built in 1901, was the home of Jennie Flood. It was built by her brother, James Leary Flood, who was the son of silver king James Clair Flood. Jennie was living in her father's Nob Hill mansion, which was damaged in the 1906 quake, so she moved here. Since 1927 it has housed ❽ **The Hamlin School** for girls. James Leary Flood left a few years later, after building a new home up the street, at No. 2222, for himself and his wife. The second Flood estate, consisting of a nearly identical pair of massive villas, was completed in 1915. It is now the outrageously posh home of the ❾ **Schools of the Sacred Heart,** a Catholic academy.

Having just passed Webster Street, double back and turn right (south). The house at 2550 Webster is the ❿ **Bourn Mansion,** a dark brick fortress with fantastic chimneys. It was built in 1896 for William Bowers Bourn, inheritor of the Empire Gold Mine, the richest in the state. The house was not Bourn's home—just a luxurious pit stop for entertaining guests while he was in town. Willis Polk was the architect. In the 1970s, the home was purchased by eccentric Arden Van

Upp and a partner, who threw rock-and-roll parties, filmed porn movies, and wreaked all manner of havoc that caused the neighbors to whisper—not the least of which was Van Upp's teenage belly-dancing daughter, Tammy, who made coast-to-coast headlines for undulating with a 6-foot-long python they kept at the house. Neither Van Upp nor the house aged well, and both fell into a state of disrepair. It sold for less than $3 million in 2010—a mere pittance for the size and location. Outward appearances indicate that it now enjoys a more mundane life.

Turn right at Pacific Avenue and turn left onto Fillmore Street, the principal commercial street of Pacific Heights. It's lined with clothing boutiques, beauty salons, restaurants, and cafés. Recommended places to stop for dinner are ⓫ **Jackson Fillmore,** an intimate little Italian spot, and the ⓬ **Elite Cafe,** a classy New Orleans–inspired gathering spot with an oyster bar and a decent Cajun-Creole menu. Both eateries have been around for more than three decades and are deservedly renowned.

Turn left at California Street. The corner of California and Webster is dominated by the magnificent ⓭ **Temple Sherith Israel,** one of the pillars of the city's well-established Jewish community. The congregation dates back to the 1850s, and this awesome temple went up in 1904. It is more spectacular inside than out, with a frescoed inner dome and beautiful stained glass windows conducting a brilliant spectrum on sunny days. Albert Pissis was the architect.

Three blocks down, at 1990 California, the ⓮ **Atherton House** looks humble, considering the size of the Atherton family's fortune. Faxton Atherton owned a huge estate that spanned the peninsula south of San Francisco. (The tony suburb of Atherton is named for him.) After his death, his widow, Dominga, built this house in 1881 and lived there with her son, George, and his wife, Gertrude. George boarded a sailing ship for Chile to try and accrue his own wealth but died of kidney failure at sea. According to numerous accounts, including the *San Francisco Landmarks* book, the captain stuffed George's body into a rum barrel for preservation and then mailed it to the family back home. While George was eventually given a proper burial, many think his spirit never left the premises, and the Atherton House is another site frequented by paranormal students eager to learn more about mysterious noises and apparitions. Across the street at 1969 California, the Tudor Gothic Revival ⓯ **Tobin House** appears to have been chopped in half, with an arch ending at its midpoint against the neighboring building. Michael de Young (founder of the *San Francisco Chronicle*) commissioned Willis Polk in 1915 to create two mirroring adjacent homes for his daughters Constance and Helen. The latter, however, decided she didn't want to live quite so close to the family, and the second home was never built, leaving this architectural oddity.

From the Tobin House, it's just a few blocks back to Van Ness Avenue.

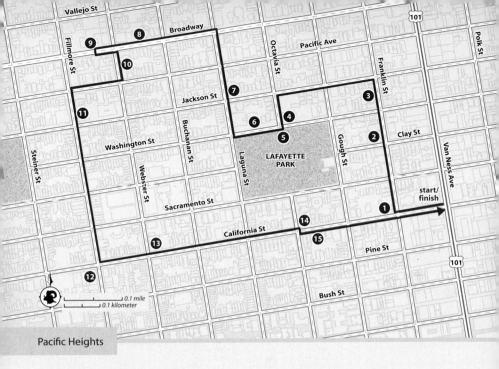

Pacific Heights

Points of Interest

1. **Coleman Mansion** 1701 Franklin St. (private residence)

2. **Golden Gate Spiritualist Church** 1901 Franklin St.; 415-885-9976, ggspiritualistchurch.org

3. **Haas-Lilienthal House** 2007 Franklin St.; 415-441-3000, haas-lilienthalhouse.org

4. **Spreckels Mansion** 2080 Washington St. (private residence)

5. **Lafayette Park** Gough and Washington Sts.; 415-831-5500, sfrecpark.org/destination/lafayette-park

6. **Phelan Mansion** 2150 Washington St. (private residence)

7. **Whittier Mansion** 2090 Jackson St. (private residence)

8. **The Hamlin School** 2120 Broadway St.; 415-922-0300, hamlin.org

9. **Schools of the Sacred Heart** 2222 Broadway St.; 415-563-2900, sacredsf.org

10. **Bourn Mansion** 2550 Webster St. (private residence)

11. **Jackson Fillmore** 2506 Fillmore St.; 415-346-5288, jacksonfillmoresf.com

12. **Elite Cafe** 2049 Fillmore St.; 415-346-8400, theelitecafe.com

13. **Temple Sherith Israel** 2266 California St.; 415-346-1720, sherithisrael.org

14. **Atherton House** 1990 California St. (private residence)

15. **Tobin House** 1969 California St. (private residence)

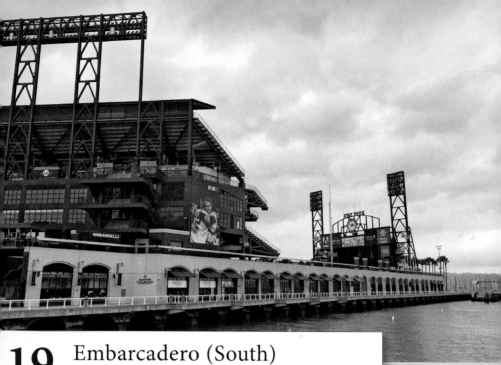

19 Embarcadero (South)
The Docks of the Bay and a Ballgame Bonus

Above: *Home of the Giants, AT&T Park nestles next to the waters of McCovey Cove.*

BOUNDARIES: Mission St., Spear St., Embarcadero South, King St.
DISTANCE: 2.75 miles
DIFFICULTY: Easy
PARKING: Off-street parking at 50 Howard St.; metered street parking limited to 2 hours
PUBLIC TRANSIT: Embarcadero BART station; F streetcars (street level); J, K, L, M, N, S streetcars
    (underground); 1, 2, 7, 14, 21, 71 Muni buses

In recent years, the waterfront south of Market Street, like much of San Francisco, has changed dramatically. The development of luxury condominiums, high-rise office towers, and the Giants' home base—AT&T Park—has brought new life to an area long ago abandoned by the shipping industry, which moved across the bay to Oakland in the late 1950s. The spanking-new NBA Warriors stadium will continue this trend.

Public art adds color and interest, as do restaurants and bars that get lively before and after baseball games, which are good times to take this walk (see the Sporting Green section of the *San Francisco Chronicle* for a schedule). Here and there are remnants of the Embarcadero's long-gone stevedore days.

On this tour we'll take a close look at the ongoing development of this precious strip of real estate, meander along the historic waterfront, pass the ballpark, and enjoy a stroll around the European-style park that played host to the first tech boom.

Walk Description

Start at the ❶ **Rincon Annex Post Office,** at the corner of Mission and Spear Streets. It's no longer a post office, and as you can see from the street, the modern Rincon Center rises up over the building's back side. The historic post office, an Art Deco beauty dating to 1939, has been preserved in near-pristine condition and now serves as a unique foyer to the office tower. It was saved from demolition in 1978 primarily to protect the murals that grace the interior. Step inside for a look. From 1946 to 1948, Russian-born Anton Refregier painted 27 scenes depicting California history. Some common threads address concerns about freedom of speech and worship, for as Refregier worked on the murals such liberties were threatened in Europe, where Communism was spreading, and also in America, where anti-Communist paranoia had the country in its grip. Refregier's unromanticized scenes are populated by serious, often somber characters. Pass through the lobby into the newer Rincon Center, and you'll reach a large, classy food court, with tables and chairs arranged around a "rain column"—water pours from the ceiling, several floors above, expands as it falls, and then appears to collapse neatly as it hits a stone platform on the floor. Your best choice for a light bite here is ❷ **Yank Sing,** one of the best dim sum places in the city.

A block east down Mission Street, at Steuart Street, the ❸ **Audiffred Building** looks like no other San Francisco landmark. It was built in 1889 by Hippolyte d'Audiffred, a French immigrant who in San Francisco sold charcoal to Chinese laundries and parlayed his earnings into real estate. He is believed to have designed this building himself, although he had no training as an architect. Consequently, the Audiffred Building is an unusual amalgam of styles—a New England–style brick structure with Victorian and Gothic details, capped with a mansard roof reminiscent of d'Audiffred's native France. The ground floor was originally occupied by the Bulkhead Saloon, popular with sailors and wharf hands, and the Coast Seamen's Union kept offices upstairs. Local legend maintains the building survived the 1906 fires thanks to a savvy barkeep, who bribed the fire department with a cart of wine and whiskey. The surrounding buildings all burned to the ground while drunk firemen trained their hoses on the Audiffred Building. During the early 1950s, the upper floors served as artist lofts, and poet Lawrence Ferlinghetti (who also paints) was among the creative souls who rented space here. Today, the ground floor is occupied by Chef Nancy Oakes's excellent ❸ **Boulevard Restaurant**, and its interior design is redolent with Belle Époque details. The restaurant jumps during the weekday lunch hour, when free-spending office workers pour into its swank booths, and its bar is always a lively spot for a classy cocktail.

Across Mission Street is a monument to the striking longshoremen who were gunned down by police during a demonstration in 1934. It was on this corner that police fired into the crowd, killing Howard Sperry and Nick Bordoies.

Continue around the Audiffred Building and turn right onto the Embarcadero. The ❹ *Aurora fountain* at the corner of Howard and Steuart is the work of the late artist Ruth Asawa (1926–2013). The child of Japanese immigrants, Asawa was frequently inspired by origami paper-folding techniques. With multiple public art displays around the city, she was nicknamed the Fountain Lady. Farther along the Embarcadero at No. 250 is the headquarters for ❺ **Gap,** the well-known purveyors of casual clothing. The company was founded in 1969 by Donald and Doris Fisher and has grown to include more than 3,500 stores. Gap (originally *The* Gap) began by marketing inexpensive blue jeans for teenagers; the name refers to the so-called generation gap of the late 1960s. Peer through the building's glass doors for a look at Richard Serra's huge metal sculpture,

Pier 14 stretches proudly as the Bay Bridge does the same in the distance.

The *Phoenix* fireboat has been part of the city's maritime firefighting crew since the 1950s.

which dominates a five-story atrium. It's called *Charlie Brown*, although it bears no resemblance to Charles M. Schultz's prematurely bald cartoon character.

Cross the Embarcadero at Folsom Street for an up-close look at **6 *Cupid's Span***, Coosje van Bruggen and Claes Oldenburg's 60-foot-high representation of the little cherub's bow and arrow, looking as if it fell from the sky and embedded itself into the ground here.

Continue walking along this side of the Embarcadero. By now, you're already enjoying a wonderful perspective of the Bay Bridge, which you'll soon be walking under. On the way, at Harrison Street, you'll pass the Hills Bros. Coffee Building, with its huge, eye-catching neon sign. Just as you reach the shadow of the bridge, take note of the **7 Pier 22½ fire station,** where two antique fireboats are docked. *Phoenix*, which was built in 1954, was used to pump water out of the bay to douse fires in the Marina after the 1989 earthquake. Afterward, Marina residents donated funds to purchase *Guardian*, a lovely vessel built in 1951.

The underbelly of the Bay Bridge is an awesome sight. The size of the bridge and the effort that went into building it are difficult to comprehend, especially from this informed vantage point. The bridge hits land at the southern side of Rincon Hill, which in the 1850s and '60s was the city's most fashionable neighborhood. It was here that the first millionaires of the gold rush city built their magnificent mansions. There's no sign of the hill's former splendor, as the area declined following development of Nob Hill in the 1870s. After more than a century of neglect, compounded by construction of the bridge in the 1930s, new condominiums and offices, including the 60-story One Rincon Hill, are going up in this part of town, making Rincon Hill once again a desirable address.

On down the Embarcadero, at Pier 28, you'll spot an old tavern left from the waterfront's heyday. Called the **8 Hi Dive,** it's a smart little joint where you might enjoy a beer and a view of the bay. At Pier 30, in an unprepossessing little shack suspended over the water, is **9 Red's Java House,** a classic once patronized by old salts and longshoremen. It still attracts average Joes today, along with suited office workers. Head on in to this historic joint. In back, toward the loo, the walls are covered with photos by Bruce Steinberg, taken in 1971. These include shots of Red himself, looking every bit the wiry and fierce-tempered grill chef. He doubtless ran an orderly establishment. Red is no longer around, but you can still order a greasy cheeseburger on sourdough and a cold bottle of Bud for $10 and some change.

Immediately to the south is the **10 Brannan Street Wharf,** a waterfront park that replaced the slowly rotting Pier 36 in 2013. The green lawn, benches, and interpretive displays are a welcome change from the previously fenced off area. The son of the late soul singer Otis Redding was on hand to croon "Sittin' on the Dock of the Bay" at the ribbon cutting.

Moseying on down the waterfront, keep your eyes peeled for the historical marker at the far end of Pier 30, which lists the names of 23 men who died while building the Bay Bridge.

11 AT&T Park begins to exert its gravitational pull here, especially before games, when a stream of pedestrians will be headed in its direction. Approach along the bay, through South Beach Harbor, where sailboats and yachts are docked. The huge Coke bottle and antique mitt loom over the left-field bleachers. Follow the curve of the stadium to where the right field arcade overlooks McCovey Cove. Along this side of the ballpark, an iron gate permits a view to nonpaying fans, who are allowed to stand and watch part of the game from the field level, just a few paces beyond the right field warning track. Staff clear the area every three innings to make room for a fresh crowd. Every few months or so one of the ballplayers launches a titanic home run that plops into McCovey Cove, and it's usually a race between kayakers and dogs to see who can retrieve the ball.

Walking in the same direction around the ballpark leads to a statue of Juan Marichal, the legendary Dominican pitcher (from 1960 to 1973) whose menacing, high-kick delivery was a beautiful sight to Giants fans. A little ways farther is Willie Mays Plaza, with a statue of the greatest ballplayer to wear a Giants uniform. (Some say he was the greatest, *period.*) For two decades Mays hit for power, stole bases, and played the outfield with extraordinary ability, intuition, and spirit. He began his career with the New York Giants in 1951, coming to San Francisco when the team relocated in 1958.

Continue circling the stadium on King Street and turn left on Second Street. After crossing Townsend, you'll reach independent bookseller and publisher **⑫ Chronicle Books**'s headquarters and retail store, nested in an old maritime machine shop and warehouse. Peek in to check out the latest offerings from this innovative literary house that has been serving up stories since the 1960s. Farther up on Second and across the street is the much-lauded **⑬ 21st Amendment Brewery,** which has been "celebrating the right to be original" since 2000 and is now one of the nation's largest craft breweries. It's a fine place for pub grub and a pint from constantly rotating taps. The name stems from the amendment that repealed prohibition. Before the 1920s, more than 40 breweries operated within the city's limits (and there were far fewer people then!); 21st Amendment is doing its part to honor San Francisco's brewing legacy.

If you've paused for a pint, cross Second Street and head straight onto South Park, a secluded city block shaped like a racetrack. The street loops around a pleasant green with a playground and spacious lawn that attracts more dogs than children. The street is a mix of Victorian residences, converted warehouses, and contemporary lofts that reveal much, but not all, of South Park's history. In the 1850s, an Englishman named George Gordon,developed the land here as an exclusive community in the style of a London square. Elegant homes were built and gold rush millionaires moved in. South Park's heyday lasted little more than a decade, as the rest of the South of Market area spread out and the working poor closed in on this tony little haven. By the time Jack London was born around the corner from here, in 1876, South Park was the home of immigrants and longshoremen. The 1906 quake and fire destroyed the block, and many of the apartments and warehouses built in the quake's aftermath remain. Among these are the former Sherman-Clay & Co. piano warehouse near the southeast corner. In the 1970s and '80s, the street began attracting artists and soon acquired a postindustrial cachet. By the late '90s, South Park was considered the heart of San Francisco's "Multimedia Gulch," as dozens of startup companies set up shop in the surrounding blocks drawn by flexible office space and low rent. That all ended abruptly in the early 2000s, but this quiet enclave retains a lively and interesting feel. **⑭ Caffè Centro,** serving panini and hot Italian plates, is a great way to embrace the European vibe.

When you've had your fill of South Park, traverse to the far end and make a right on Third Street to make your way back toward the ball park. Shortly after Willie Mays Plaza, you'll cross the Lefty O'Doul Bridge, named for Francis "Lefty" O'Doul, a ballplayer and San Francisco native who won the National League batting crown in 1929 with a remarkable .398 average. O'Doul managed

Backstory: The Historic F Lines—Moving Forward, Looking Back

You've likely noticed the classy vintage streetcars moving along steel rails down Market Street and along the Embarcadero. Providing old world glam to public transit, these beloved heritage cars almost never came to exist.

San Francisco's Market Street is no stranger to traffic. First there were steam trains, then horse-drawn carriages, followed by cable cars. When the 1906 earthquake destroyed the cable system, the city rebuilt Market Street with newfangled electric streetcars. But times and fashion change. With the advent of BART in the 1960s and other underground transit options later on, it seemed that streetcars would soon be a thing of the past.

In 1982, however, the iconic cable car system was completely shut down for an overhaul that lasted nearly two years. Worried that this would disappoint tourists, the idea was born to create an alternative historical rail attraction: the San Francisco Historic Trolley Festival. The city rolled out a handful of vintage streetcars, including the very first car from 1912, for limited service on weekends, and the measure was a smashing success. So great was the enthusiasm for the trolley festival that it was extended far after the cable cars were up and running.

After the 1989 earthquake forced the removal of the Embarcadero freeway, new life was breathed into the waterfront, now liberated from the shadow of a giant cement overpass. Thus, in 1995, the F streetcar line was born. Today it serves more than 20,000 riders daily.

Hailing from as far away as Moscow, Osaka, and Melbourne, abandoned streetcars have been renovated and given a serious spit shine; the oldest car in the fleet was built in 1895. You never know which streetcar will roll up, and locals eagerly anticipate favorites like the open-air boat-tram from Blackpool, England, and the streetcar from New Orleans named—you guessed it—Desire. And unlike the cable cars, streetcars cost the same to ride as a regular bus. Hop on and these museums in motion will inspire you to celebrate the past while whisking you to the future.

the San Francisco Seals, of the Pacific Coast League, from 1935 to 1951. The bridge named for him is a charmer, a Strauss trunnion bascule span built in 1933 that crosses narrow Mission Creek.

Once across the bridge, hook left and walk along McCovey Cove on the opposite side from the ballpark. This is **⑮ China Basin Park.** You'll reach a statue of Willie McCovey (1938–2018), the slugging first baseman who was known as "Stretch" for his great size and for his ability to reach for wild throws to first. McCovey began his career in 1959 and retired in 1980. Also in the park is a perfect T-ball field with a pint-size diamond for pipsqueak players.

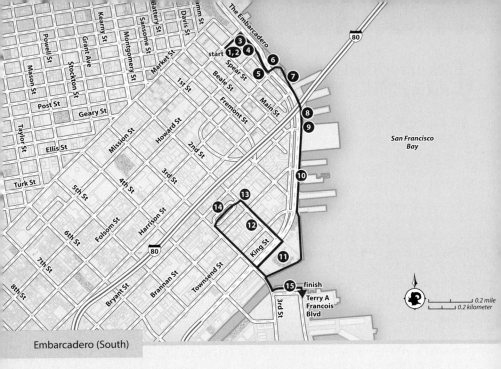

Points of Interest

1. **Rincon Annex Post Office (former)** 101–199 Mission St. (no published phone number or website)
2. **Yank Sing** 101 Spear St.; 415-781-1111, yanksing.com
3. **Audiffred Building and Boulevard Restaurant** 1 Mission St.; 415-543-6084, boulevardrestaurant.com
4. *Aurora* **Fountain** 188 Embarcadero
5. **Gap Headquarters** 2 Folsom St.; 800-333-7899, gap.com
6. *Cupid's Span* Rincon Park, Embarcadero and Folsom St.; oldenburgvanbruggen.com
7. **Pier 22½ Fire Station** 399 Embarcadero; 415-558-3200, sf-fire.org/fire-station-locations
8. **Hi Dive** Pier 28½, Embarcadero and Bryant St.; 415-977-0170, hidivesf.com
9. **Red's Java House** Pier 30, Embarcadero and Bryant St.; 415-777-5626, redsjavahouse.com
10. **Brannan Street Wharf** Piers 30–38, Embarcadero and Brannan St.
11. **AT&T Park** 24 Willie Mays Plaza (corner Third and King); 415-972-2000, mlb.com/giants/ballpark
12. **Chronicle Books** 680 Second St.; 415-537-4200, chroniclebooks.com
13. **21st Amendment Brewery and Restaurant** 563 Second St.; 415-369-0900, 21st-amendment.com
14. **Caffè Centro** 102 South Park St.; 415-882-1500, caffecentro.com
15. **China Basin Park** Terry A. Francois Blvd. and Third St.; 415-274-0400, fport.com/parks-and-open-spaces

20 SoMa
From Publishing Past to High-Tech Future

Above: *St. Patrick Church and the Marriott Marquis from Yerba Buena Gardens*

BOUNDARIES: Market St., Fourth St., Second St., Natoma St.
DISTANCE: 1.5 miles
DIFFICULTY: Easy
PARKING: Fifth and Mission garage
PUBLIC TRANSIT: Powell St. BART station; 30, 45 Muni buses; Market St. buses and streetcars

South of Market (SoMa) has been in a state of metamorphosis for decades, and it doesn't show any signs of stopping. The area around Yerba Buena Gardens, once a grid of skid rows, is now firmly established as a zone of conventions and culture. Moscone Center and the San Francisco Museum of Modern Art (SFMoMA) anchor the district. Farther to the west by just a few blocks, however, traces of the neighborhood's down-at-the-heels past remain. Taking it all in makes for an interesting study in contrasts as the transformation of SoMa continues apace. From the residential hotels and seedy underbelly of Sixth Street to the looming Salesforce Tower and Transit

Center, this walk highlights San Francisco's old and new wealth, as well as the vibrant and growing arts district that separates the two.

Walk Description

Start at the corner of Fifth and Mission Streets, the home of the **❶** *San Francisco Chronicle*. The "Voice of the West" has occupied this building since 1924. By the paper's own account, it was founded in 1865 by brothers Charles and Michael de Young, who were teenagers at the time and in possession of a single $20 gold piece, which they borrowed. The paper quickly established itself as a legitimate news source when it scooped the city's other dailies with the news of Abraham Lincoln's assassination. It was the city's only afternoon paper, and in the age of the telegraph the timing worked in the favor of the "Chron." Miraculously, the paper has weathered seismic shifts in journalism, delivering a mix of breaking news and in-depth reporting via online and print outlets. Still, many locals love to complain about its coverage.

Turn left down Mint Street, an alley behind **❷ The San Francisco Mint.** The sandstone building is in good shape, considering that it was built in 1874 and survived the 1906 quake and fire.

SFMoMA combines Mario Botta's 1995 building *(foreground)* with a 2016 extension.

Lovingly referred to as The Granite Lady, it supposedly once held nearly a third of the entire nation's money at its peak. It operated as a U.S. Mint until 1937 but these days is used mainly as an event space and wedding venue. A large-scale restoration project, headed by the San Francisco Museum and Historical Society, is moving slowly at press time.

Mint Street leads to Jessie Street, which along the mint's left flank has been made into a public square, with a stone patio and orange plastic chairs strewn about for conversation or people watching. A number of cafés and restaurants have opened around this plaza, and during the lunch hour outdoor tables are set up in the shadow of the old mint building, bringing life to a once-neglected alleyway. **❸ Blue Bottle Coffee**, on the ground floor of the 1912 San Francisco Provident Loan Association building (which appears in *The Maltese Falcon*), is an impeccably caffeinated laboratory where single-source coffees burble in siphon pots. (Needless to say, San Francisco's obsession with coffee reaches ceaselessly for new levels of intensity.)

The next block of Mission Street is defined by a block-long parking garage on one side and the sleek glass back of Bloomingdale's department store on the other. At the end of the block, a partial view opens up on the Yerba Buena Center for the Arts, the result of a 30-year project to transform 87 acres of dilapidated hotels into a shopping, convention, and cultural district.

More than a century ago, SoMa was known as South of the Slot, for the cable car slot that ran down Market Street. It was home to immigrant families and to migrant workers, a considerable proportion of whom were seasonal laborers who mined the foothills and cleared Sierra forests. Between jobs or during the winter, they meandered back to the city, where they flooded into SoMa's bounty of residential hotels. When gold rush–era fires and the 1906 quake destroyed parts of San Francisco, SoMa itinerants came in handy for the rebuilding effort. More often, though, they were forced to stretch meager savings over fruitless winters. They ate cheap meals in diners and found their entertainment in pool halls and theaters. Free lunches could be had in saloons and at rescue missions. Many had a propensity to drink and went broke before the arrival of spring. Able-bodied men were often reduced to panhandling. The injured and aged had little hope of ever seeing a paycheck again. The Great Depression broke many a man's back here, and the neighborhood declined and never recovered. By the mid-60s, SoMa, like the Tenderloin to the north, was a grid of skid rows, its residents largely subsisting on monthly relief checks. The city's Redevelopment Agency fixed its eye on the area. They met with resistance from tenant groups, but in the end the agency had its way, sweetening the deal with museums and the promise of cash trickling down from conventions at Moscone Center. Demolition of block after block began in the late 1970s and, along with Ronald Reagan's policy of slashing federal aid to urban programs, coincided with a dramatic jump in the city's homeless population.

Note the office at 814 Mission, former home of the ❹ *Daily Evening Bulletin,* which once boasted the highest circulation of any paper in the city. Founded by James King of William in 1855, King used the paper to wage against political corruption. His success was short lived, however, as a year later he was gunned down in broad daylight by city supervisor and rival newspaper editor James Casey who was angry about a critical piece the paper had run about him. The San Francisco Committee of Vigilance responded by taking matters into its own hands and hanging Mr. Casey. No easy business, this journalism.

Continue east on Mission Street. Cross Fourth Street and continue a few steps down Mission to Yerba Buena Lane on your left, a pedestrian route that cuts directly to Market Street. The walkway links the San Francisco Marriott Marquis hotel, the Contemporary Jewish Museum, and St. Patrick's Church. The gleaming tower of the ❺ **Marriott Marquis** is a much-reviled piece of architecture that fatefully opened on the day of the 1989 Loma Prieta earthquake. Sound construction ensured that only one window was broken; it couldn't, however, protect the building from the rapier wit of *Chronicle* columnist Herb Caen, who likened it to a jukebox and famously complained that the glare blinded him in his office. (Truthfully, though, San Franciscans would probably appreciate it if it looked more like a jukebox and less like a hotel.) The ❻ **Contemporary Jewish Museum** occupies a historic power substation, with modifications designed by architect Daniel Libeskind, who found time to draw these plans while winning the contract for the new World Trade Center towers in New York City. The building's facade, designed by Willis Polk in 1907, survives in its entirety, with Libeskind's off-kilter cubes, colored a somber shade of night blue, jutting above the roof and adjoining the west side of the building. The museum itself has galleries devoted to art, history, and ideas, all relating to the Jewish people. It's also home to the excellent ❼ **Wise Sons Jewish Delicatessen,** serving up bagels, salads, and matzo ball soup; museum admission isn't necessary to have a little nosh. ❽ **St. Patrick Church,** originally the parish of Irish Catholics who lived South of the Slot, was built in 1872. Step inside for a look at the stained glass windows. Some members of the now-predominantly-Filipino congregation may be lighting votive candles or crawling, in a display of humility, up the aisles toward the altar. Across Jessie Square from the church, a four-story glass cube will be the new digs for the ❾ **Mexican Museum.** The Smithsonian affiliate museum is the oldest in the country focused solely on Mexican, Chicano, and Latino art. Its new multimillion-dollar building—which will have seven times the space of its current Fort Mason home—promises to provide rich artistic, cultural, and educational experiences when it opens in 2020.

On the other side of Mission Street, the Metreon shopping center opened at the height of the dotcom frenzy, promising to be a beacon of cool technology, hence the late-1990s vibe. Many of the original shops, including showcases for Sony and PlayStation products, barely survived the '90s, and the place no longer seems to be the wave of the future. But there's a decent food court if you're hungry, plus a bookstore and a busy multiplex cinema. Walk through the Metreon and exit through the doors on the east side, facing Yerba Buena Gardens; then follow the meandering path that borders the Metreon on your left. The park is essentially an undulating lawn and a few trees, but it's a lovely urban space enhanced by an attractive skyline.

Wander over to the elegant ❿ **Martin Luther King Jr. Memorial**, where a series of waterfalls pounds rocks below and drowns out your thoughts. Walk behind the falls to fully experience this reflective monument. From May to October, on weekends and some weekdays, a stage is set up on the lawn for live music and dance performances. Acts range from puppeteers to opera singers,

The Martin Luther King Jr. Memorial is the US's second largest monument dedicated to this great leader.

and admission is free. If you take a detour to the upper level, continuing up the path to the right of the MLK Jr. Memorial, you'll find a raised walkway crossing Mission Street that brings you to a vintage carousel, an ice-skating rink, a bowling alley, a playground, and the Children's Creativity Museum, a space dedicated to innovative art and technology for the under-12 set.

The **⓫ LeRoy King Carousel,** designed by master carver Charles I. D. Loof (who designed Coney Island's first carousel), was originally slated for delivery to a small Market Street park in 1906. The earthquake changed that, and it was rerouted to Seattle's Luna Park instead. The miraculous carousel somehow survived the great Luna Park fire of 1911 and bounced around various locations until finally landing here in 1998.

The **⓬ Yerba Buena Center for the Arts,** with exhibit spaces and a performing-arts center, takes up the Third Street side of the park. It emphasizes the work of living artists in all media, mostly with a local angle; admission is $10. With the arts center at your back, head toward the giant fountain bordering Third Street and take the crosswalk directly to the **⓭ SFMoMA.** Designed by Mario Botta, the museum moved to these new digs in 1995 after residing in the Civic Center for many decades. In 2013 the museum closed for a three-year, $305-million expansion of 10 additional floors, nearly tripling the gallery space. Upon its reopening in 2016, *The New York Times* raved that the renovation "bumps this widely respected institution into a new league, possibly one of

140 New Montgomery is replete with Art Deco glam.

its own." It's an immensely popular museum, and the lauded Fisher Collection, bequeathed by Gap founders Doris and Donald Fisher, adds real depth. Its photography collection is excellent, and fine traveling exhibits stop here regularly. Inside the museum are a variety of dining options from the casual Sightglass Coffee to the Michelin-starred In Situ. Admission to the museum (which is closed Wednesdays) is $25, but there are some free installations on the first two floors, including an immense Richard Serra piece, *Sequence,* that you may walk through.

Follow Third Street back to Mission Street, and turn right. On the next block, between Third and New Montgomery, are two notable museums. First is the ⓮ **Museum of the African Diaspora (MoAD),** which showcases the work of African and African-descended artists ($10 admission; closed Monday and Tuesday). Across the street is the ⓯ **California Historical Society,** a research facility with a huge library and a collection of historical photos, maps, and artifacts. It plucks gems from its collections for display in the back gallery ($10 admission; closed Monday). This is a fabulous place to pick up unique and interesting California and San Francisco gifts.

At New Montgomery turn right. The striking Art Deco high-rise at 140 New Montgomery (at the corner of Minna Street) is the former ⓰ **Pacific Telephone & Telegraph Building,** designed by Timothy Pflueger and James Miller and built in 1925. A striking symbol of the telecommunications age, it was San Francisco's first and tallest skyscraper for three years. Today the building's main occupier is the online review business Yelp, and a step inside the lobby reveals a beautiful $60-million restoration, including unicorns and phoenixes gracing the ceiling, said to be adapted from a Chinese brocade. You will also see Art Deco nods to the original tenants.

Return to Mission Street and continue heading south toward the waterfront crossing Second Street. Community activists are actively trying to rebrand this area as the East Cut. Longtime San Franciscans know this area as Rincon Hill, one of the original storied seven hills of San Francisco. Following the gold rush, this was an upscale and sought-after neighborhood, where sea captains and upper-crust merchants settled to escape the bawdy Barbary Coast. But an ill-fated urban planning decision of 1869 was the beginning of the end, when the hill was leveled along Second Street to improve access to the southern waterfront. The 1906 earthquake and subsequent fires were the nail in the coffin, as families fled to higher addresses with better views. Adding insult to injury, the 1950 construction of the Embarcadero freeway essentially surrounded the area with concrete and cut it off from the Financial District. But when the 1989 Loma Prieta earthquake hit, leading to the removal of the damaged freeway, development eyes turned once again to the forgotten area. With glass towers sprouting up seemingly overnight, the area is definitely changing; whether the name sticks remains to be seen.

About two-thirds of the way down Mission from Second Street, look for the stairway past the 100 First Garage. This leads you up to the **🕖 100 First Street Rooftop Garden,** an open sun terrace with plenty of benches, water features (including art meant to evoke ocean waves), and greenery. This is one of many privately owned public open spaces, or POPOS, that are hidden gems of the downtown area. In 1985, zoning regulations changed to control growth and also assure that new development provided for public open space; as a result, more than 60 POPOS dot downtown and the Financial District. While there are plaques designating each area, they are often small and rather hidden.

Back on Mission Street, you'll soon find yourself among the city's newest and tallest designer skyscrapers. As of 2018, the looming **🕘 Salesforce Tower** has wrested the "tallest building" designation from the Transamerica Pyramid by reaching 1,070 feet into the fog. Designed by Pelli Clarke Pelli, the tower is built on landfill (tall ships and old anchors are likely underfoot), and developers needed to drive the foundation piles nearly 300 feet below ground to hit bedrock. The top nine stories of the building are devoted to an electronic LED art piece, the brainchild of local artist Jim Campbell. As with all things new in San Francisco, the reaction has been mixed. John King, urban design critic for the *Chronicle,* has decried its "lack of visual swagger," while other locals have been less restrained about what they perceive as the demise of the classic San Francisco skyline. It's worth noting, though, that more than 40 years ago the venerable architecture critic Wolf von Eckardt lambasted the unveiling of the Transamerica Pyramid as "hideous nonsense" that would desecrate one of the most breathtaking skylines of the world.

Across Fremont Street, the **🕘 Millennium Tower** has gained notoriety for an altogether different reason: it's sinking. When it first opened in 2009, the tower was hailed as one of the top 10 residential buildings in the world by *Worth Magazine.* Accolades were flying, and high-profile residents like NFL Hall of Famer Joe Montana and Giants outfielder Hunter Pence brought prestige to the multimillion-dollar luxury condos. But then things shifted—literally. While it's common for buildings of this size to settle to some degree, the pace and degree to which the Millenium

Tower is moving are rather unprecedented: within less than a decade, it has sunk 17 inches and tilted more than 14 inches toward Fremont Street. The problem seems to arise from its heavy concrete (versus steel) frame and the fact that the building's engineers chose not to drill into bedrock. Not surprisingly, a huge legal battle is ensuing with fingers being pointed everywhere, and the structural solutions being bandied about are more expensive than the building of the tower itself. An art-filled atrium is located on the ground floor, should you want to take a gander inside.

The crown jewel of all this tech-industry growth is the ⓴ **Salesforce Transit Center and Park,** a $2-billion-plus endeavor that accommodates buses, MUNI, and, we hope, the eternally

Lofty Salesforce Tower is reflected in the gleaming windows of Millennium Tower.

delayed high-speed rail between San Francisco and Los Angeles. Excavation for the project was vast and unearthed a variety of archaeological treasures, including an 11,000-year-old woolly mammoth tooth that was donated to the California Academy of Sciences, and a glittering nugget from the gold rush. The rooftop park is a beauty to behold, with 5.4 acres of greenery that include an amphitheater, playground, cafés, and restaurants. While there are more pragmatic ways to access the garden, we encourage you to board the 20-person gondola from the corner of Fremont and Mission Streets to enjoy the end of this walk.

Points of Interest

❶ *San Francisco Chronicle* **Building**   901 Mission St.; 415-777-1111, sfchronicle.com

❷ **The San Francisco Mint**   88 Fifth St.; 415-608-2220, thesanfranciscomint.com

❸ **Blue Bottle Coffee**   66 Mint St.; 415-495-3394, bluebottlecoffee.com

❹ *Bulletin* **Building (former)**   814 Mission St. (no published phone number or website)

❺ **San Francisco Marriott Marquis**   780 Mission St.; 415-896-1600, tinyurl.com/sfmarquis

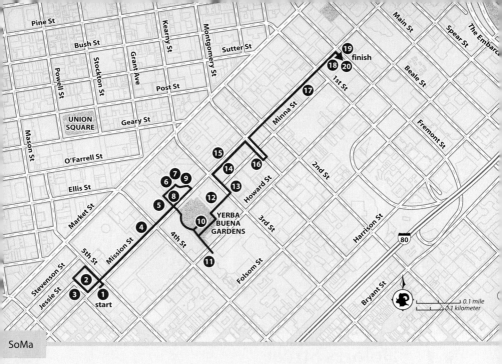

SoMa

6 Contemporary Jewish Museum 736 Mission St.; 415-655-7800, thecjm.org

7 Wise Sons Jewish Delicatessen 736 Mission St.; 415-655-7887, wisesonsdeli.com

8 St. Patrick Church 756 Mission St.; 415-421-3730, stpatricksf.org

9 Mexican Museum 706 Mission St.; 415-202-9700, mexicanmuseum.org

10 Martin Luther King Jr. Memorial Yerba Buena Gardens, 750 Howard St.; 415-820-3550, yerbabuenagardens.com

11 LeRoy King Carousel 221 Fourth St.; 415-820-3320, creativity.org/visit/childrens-creativity-carousel

12 Yerba Buena Center for the Arts 701 Mission St.; 415-978-2787, ybca.org

13 San Francisco Museum of Modern Art (SFMoMA) 151 Third St.; 415-357-4000, sfmoma.org

14 Museum of the African Diaspora 685 Mission St.; 415-358-7200, moadsf.org

15 California Historical Society 678 Mission St.; 415-357-1848, californiahistoricalsociety.org

16 Pacific Telephone & Telegraph Building (former) 140 New Montgomery St.; 140nm.com

17 100 First Street Rooftop Garden 100 First St.; sfpopos.com

18 Salesforce Tower 415 Mission St.; salesforcetower.com

19 Millennium Tower 301 Mission St. (no published phone number or website)

20 Salesforce Transit Center and Park 425 Mission St.; sfmta.com/projects/salesforce-transit-center

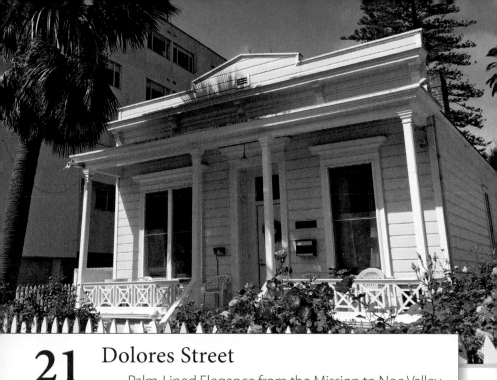

21 Dolores Street
Palm-Lined Elegance from the Mission to Noe Valley

Above: *One of the twin Tanforan Cottages, the oldest residences in the Mission District*

BOUNDARIES: Market St., Valencia St., 24th St., Sanchez St.
DISTANCE: 2.5 miles
DIFFICULTY: Strenuous (uphill climbs)
PARKING: Street parking is limited to 2 hours except on Sunday. The Market and Noe Garage (261 Noe St.) is 3 blocks from the start of this tour. *Don't* park at the Safeway store across the street, which is monitored.
PUBLIC TRANSIT: F streetcar; J Church train; 22 Muni bus

Dolores Street is luxuriant without being snooty, grand without being opulent. For some 2 miles, the street's palm-shaded medians follow a straight and gracefully undulating path along the eastern edge of the Mission District. Fans of architecture will note that the surviving Victorian homes tend to be on the west side of the street, while the newer Edwardians reside on the east side; this is largely because the 1906 fire consumed the east side but spared the west. Speaking of fire, the Phoenix palms that are planted along the meridian seem a nod to San Francisco rising from the ashes following the disastrous quake (although San Francisco's adoption of the phoenix as the city symbol predates the event).

This walk takes in Mission Dolores, panoramic vistas from Dolores Park, and inviting tangents up and down some of San Francisco's finest rows of 19th-century houses. It skirts the fringes of the Castro District and Noe Valley. Apart from the mission itself, however, this tour is not hugely concerned with landmarks or history—it's simply one of the most beautiful walks in the city. We won't faithfully walk every block of Dolores Street, opting instead to venture into the roller-coaster blocks of the Liberty Hill District and the northern rim of Noe Valley.

Walk Description

Start at the corner of Dolores and Market Streets, where the *California Volunteers* statue appears to be poised to ward off an invading army. The statue is worth a moment's appreciation, for it was created by Douglas Tilden, one of the city's finest artists at the turn of the 20th century, earning him the moniker Michelangelo of the West. It's very dramatic, with its cavalryman jabbing the air with his sword as his horse tramples a fallen soldier who helplessly tries to aim his gun.

Walk down Dolores Street. Once you cross 14th Street, the street begins to take on a more elegant character. Most of the buildings on either side of the street are apartments. The palms in the medians are a popular pit stop for wild parrots. (The flocks here do not mingle with the flocks that habituate Telegraph Hill and parks in the north half of the city.) Pause in front of the twin yellow homes with Classical Revival facades at 214 and 220 Dolores St. These are the ❶ **Tanforan Cottages,** noted for being the oldest residential buildings in the Mission District and among the oldest in all of San Francisco, built in 1853 and 1854, respectively. The redwood structures are believed to have been originally constructed as farmhouses by the Tanforan ranching family—almost unfathomable when you consider the current surroundings. At present, the cottage at 220 provides housing and care for formerly homeless individuals coping with HIV-related illness as part of Dolores Street Community Services, and 214 is also a nonprofit residential treatment facility.

At 16th Street, the huge ❷ **Mission Dolores Basilica** rises into view, and behind it is the humble mission itself. Mission Dolores, built of 4-foot-thick adobe walls and a clay-tile roof supported by wooden beams, is the oldest building in San Francisco, having been completed by 1791. When the mission was founded, in 1776, it originally stood about a block and a half east of here, on the shore of Laguna de los Dolores, an inland waterway that was later filled in. The Spanish missionaries conscripted local American Indians to do their building for them, more or less in exchange for saving their souls. The surrounding lands were farmed by Indians, along with Spanish families, though the settlement remained very small. The much larger Basilica was built after the 1906 fires destroyed an earlier cathedral on the site. Pope John Paul II said Mass here on September 17, 1987. By all means, pay the $7 admission and take a self-guided tour to admire the painted ceiling (originally done with vegetable dyes by the Ohlone Indians), the stained glass, and the diorama depicting the area when the mission was first built. The small, peaceful cemetery is another highlight, in part because it is the only nonmilitary cemetery within the city limits. Most of the names have worn off of the ancient headstones, but interred here is an intriguing mix of dignitaries, paupers, and ordinary folks from the 18th and 19th centuries.

Two blocks down Dolores Street, Mission High School's bell towers are a nice complement to Mission Dolores. Built in the Mission Revival style, the school was completed in 1924. Author Maya Angelou and rocker Carlos Santana are alums.

Just off the corner of Dolores and 18th Street, you can get in line for ice cream at the ❸ **Bi-Rite Creamery,** an exceedingly popular spot for heaping scoops of traditional and soft-serve ice creams and sorbets made in small batches. Everything is organic and locally sourced, and the flavors are exquisite and unique: try a scoop of orange cardamom, honey lavender, or the signature salted caramel. For something more substantial, try to grab a sidewalk table across the street at ❹ **Dolores Park Cafe.**

The Little Giant hydrant is one of the few that kept pumping after the 1906 earthquake.

For the next few blocks, Dolores Park slopes up from the western side of the street. What was at one time a Jewish cemetery and then a camp for more than 1,600 earthquake refugees is now an amphitheater-like bank of green, with tennis courts, a soccer pitch, a playground, and lawns that are very popular among dog walkers and sunbathers. Having undergone a major renovation between 2012 and 2016, Dolores is truly a crown jewel of the San Francisco park system. Continue on the sidewalk for a block; then follow the asphalt walkway up through the park toward the statue of Miguel Hidalgo, liberator of Mexico in 1810 (which, of course, included

Backstory: The Fireplug Worth Its Weight in Gold

Many visitors to San Francisco fear the Big One—the earthquake that will set the ground shaking and bones rattling. But truthfully, it wasn't the 1906 quake that brought San Francisco to its knees, but the subsequent three days of fires, caused by ruptured gas lines, that destroyed 80% of the city.

Firefighters and their workhorses were exhausted as they came upon countless broken water mains and a dwindling supply to combat the raging infernos. San Francisco was literally going up in smoke. In many areas it seemed that all hope was lost, but one little fire hydrant changed all that in the Mission. The squat little plug at the corner of 20th and Church Streets miraculously kept working when all the others stopped. Likely drawing water from an underground spring, the so-called Little Giant kept pumping. Hundreds of neighbors pushed a pump wagon up and down the 20th Street hill more than 10 times, when the horses were too spent to continue. They would fill the tanks and then feather the brakes while rolling the wagon downhill to resupply the waiting engines.

To commemorate this historic feat, every year on April 18 at 5:12 a.m.—the anniversary of the quake— the fire hydrant gets a fresh coat of gold paint and a wreath of flowers. In 2012 it was accidentally painted silver, but that was quickly remedied.

California at the time). Beyond the Hidalgo statue, cross the pedestrian bridge, which clears the Muni J Church streetcar tracks, then make a left onto the sidewalk just below Church Street. The corner of Church and 20th forms the southwest corner of the park and one of the great lookout points in SF. The J Church train is a pleasure to ride (you might want to catch one at the end of this walk) for views like this, as well as for the curving course the tracks follow through the backyards of the neighborhood. It's worth crossing over to the other side of Church and 20th to pay tribute to the ⑤ **Golden Fire Hydrant** (see Backstory, above).

Turn left on 20th Street, following the southern edge of the park, and then turn right on Dolores. A block down, turn left on Liberty Street. The south side of the block is a fine row of historic houses, all very different in style and all in tip-top shape. At Guerrero Street, turn right. On the corner of 21st Street, the house at 900 Guerrero is a stunner built by John Daly, an exceedingly successful dairy farmer, in 1895. Daly owned a huge tract of land south of the city. Parts of Daly City, named for him, were developed on land that had been his farm. The house here is in excellent condition, although it is no longer a single-family home.

Turn left on Hill Street. On the north side of the block is an impeccable row of nearly identical Stick-style Victorians, all built in the 1870s and '80s. These were originally middle-class homes.

Turn left on Valencia and you'll walk by ⑥ **Ritual Roasters,** a coffeehouse that many credit for introducing "third wave" coffeemaking techniques to San Francisco and starting a virtual revolution in how the city takes its coffee. Many other roasters have followed suit, and caffeine artistry and consumption have been taken to a new (and incredibly expensive) level. Grab a cup to fuel you up the hill, and turn left again on 21st Street, which we'll follow past Dolores Street up to Church Street. At Church turn right; then turn left on Liberty Street. It's a steady climb to the top. Stay on the north side of the street, where you can see the gardens that appear to be thriving along the median—hopefully, the sight of plants will make the uphill trudge easier to bear. At the top of the block, take the steps leading to Sanchez Street, and turn left.

A block up, the corner house at 3690 21st St. is a gingerbread cottage straight out of a Disney movie. It's called Casa Ciele ("sky house" in Spanish)—which ought to feel appropriate enough after you've hiked to this point.

It's all downhill from here, in a purely topographical sense. Follow Sanchez several blocks to 24th Street, Noe Valley's main drag. The street, which has a villagelike feel, mostly serves the needs of the affluent young families that call Noe Valley home. To your right, you'll find all manner of window shopping, including high-end children's clothing, two excellent independent bookstores, shoe shops, cafés, salons, and art supplies. Near Sanchez, ⑦ **Folio Books** offers a few more titles aimed at adults and features author events and a celebrated staff of dyed-in-the-wool book lovers. ⑧ **Noe Valley Bakery,** a neighborhood mainstay since 1994 that offers everything from artisan fig bread to specialty birthday cakes. At the intersection of 24th and Castro, ⑨ **Charlie's Corner Bookstore** caters to younger readers with story time in English, Spanish, and French and a great selection of titles to read under the massive "tree" in their shop. Across from Charlie's Corner and just up Castro Street, ⑩ **Contigo** features Spanish and Catalonian tapas (small plates) and is beloved for its Tuesday-night paella special. A neighborhood dinner favorite, ⑪ **Firefly,** on the corner of Douglass Street, is deservedly celebrated for its New American cuisine.

To get back to where we started, walk back down to Church Street and hop on a J train for a scenic ride. En route, you'll pass ⑫ **The Dubliner,** a decades-old Irish pub that couldn't be friendlier or more down-to-earth. Duck in for a happy hour pint; you may find yourself staying for live music or a hand at trivia. To get back to where we started, walk down to Church Street and hop on a J train for a scenic ride.

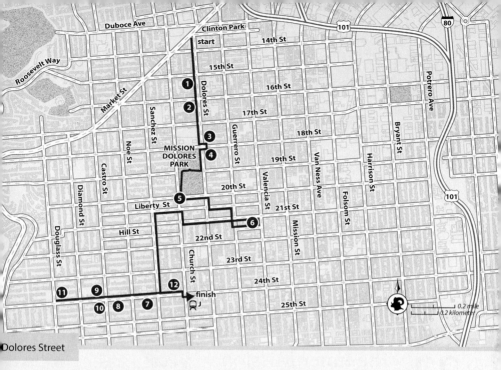

Points of Interest

1. **Tanforan Cottages** 214 and 220 Dolores St. (private residences)
2. **Mission Dolores Basilica** 3321 16th St.; 415-621-8203, missiondolores.org
3. **Bi-Rite Creamery** 3692 18th St.; 415-626-5600, biritecreamery.com
4. **Dolores Park Cafe** 501 Dolores St.; 415-621-2936, doloresparkcafe.com
5. **Golden Fire Hydrant** Corner of 20th St. and Church St.
6. **Ritual Roasters** 1026 Valencia St.; 415-641-1011, ritualroasters.com
7. **Folio Books** 3957 24th St.; 415-821-3477, foliosf.com
8. **Noe Valley Bakery** 4073 24th St.; 415-550-1405, noevalleybakery.com
9. **Charlie's Corner Bookstore** 4102 24th St.; 415-641-1104, charliescorner.com
10. **Contigo** 1320 Castro St.; 415-285-0250, contigosf.com
11. **Firefly Restaurant** 4288 24th St.; 415-821-7652, fireflysf.com
12. **The Dubliner** 3838 24th St.; 415-826-2279, dublinerbarsf.com

22 The Inner Mission
San Francisco's Latin Heart

Above: *Simone Star's Balmy Alley mural* Antepasadas (Ancestors) *is just one of the many striking artworks celebrating Latin culture and heritage in the Mission.*

BOUNDARIES: 16th St., Dolores St., 25th St., York St.
DISTANCE: 2.25 miles
DIFFICULTY: Easy
PARKING: Off-street parking is available on the corner of Valencia and 18th Sts.
PUBLIC TRANSIT: 16th St. and 24th St. BART stations; 14 Muni bus

San Francisco's most colorful, diverse, and creative neighborhood is the Mission. This broad, flat district is populated by Latino families, artists, hipsters, and a growing number of white-collar workers. Amid the bars, bodegas, taquerías, and upscale restaurants are many buildings distinguished not so much by the businesses operating there but by the art on the exterior walls. Murals—some in the tradition of Diego Rivera, others drawing on contemporary pop culture—are ubiquitous throughout the Mission. There are far too many works of art to take in on a single walk. This walk passes many of the key murals and ducks into a few shops to get a feel for the neighborhood. Take your time, slow down, and breathe it all in.

Our walk concentrates on the Latin-infused side of the Mission—the *corazón,* if you will. To sample the neighborhood's latest trends and tastes, head to the 2-mile stretch of Valencia Street between Cesar Chavez Street and Duboce Avenue. Known as the Valencia Corridor, this is a treasure trove of coffeehouses, bars, parklets, and restaurants, with nary a chain to be found.

Walk Description

Start at the corner of Mission and 16th Streets, which is convenient if you're arriving on a BART train. Unfortunately, this busy intersection often feels like the end of the line for a growing number of addicts and homeless, but thanks to the station, there's plenty of foot traffic. Walk a block east on 16th and you'll reach the ❶ **Redstone Building,** at No. 2940. This building, also called the Temple of Labor, was a meeting hall for labor unions and played a pivotal role in the 1917 United Railroads Streetcar Strike. These days the building houses theater groups and nonprofits. During business hours, enter to view the murals that cover every inch of wall in the lobby and hallways. The murals, including works by Barry McGee, Rigo, Aaron Noble, John Fadeff, and Sebastiana Pastor, were unveiled in 1997. Many of the works here echo the styles of the Depression-era artists who contributed pro-labor murals in Coit Tower and elsewhere in the city. The artists who worked on the Redstone Building are all associated with the Clarion Alley Mural Project (CAMP), and we'll see more of their works on the next stop of this tour. Across the street, you'll notice the ornate exterior of the ❷ **Victoria Theatre,** San Francisco's oldest operating theater. Originally home to vaudeville acts upon its construction in 1908, the theater has changed with the times and the neighborhood. Cycling through various identities as a movie theater, Spanish-language cinema, burlesque house, and others, the Victoria now hosts film fests and various live events.

Return to Mission Street and, after crossing, turn left on Mission and right onto narrow ❸ **Clarion Alley.** Without its continuous murals, Clarion Alley would just be a gritty alley inviting illicit activities. The alley's transformation began in the early 1990s, when artists living in an artists' loft midway up the block formed CAMP. The original group included Rigo, Aaron Noble, and Vince Oresman, among others, and some of their early works still survive on the alley's continuous wall of backyard fences and garage doors. Many other artists have joined them since. (Rigo and Noble have moved on, and the warehouse they worked in has since been demolished.)

The murals here on Clarion reflect the influence of pop art, comic books, outsider art, and graffiti. Critics sometimes categorize the Clarion painters, along with other Mission District artists, as the Mission School. Sometimes their diverse styles are lumped into a catchall description:

The Art Deco New Mission Theater

"urban rustic." Near Mission Street, a work by Brian Tripp, an American Indian artist, represents just one of many cross-cultural connections established by Clarion Alley painters. The Mission Mural movement began as predominantly Latin American, with an obvious concern for immigration issues and the Reagan-era wars in Central America. Here the concept has broadened to embrace a postpunk and hip-hop street aesthetic. A lot of the work, such as Matso's mural of ghosts emerging from the downtown skyline, are both political and cartoony. Clarion is a permanent work in progress. Over the years, weather has faded some of the older murals, while fresh new murals are continually introduced. Of late, taggers have had a hand in modifying the murals—Julie Murray's realistic elevator painting, midway up the block, is almost completely obscured. (Not surprisingly, Murray has also painted movie sets for a living.) More murals are located one block north along Sycamore Street.

At Valencia Street turn right and then turn left at 17th Street. Make a left at Dearborn Street. At Bird Street, you'll notice the ❹ **Dearborn Community Garden** spanning both sides of the road. Here, more than 40 plots are carefully tended by neighboring gardeners on what was once a parking lot for a Pepsi bottling plant. As you approach 18th Street, the spectacular ❺ **Women's Building** comes into view. The mural on the building, called *Maestrapeace*, wraps like vines around two sides of the building. It was painted in 1994 by seven women artists, and thematically the painting celebrates women of all cultures. Walk a little ways up Lapidge Street to enjoy the inspiring artwork on the building's east side.

Return to 18th Street and turn right. Then right again to follow Lexington to 19th Street and turn left. Across the street you'll see the Precita Eyes Mural *Vamos Gigantes* showcasing local pride. Turn right onto Mission Street, one of San Francisco's liveliest and most interesting streets. Amid the taquerías and tiendas you'll see signs of the street's pre-Latino past, from a time when this was a largely Irish neighborhood. Some blocks are dominated by the faded and rusted beacons of grand old movie palaces that closed down decades ago. Not all cinematic hope is lost, however. ❼ **Foreign Cinema** has been showcasing movies on its elegant outdoor patio since 1999. Tables have drive-in-style speakers, but the real star of the show is the award-winning cuisine. Next door, new life was breathed into the ❽ **New Mission Theater,** as the old Art Deco masterpiece was restored to glory in 2015 by the Austin-based Alamo Drafthouse group that brings food and drink to your cinematic experience. To get a real feel for the street, though, have a veggie burrito at ❻ **Taquería Can-Cun** (between 18th and 19th Streets) or a carnitas taco at ❾ **La Taquería** (between 24th and 25th Streets). If you're not ready for a full meal yet, head left on 22nd to the corner of Capp Street for a quick side trip to family-owned ❿ **La Copa Loca,** where an Italian gelato maker mixes the flavors of Central and South America with creamy scoops incorporating guanabana, tamarind, dragon fruit, lucuma, and other exotic tastes.

Returning to Mission Street, continue and turn left at 23rd Street. A few doors down, a barber shop is completely covered by ⓫ *La Lucha Continua (The Struggle Continues)*, a mural composed of portraits of political and multicultural icons such as Pancho Villa, Martin Luther King Jr., Madame Nguyen Thi Binh, Mohandas Gandhi, Sitting Bull, and Che Guevara. The mural was supervised by Susan Greene but was a collaborative effort (as are many murals) that resulted in a rich variety of styles in the portraits.

Return to Mission and turn left. Continue on for a block and turn left onto leafy 24th Street, lined with shops, restaurants, and cantinas almost all catering to the Latin American community.

La Palma Mexica-Tessen serves delicious and authentic Mexican food.
Photo: SanFranAnnie/Flickr (creativecommons.org/licenses/by-sa/2.0)

Backstory: Kinky Stuff

In December 2006, a historic building in the Mission District was sold: the old San Francisco Armory, a huge pile occupying an entire city block at 1800 Mission St., designed to resemble a Moorish castle. The buyer, Kink.com, is a producer of bondage films. So just when people were starting to worry that the Mission was getting less interesting, along came the porn industry to the rescue!

The building is strikingly well suited to its current purpose. It has a menacing medieval exterior, and the last surviving stretch of Mission Creek runs through its dungeonlike basement. According to filmmaker James Mogul, the boiler room was tailor-made for a film set.

Kink has also hosted art festivals, open to the public and suitable for all ages, so occasionally you can see what the building's interior is like without consenting to appear in a movie. Kink's ownership has also entertained the idea of developing condominiums in the building, but with a catch: each unit would come equipped with cameras that could capture the residents' private moments on film. These days, the best way to get a feel for the vibe is to nurse a swank cocktail across the street at the **Armory Club** (1799 Mission St.; 415-431-5300, armoryclub.com), an atmospheric lounge that feels like a Victorian gentlemen's club.

This is the true heart of the neighborhood. While murals abound, be sure to stop at the corner of 24th Street and South Van Ness to admire ⑫ *La Rumba No Para (The Party Won't Stop)*, by artist Carlos "Kookie" Gonzalez in collaboration with Precita Eyes Muralists. The mural honors Chata Gutierrez (1953–2013), a DJ and community activist who championed Latin music with her radio show *Con Clave*. So beloved was Chata that the neighborhood raised funds to help her with her cancer treatments. Next to Chata, above the House of Brakes, is an homage to Carnaval San Francisco, a pulsating multicultural block party rife with costumed dancers, drumming, live music, and all manner of pageantry that the Mission throws every year over Memorial Day.

Just past Shotwell, you'll come to the first of two great bookstores that each feature art galleries as well; a testament to the neighbohood's rich independent art scene. The first is the worker-owned ⑬ **Adobe Books & Arts Cooperative,** a comfy spot with new and used titles and a plethora of author and community events. A few blocks down, you'll find ⑭ **Alley Cat Books and Gallery,** another funky, freewheeling bookstore offering titles in Spanish and English and showcasing local artists. Across the street from the bookstore, turn right onto ⑮ **Balmy Alley,** the Mecca of the Mission District's mural arts scene. It's your classic back alley lined with garage doors and backyard fences, but the entire length of it is covered with colorful murals. Balmy predates Clarion Alley by nearly two decades. Some of the oldest murals on the block were painted in the 1970s by Ray Patlán and a group of women artists who called themselves Las Mujeres Muralistas—painters who favored the Mexican folk styles that inspired Diego Rivera and José Clemente Orozco. At the time, their collectivist politics, florid color schemes, and phantasmagoric compositions also would have meshed fairly easily with the psychedelia of the Haight and the idealism of hippie communes. The machine guns are more Latin revolutionary than flower power, however.

As you enter the alley from 24th Street, Susan Cervantes's mural of a woman giving birth is sure to grab your attention, followed by older murals inspired by Aztecan imagery and a mural depicting *campesinas* wielding AK-47s. New murals appear all the time. Some of the more contemporary works are by artists cut from the Clarion Alley cloth, and while not apolitical, these are stylistically less tied to the traditions of the Latin American left. Some works make use of stencils, while others are inspired by cinema and comics. Toward the end of the block, a mural pays homage to classic Mexican film stars, including the comedian Cantinflas, painted by Rigo. A native of Portugal, Rigo is one of the city's better known contemporary artists, having made a visible impact on South of Market with prominent murals such as *One Tree* and *Inner City Home*. Here, in a more collaborative spirit, his work blends with the work of others. His *Cantinflas* shares the spotlight with an alluring dancing woman, painted by Carolyn Castaño. Walk to the end of the block and double back, taking in the art along both sides of the alley, and continue east down 24th Street.

Half a block down, at No. 2981, is ⑯ **Precita Eyes Mural Arts and Visitors Center,** which is a great place to learn about the local mural arts scene. Founded in 1977 by muralist Susan Cervantes, Precita Eyes has overseen many important commissions throughout the neighborhood, including along Balmy Alley, and the center's educational wing has produced many of the Mission's artists. The shop sells postcard photos of murals and T-shirts with murals on them. Anyone wishing to delve deeper into the culture can gather books and information here. Precita Eyes also organizes walking tours of the neighborhood's public art, sometimes led by local muralists.

Across the street, past Alabama Street, are a couple of very traditional Latino markets and

Independent bookstores like Alley Cat Books and Gallery abound along 24th Street.

Head to an authentic *panadería* to satisfy your sweet tooth with specialties like the *niño envuelto* (jelly roll).

panaderías (bakeries). **17 Casa Lucas,** at No. 2934, is a colorful shop that's useful if you're in need of a piñata or a bottle of guava juice. On the corner of Florida Street, at No. 2884, **18 La Palma Mexica-Tessen** is a classic purveyor of over-the-counter snacks, including excellent tamales and tacos. Grab a pack of hand-patted corn tortillas for an authentic treat. Sometimes you can spot women making them in the back of the shop.

At the corner of 24th and Bryant Streets, **19 Galería de la Raza** is a neighborhood institution that was founded in 1970 by artists involved in the Chicano civil rights movement. The gallery is an interdisciplinary space where art is exhibited and performances are staged. The gallery often showcases provocative and controversial art that usually casts perspective on topical issues such as illegal immigration.

A block down 24th Street at York Street, you can end your tour over a milkshake at **20 St. Francis Fountain,** a classic ice cream parlor that's been dishing out scoops since 1918 and shows no signs of stopping. (They haven't bothered to maintain museum-quality decor, but hey, the place is more comfortable for it.) You can also get a burger or BLT if you haven't already filled up on delicious Mexican food.

Points of Interest

1 Redstone Building 2940 16th St.; 415-820-1698, rlta.org

2 Victoria Theatre 2961 16th St.; 415-863-7576, victoriatheatre.org

3 Clarion Alley clarionalleymuralproject.org, info@clarionalleymuralproject.org

4 Dearborn Community Garden Dearborn St. and Bird St.; 415-431-7363, sfparksalliance.org /our-parks/parks/dearborn-community-garden

5 Women's Building 3543 18th St.; 415-431-1180, womensbuilding.org

The Inner Mission

6 **Taquería Can-Cun** 2288 Mission St.; 415-252-9560, taqueria-cancun.cafes-world.com

7 **Foreign Cinema** 2534 Mission St.; 415-648-7600, foreigncinema.com

8 **New Mission Theater** 2550 Mission St.; 415-549-5959, drafthouse.com/sf

9 **La Taquería** 2889 Mission St.; 415-285-7117, facebook.com/lataqsf

10 **La Copa Loca** 3150 22nd St.; 415-401-7424, lacopalocagelato.com

11 *La Lucha Continua* Mural 3260 23rd St.; tinyurl.com/laluchacontinua

12 *La Rumba No Para* Mural 24th St. and South Van Ness Ave.; 415-285-2311, precitaeyes.org

13 **Adobe Books & Arts Cooperative** 3130 24th St.; 415-864-3936, adobebooks.com

14 **Alley Cat Books and Gallery** 3036 24th St.; 415-824-1761, alleycatbookshop.com

15 **Balmy Alley** Parallel to Treat Ave. and Harrison St. between 24th and 25th Sts.; balmyalley.com

16 **Precita Eyes Mural Arts and Visitors Center** 2981 24th St.; 415-285-2287, precitaeyes.org

17 **Casa Lucas Market** 2934 24th St.; 415-826-4334 (no website)

18 **La Palma Mexica-Tessen** 2884 24th St.; 415-647-1500, lapalmasf.com

19 **Galería de la Raza** 2857 24th St.; 415-826-8009, galeriadelaraza.org

20 **St. Francis Fountain** 2801 24th St.; 415-826-4200, stfrancisfountainsf.com

23 Mission Bars
A Tavern for Every Taste

Above: *Knock down some pins while enjoying a brew and a burger at the Mission Bowling Club.*

BOUNDARIES: Duboce St., Valencia St., Folsom St., 22nd St.
DISTANCE: 2.5 miles
DIFFICULTY: Easy
PARKING: Street parking can be difficult to find day or night. There is off-street parking at the corner of 18th and Valencia Sts.
PUBLIC TRANSIT: 16th St. BART station; F streetcar

As the sun goes down on the Mission District, the neighborhood's vibrant murals fade into the shadows and irresistible artificial light splashes out onto sidewalks from the barrooms. This is one of the city's very best nightlife zones. The entertainment options are varied and of high quality, with a healthy mix of dives, supper clubs, and live-music venues. This tour selects several scattered spots, and you'll no doubt want to whittle it down a bit to avoid passing out somewhere. A lot of ground is covered, and some of the streets are a bit dodgy at night. Use good sense while walking down dark blocks. You might also want to break a cardinal rule of walking tours and call on a taxi or ride share to bridge the gaps now and then.

Walk Description

If you're starting out in late afternoon or early evening head to ❶ **Zeitgeist,** where bikers and heavily tatted rockers hang out, at the corner of Valencia Street and Duboce Avenue. The draw here is the outdoor beer garden—actually nothing more than a graveled lot with picnic tables and a freeway ramp looming above it. Yet somehow, in the twilight on a warmish evening, this is one of the best places to be in San Francisco. You needn't be a local or a biker or have any street cred to fit in here. You can grab a greasy burger and similar fare from a window next to the pool table. Bring a deck of cards, and make yourself at home.

Before you get too comfortable, though, head down Valencia Street several blocks to the ❷ **Elbo Room,** between 17th and 18th Streets. If you're short on time or you'd rather not walk too far, this is a great place to start your journey. The bar has been operating in some capacity or other since the end of Prohibition, but it's been a Mission District mainstay since the early 1990s. If you can snare a stool at the sexy, curvaceous bar, then you deserve a suave cocktail of some kind. When things get cranking here—9 or 10 p.m., usually—it can be difficult to get anywhere near a bartender or server. Bands (rock, Latin, miscellaneous) and DJs work the room upstairs. Have an early drink, return to 17th Street, turn right, and mosey on.

Next stop is the ❸ **Uptown,** at 17th and Capp Streets. This is one of the city's great dives. It doesn't look particularly welcoming from the outside (extra points for that), and the location isn't great (more extra points), but step in and you'll have a hard time leaving. The old Formica booths and cool lighting are almost too perfect, but the place is real, very low-key, and more of a local hangout than most of the Mission's hipster joints. Play some pinball or shoot some pool before moving on.

Down a block and across the street, the ❹ **Mission Bowling Club** offers six bowling lanes, a full bar, and one of the best upscale burgers the Mission has to offer. Lanes are usually reserved in advance, but you might get lucky if you show up early. Otherwise, check out the retro bowling art, grab a beer at the bar, and head back out. A little farther down, on the desolate corner of 17th and Folsom Streets, is the unassuming ❺ **Rite Spot Cafe.** From the outside the bar appears to have been closed for years—it's a great look. But inside you'll find a sleepy, candlelit, self-described dive that feels a little like stepping back in time. Truthfully, it's a supper club, with a long bar, a rickety piano, a mess of tables and barely enough space for the band, making for an intimate experience.

A classic supper club, the Rite Spot hosts everything from live jazz to trivia nights.

The calendar is eclectic, offering everything from top-notch soul and blues to trivia and comedy nights. As for the food, try the chicken cacciatore sandwich slathered in melted cheese and mayonnaise.

From the Rite Spot, follow 17th Street to Alabama Street and turn right. When you hit 20th, turn left to duck into the former warehouse that now houses one of the city's best cocktail bars, ❻ **Trick Dog.** The clever novelty menus change every six months (they've been everything from in-flight safety cards to a book of paint swatches), but there's nothing gimmicky about their award-winning cocktails. As you head back the way you came on 20th, you'll come upon the ❼ **Atlas Cafe,** which has been holding down this corner since 1996. The Atlas is a low-key, slightly arty coffee shop with an upbeat vibe. You can order beer, pizzas, and tasty sandwiches here. The only drawback is the place closes at 10 p.m. If it's a Thursday night around 8 p.m., definitely make this stop, since that's when the Atlas features live bluegrass music. On Saturday afternoons, from 4 to 6 p.m., it's ragtime.

Continue on 20th Street to Mission Street. The next couple of blocks have enough bars for a full weekend bender. Just north on Mission, off 20th, you can't miss ❽ **Bruno's** bold, lit-up sign. It opened in the 1940s as a clubby Italian American restaurant with sleek lines, mood lighting, and plush Naugahyde booths. In the 1990s the place benefited from renewed interest in mid-20th-century swank and highball culture. An intimate jazz room was added. After a 2006 remodel, Bruno's is still a classy place for cocktails, but the musicians have been replaced by DJs, and they're open to the public only on Friday and Saturday (other nights are reserved for events).

Turning around and heading south to the next block of Mission, between 20th and 21st Streets, one of the Mission's finest dives, ❾ **Doc's Clock,** moved a block from its original haunt after a landlord dispute. They did, however, keep their iconic sign—walk across the street for a good look, as it's a real beauty that promises good times within. The new venue is little changed, and they still plan interesting events, such as Doggie Happy Hour (bring your pooch), Barbie Mutilation Night (!), and film screenings by local filmmakers. No cover.

A block farther and across the street, you'll see a line on the sidewalk for folks clamoring to hit the rare rooftop bar at ❿ **El Techo,** above the restaurant Lolinda. If you can score a spot, you'll find Latin American street food, amazing views, and heat lamps and wind breaks (it is San Francisco, after all).

When you get to 22nd, turn left to hit ⓫ **Urban Putt,** an artful indoor take on minigolf housed in an abandoned mortuary. The course is steampunk-zany, featuring local landmarks like painted Victorians shaking in an "earthquake" and an "underwater" hole, among others. A full bar and tasty eats in the adjoining restaurant round out the experience.

After a few holes in one, head back the way you came to hit the ⓬ **Make-Out Room,** just off the corner of 22nd, an idiosyncratic watering hole that's been a neighborhood stalwart for more than a decade now. With dim lighting and an assemblage of Formica tables scattered over a concrete floor, it's nothing fancy, but disco balls and hanging streamers add a certain amount of festivity. Many nights after 8 p.m. it features live bands—everything from cowpunk to indie rock—and charges a cover.

If the music scene at the Make-Out doesn't steam your glasses, head up the block on 22nd Street to the down-to-earth ⓭ **Latin American Club** for quirky art, pool tables, and a friendly mass of tourists and locals alike. Beware the pint-glass margaritas—they can be deadly.

Our final spot is the ⓮ **Lone Palm,** awash in old-school charm. Martinis, tea lights, and small tables draped with white linen invite whispered conversation, but this place still manages to feel a bit like a back-alley joint. Even better: free bar snacks on every table. Enough said.

Free snacks, stiff martinis, and candlelit tables make the Lone Palm a perennial favorite.

Mission Bars

Points of Interest

1. **Zeitgeist** 199 Valencia St.; 415-255-7505 (no website)
2. **Elbo Room** 647 Valencia St.; 415-552-7788, elbo.com
3. **Uptown** 200 Capp St.; 415-861-8231, uptownnightclub.com
4. **Mission Bowling Club** 3176 17th St.; 415-863-2695, missionbowlingclub.com
5. **Rite Spot Cafe** 2099 Folsom St.; 415-552-6066, ritespotcafe.net
6. **Trick Dog** 3010 20th St.; 415-471-2999, trickdogbar.com
7. **Atlas Cafe** 3049 20th St.; 415-648-1047, atlascafe.net
8. **Bruno's** 2389 Mission St.; 415-643-5200, brunossf.com
9. **Doc's Clock** 2417 Mission St.; 415-824-3627, docsclock.com
10. **El Techo** 2516 Mission St.; 415-550-6970, eltechosf.com
11. **Urban Putt** 1096 S. Van Ness Ave.; 415-341-1080, urbanputt.com
12. **Make-Out Room** 3225 22nd St.; 415-647-2888, makeoutroom.com
13. **Latin American Club** 3286 22nd St.; 415-647-2732, tinyurl.com/latinamericanclubsf
14. **Lone Palm** 3394 22nd St.; 415-648-0109, tinyurl.com/lonepalmsf

24 Potrero Hill and Dogpatch
Small-Town Vibe, Big-City Views

Above: A barn turned acclaimed restaurant, Piccino anchors Dogpatch's burgeoning culinary scene.

BOUNDARIES: 17th St., San Bruno Ave., 22nd St., Terry A. Francois Blvd.
DISTANCE: 2 miles (Potrero Hill only), 3.5 miles (Potrero Hill and Dogpatch)
DIFFICULTY: Moderately strenuous
PARKING: It's fairly easy to find, but keep an eye out for street cleaning and 2-hour-time-limit zones.
    If you're willing to head farther away from 18th St., you can find unlimited parking.
PUBLIC TRANSIT: 22 Muni Bus

Potrero Hill has long been a secret among locals, beloved for its sunny weather, great views, charming restaurants and bookstore, and small-town feel. What was once the grazing area for cows and goats from Mission Dolores (*potrero* means "pasture" in Spanish) is now a place where neighbors greet each other at the coffee shop, water bowls are left outside stores for local pooches, and parking is plentiful.

To the east, Dogpatch was always the more industrial neighbor to Potrero, a former shipyard and manufacturing area that boasted an eclectic mix of warehouses, single family homes, and a smattering of restaurants and bars. Long a mecca for waves of immigrants seeking work in the waterfront industries, Dogpatch was traditionally a solidly working-class community with the bars and affordable housing to prove it. But the secret is out on both these enclaves, and today they are two of the hottest neighborhoods for new restaurants, art initiatives, and a boom of housing redevelopment. Walk them now and then visit again in five years to see what's changed.

This walk will take us up and down the steep hills of Potrero with great views of the downtown skyline, past community gardens, the city's *real* crookedest street, charming commercial districts, and down into historic Dogpatch where hip restaurants and an artistic nod to its shipbuilding past awaits.

You can turn this into a shorter loop just through Potrero Hill, or you can continue on through Dogpatch and end at a funky waterfront restaurant that's a far cry from the slicker spots along the Embarcadero.

Walk Description

Begin at the corner of 18th Street and Texas Street, where a whole host of sweet mom-and-pop stores await perusal. There's usually a line out the door at ❶ **Plow,** a brunch spot sought after for its crispy fried potatoes and amazing egg dishes. Crossing Texas and heading west on 18th

Farley's coffeehouse has long been a community anchor.

Street, you'll come to ❷ **Farley's,** where they've been offering "community in a cup" at this location since 1988. A true neighborhood hub, Farley's hosts live music, local art, and the shady parklet outside invites long conversations over coffee.

The next two blocks of 18th firmly cement the small-town vibe with flower shops, bistros, a smattering of delicious restaurants, and a fantastic corner bookstore, ❸ **Christopher's Books,** where the staff always have excellent suggestions. And with their signature tangy sourdough crust, ❹ **Goat Hill Pizza** has been anchoring the corner of Connecticut Street since 1975.

Turn right on Connecticut Street to head downhill two blocks. At the corner of 17th Street, the ❺ **Connecticut Yankee** is a little slice of Boston on the hill. Outdoor picnic tables, friendly staff, and excellent burgers make this a local favorite. The building has been there since 1907, and this one-time bootleg and speakeasy operation has been an institution ever since.

Turn left on 17th Street and you'll soon be passing Jackson Park, a block-long square of grass and play space that is frequently home to softball games and lunchtime sunbathers. Head left on De Haro Street and follow your nose toward the malty smell of ❻ **Anchor Steam Brewery,** one of America's first craft breweries. (Anchor used to use foggy San Francisco air to cool the beer mash on their rooftops, creating a halo of steam—hence the name.) The brewery is open for excellent public tours, but you need to reserve well in advance. If that ship has sailed, you can drown your sorrows at ❼ **Anchor Public Taps,** a taproom that serves up small-batch pints and offers food trucks in the outside courtyard.

Continue up De Haro, and where 19th meets it, head up the pedestrian stairway through the garden to your right. Follow 19th to San Bruno and turn left. Near the top of the street, you'll find the ❽ **Potrero Hill Community Garden.** The plots are maintained by residents (there are more than 50 individual plots, as well as some beehives) and you are welcome to stroll around and enjoy this slice of sublime green space overlooking the Mission and Twin Peaks (with peekaboo views of the Golden Gate Bridge).

Just past the garden, follow the sidewalk stairs leading up to McKinley Square Park instead of continuing on the sidewalk. Follow the cement path that skirts the grassy dog park and you'll reach the top of the "real" crookedest street in San Francisco: ❾ **Vermont Street.** While not nearly as well maintained (or well known) as Lombard Street (see Walk 11, Russian Hill, page 74), Vermont was deemed more crooked on an episode of the Travel Channel's *Travel 911*. An annual Bring Your Own Big Wheel race down the street is held every Easter Sunday, which is a colorful (and mildly dangerous) affair. After sneaking a peek, head back toward 20th Street on Vermont and turn right.

Pause at the corner of 20th and Kansas and try to imagine Steve McQueen careening past in a 1968 Ford Mustang. This is one of the intersections shown in the iconic car-chase scenes of *Bullitt*. Turn right on Rhode Island. ❿ **Chiotras Grocery** is a friendly deli-market with a great beer and wine selection and a small outside deck at the back where you can enjoy your nosh.

Turn left on curved Southern Heights to reach the brown-shingled ⓫ **Potrero Hill Neighborhood House,** affectionately called The Nabe, originally conceived to provide resources to the Russian immigrants who landed in this part of Potrero Hill beginning in 1905. Potrero Hill has always been more Russian than Russian Hill, and The Nabe used to offer classes in English, sewing, and cooking and served as a cultural hub. Renowned architect Julia Morgan designed the building, which was originally a two-story structure. The top floor had to be moved to accommodate the creation of Southern Heights, so it was simply lopped off and moved to the side. Today The Nabe continues to offer a whole range of social and community services.

Pass in front of The Nabe to continue along Southern Heights. When you see a small cement stairway to your left, look across the lower street to the ⓬ **First Russian Christian Molokan Church,** another testament to the Russian presence on the hill. Molokans ("milk drinkers" in Russian) were originally dairy farmers who protested, among other things, the Russian Orthodox proscription against drinking milk on holy days. This is one of the oldest Molokan churches in the United States and still has a small congregation.

Continue along Southern Heights and turn left on Wisconsin Street to head downhill. The Queen Anne Victorian at ⓭ **706 Wisconsin** is where Beat icon Lawrence Ferlinghetti lived from 1957 to 2004. The founder of City Lights bookstore (see Walk 7, North Beach, page 50), Ferlinghetti was also San Francisco's first poet laureate.

Turn right on 20th Street, and you'll soon pass the Potrero Hill Library, with one of the best views around. Continue down 20th Street, where local cafés, groceries, and corner stores add color to commerce.

When you reach the corner of 20th and Texas, you have a choice: turn left and walk two blocks to return to the start of our journey, or continue into the adjacent Dogpatch neighborhood by turning right on Texas Street to head downhill. The buildings on the hill facing you on the descent are the low-income housing projects where O. J. Simpson and actor Danny Glover grew up.

As Texas turns into 22nd, you'll pass next to the CalTrain Station that whisks passengers downtown and to the South Bay and enter the Dogpatch Historic District. There is much disagreement about where the name *Dogpatch* comes from. The area was originally populated with waves of immigrants—Scotch, Irish, and Dutch, and then Russian and Eastern European—who came to ply their trade in the shipyards and ironworks. The place-names of these microneighborhoods originally reflected a diversity of nationalities and occupations: Irish Hill, which was gradually eroded to almost nothing to provide landfill to raise Mission Bay; Dutchman's Flat; and Butcher Town, where butchers supposedly left scraps for stray dogs. With Dogpatch being one of the last areas in the city with room for development, concerned residents banded together and applied for historic status in 2003. Because the neighborhood is built on earthquake-defying serpentine rock, many of its original buildings remain intact, and the historic designation led to their preservation. This one-time residential outpost for shipbuilders, rope workers, and canners is now a hotbed of sleek restaurants and bars, but it retains an authentic grit.

Turning left on Minnesota Street, head up to see a cluster of ⓮ **Pelton Cottages** (905–913 Minnesota St.), which date from 1887 and helped Dogpatch earn its historic designation. The homes are named for local architect John Pelton Jr., who published free architectural plans in the *San Francisco Evening Bulletin* to meet a demand among working-class families for housing that was affordable yet attractive. Because most architects at the time wouldn't deign to draw up plans for such low-end homes, Pelton's Cheap Dwellings series was a revolutionary concept that both boosted newspaper sales and resulted in the construction of these forebears of today's trendy tiny houses. Surely Pelton would never have dreamed that these cottages are now worth close to $2 million apiece!

Dogpatch residents built cottages such as this from plans that were published in the local newspaper in the 1880s.

Returning to 20th, the large yellow building that houses acclaimed Italian-California restaurant ⓯ **Piccino** was once a coal-and-feed barn with an attached carriage repair. Speaking of carriage repair, peer through the tinted glass at ⓰ **Woods Division Carpentry Shop** to see where and how cable cars go to be restored and repaired. Working off 1870s blueprints and using original techniques (albeit with better tools), master carpenters take great care with the National Landmark cars, which can take up to a year to overhaul.

Continue along 22nd and turn left on Tennessee Street, although we wouldn't blame you if you made a brief pause for a handmade chocolate confection at ⓱ **Recchiutti at theLab.** Tennessee narrows down into Angel Alley, so named for the ⓲ **Hells Angels Clubhouse,** on your left at the end of the block. Having opened in 1955, this is the second-oldest chapter of the infamous motorcycle club; it gained further infamy following the disaster that ensued when they were providing security (along with the San Jose chapter) for the Altamont Speedway Concert in 1969. While they had worked many concerts before for the Grateful Dead, things got out of hand quickly at Altamont, resulting in the stabbing of one concertgoer by an Angel. Many point to this event as being the beginning of the end for the Summer of Love.

Turn left onto the pedestrian pathway. Here you will find placards detailing the history of the Tubbs Cordage Co., the west coast's largest rope supplier. Rope production requires a lot of space to twist and assemble the fibers, and there was once a 1,500-foot indoor "rope walk" that used to cut across this area toward Third Street. This explains why some of the buildings are at such odd angles. Tubbs was also responsible for providing the safety net that saved 19 men during the construction of the Golden Gate Bridge. Toward the end of the walkway, you can try your hand at a few knots.

Turn left on Third Street to glimpse the new face of Dogpatch, where undeniable change has tried to honor its working-class roots. The huge blocks-long American Industrial Center began as the American Can Company in 1915, with a plant stretching from 20th Street to 23rd Street. At one point it was the largest tin-can company in the United States. Now it's home to a smorgasbord of retailers breathing new life into this postindustrial corridor, including the ⑲ **Museum of Craft and Design.**

At ⑳ **Mr. and Mrs. Miscellaneous,** a pastry-chef duo churns out sweetly inventive ice cream flavors like candied grapefruit and Earl Grey tea alongside more-traditional flavors. Across the street diagonally, the ㉑ **Dogpatch Saloon** has been a watering hole since 1912. While the clientele has changed considerably, they keep an honorary seat open for the grizzled onetime owner, "Tugboat Annie," a woman revered for her sailor's mouth and stiff pours.

Crossing 22nd, venerated ㉒ **Serpentine,** so named for the bluish-green rock that forms the bedrock of Dogpatch, was one of the first restaurants to see the potential for Third Street. Continuing along Third Street there are too many great spots to name, and it has a European feel, with each small market offering a specialty good such as cheese, chocolate, bicycles, croissants, fresh-brewed beer, and other artisan goods.

Head all the way down Third Street to Mariposa and turn right. Cross Illinois and make your way through the parking lot to ㉓ **The Ramp,** a low-key waterfront barbecue joint with picnic tables, an outdoor bar, and live salsa music on the weekends. On sunny days, it's jam-packed with locals seeking out the unpretentious vibe and famed Bloody Marys. To return to our start, head back to 18th Street and head up the hill back to Texas Street.

Points of Interest

① **Plow** 1299 18th St.; 415-821-7569, eatatplow.com

② **Farley's** 1315 18th St.; 415-648-1545, farleyscoffee.com

③ **Christopher's Books** 1400 18th St.; 415-255-8802, christophersbooks.com

④ **Goat Hill Pizza** 300 Connecticut St.; 415-641-1440, goathillpizza.com

⑤ **Connecticut Yankee** 100 Connecticut St.; 415-552-4440, pourguys.com/connecticut-yankee

⑥ **Anchor Steam Brewery** 1705 Mariposa St.; 415-863-8350, anchorbrewing.com

⑦ **Anchor Public Taps** 495 De Haro St.; 415-863-8350, anchorbrewing.com/publictaps

⑧ **Potrero Hill Community Garden** 752 San Bruno Ave.; 415-449-0410, potrerogarden.org

⑨ **Vermont Street** Kansas St. north to Division St.

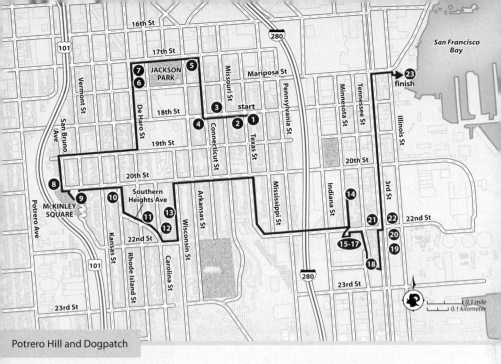

Potrero Hill and Dogpatch

25 Bernal Heights
Dogs, Parks, Slides, and Swings

Above: *The rocky wildness of Bernal Hill feels miles from downtown, but the views prove otherwise.*

BOUNDARIES: Precita Ave., Folsom St., Cortland Ave., Winfield St.
DISTANCE: 3 miles
DIFFICULTY: Moderate (long uphill stretches)
PARKING: Unrestricted street parking around Precita Park
PUBLIC TRANSIT: 24th St. BART station; 12, 14, 27 Muni buses

Bernal Heights rises up from the southern edge of the Mission, where narrow streets dead-end long before they can reach this rocky, windswept hilltop. The broad views of the Mission, Potrero Hill, the bay, and the distant downtown skyline are fantastic—but that's par for the course in San Francisco. What makes this walk especially alluring is the suddenness with which the sheltered, slightly funky Bernal Heights neighborhood turns into a rugged chunk of wilderness. The hill is home to many red-tailed hawks that glide silently about the slopes.

Backstory: Eureka? We Didn't Actually Find It!

Like the rest of San Francisco, Bernal Heights was struck by the lure of the gold rush. So in 1896, when Frenchman Victor Ressayre claimed to have found gold at the top of Bernal Hill, excitement understandably ensued. Residents flocked to the hill with all manner of excavating equipment, feverishly trying to strike it rich in their own backyard. Word spread as far south as Los Angeles, and gold-hungry hordes descended on the area, setting up makeshift stores selling beer and sundries. Alas, the excitement came to an abrupt end less than a month later, when it was discovered that quartz, not gold, had been found. Some grumbled that perhaps a savvy Ressayre—a beer salesman by trade—simply wanted to bring more commerce to the area.

Wear good hiking shoes for this walk. And if you have a dog, bring it along and free it from its leash—you'll both fit right in. Descending Bernal Hill, you will gain appreciation of the funky architecture, lively gardens, and community projects that imbue this neighborhood with such warmth and homegrown appeal.

Walk Description

Begin at ❶ **Charlie's Café,** which sits on Folsom Street across from the western end of Precita Park. You can grab a cup of coffee to fuel your uphill walk and pause for a moment to soak in the arty, community-minded vibe that characterizes this leafy, residential pocket to the north of Bernal Hill. Opened in 2001, Charlie's Café, named for its owner Charles Harb, embodies this spirit, as he greets customers by name, hangs local art on the walls, and invites neighborhood bands to cram into his tiny joint.

As you head south on Folsom, the street rises steadfastly, as though developers entertained thoughts of making it clear the hill in a straight shot. However, within two blocks, as the going gets rough the road abruptly swerves to the left. Just as suddenly, you're above the rooftops, amid the grassy, rocky terrain for which Bernal Heights is known. If it's the rainy season, wind, clouds, and mist swirl about the green face of the hill. In spring, the hill is covered with wildflowers. In summer, it's an arid scape of red rock and yellow grasses. There's a dog for just about every human up here.

Folsom curves up to Bernal Heights Boulevard. Turn right, pass the gate (which prohibits cars from entering), and you'll enter Bernal Heights Park. The road loops up a fairly easy incline around the hill. The long, straight boulevards that slice through the Mission District drop into view behind you. Down below the road, along the western side of the hill, look out for narrow,

Backstory: Bernal Heights Outdoor Cinema

Bernal Heights naturally attracts creative types, and to prove it, every fall the neighborhood showcases the works of local filmmakers in an outdoor film festival. Films are shown on Saturday nights during the months of September and October. The filmmakers usually give a talk in a local café, then everyone proceeds to a nearby park (sometimes Bernal Heights Park), where the film is shown as the sun goes down. It's a fun and social event, and so popular that they've added indoor screenings in April and June called "Face to Face with the Filmmaker."

Musician Michael Franti has shown his work in the festival, and Ralph Carney has scored films screened during the festival. The neighborhood's best known filmmaker is Terry Zweigoff, director of such delights as *Bad Santa* and *Ghost World*. So far, the festival hasn't featured Zweigoff's work. All events are free and run by generous volunteers. For information, check bhoutdoorcine.org.

unofficial trails (which at times fade beneath new grass or fallen pine needles)—these lead to hidden gardens planted by local residents on city property. The steps leading down to Esmeralda Street lead to some of these gardens.

On the south side, where the road is gated, a wide, rocky path corkscrews up toward the top of the hill. The red rock here is chert, and is the same stuff found up on Corona Heights. Follow the trail up. On blustery days, you might see several hawks hovering in place about 20 feet overhead, their wings stretched wide, adjusting perceptibly to keep the wind beneath them. The birds keep very still up there, stealthily scanning the ground for potential prey. Stand beneath them and you'll have about as good a look (without the aid of binoculars) as you could ever hope to get of wild raptors in action. If you're lucky, the Bernal Heights swing will be beckoning from the tree at the top of the hill, offering you a chance to feel the wind beneath your feet as well. It's taken down occasionally for repairs; but locals seem determined to keep it aloft, and the view from the perch is amazing.

The path loops around the summit, with unbroken perspectives of the city and the bay. Cross over the cement barricade to follow the looping dirt trail; there are ledges and lookouts and little spur trails. It's not a huge area, but you'll want to roam about a bit before returning to Bernal Heights Boulevard. A broad shale path leads down from the top. Look for Anderson Street and stroll on down past a hodgepodge of residential architectural styles. Bernal Heights was never a wealthy district, although today these homes sell for a pretty penny (as do all homes in San Francisco). The narrow streets, many of which curve abruptly to avoid steep grades, give the area an offbeat, Montmartre-like feel.

Follow Anderson down to Cortland Avenue, the main commercial strip. Make a right; you'll find good places to eat, coffee shops, and a bookstore. Bernal doesn't generally draw much business from out-of-towners or even from people who live elsewhere in the city, making this a very neighborly sort of urban backwater. That's not to say it's backwards. Fine restaurants here include **❷ Moki's Sushi and Pacific Grill,** for pan-Asian delights, and the family-friendly **❹ Bernal Star,** where they serve up gourmet burgers (including lamb, buffalo, and wild boar!) and screen movies on their heated back patio. One of the first lesbian-owned, lesbian-operated, and lesbian-welcoming bars in the city, the historic **❸ Wild Side West** had a rough ride initially, as empty toilets and junk were left on the street in front of their newly minted bar. Undeterred, the plucky owners turned the refuse into funky art in their magical downstairs beer garden, and decades later the bar is a cornerstone of the neighborhood. Drawing a friendly mixed crowd, the Wild West Side is known for being the best watering hole on the hill.

As Cortland begins to descend back down to Mission Street turn right on Elsie Street. Just off the corner, note the 19th-century barn that was converted into a house ages ago. Two blocks down, Virginia curves up to meet Elsie. Follow it and you'll see some of the neighborhood's finest Victorian homes. Local residents are cultivating a garden along the right side of the road, beneath the curved retaining wall. A block down, turn right on Winfield Street, which runs in a straight line to the north side of the hill. Where Winfield Street hits Esmeralda Street, a community mosaic points the way to the **❺ Esmeralda Slide Park,** where a slick 35-foot slide runs down a beautiful community garden. At its inauguration in 1979, then-Mayor Dianne Feinstein took a giggling ride down; we recommend that you grab a piece of cardboard and do the same.

Continuing along Winfield Street, take a left turn on Coso Avenue and you'll soon reach pretty Mirabel Avenue. Mirabel dead-ends at Shotwell Street, and a small set of stairs will lead you down to Bessie Street, meandering past the funky artful homes that characterize Bernal as you make your way back to the expansive lawn and sweet playground of Precita Park, once the stomping grounds of Carlos Santana. After all that climbing, you deserve a drink or an ice cream at the **❻ Precita Park Cafe,** across the street from the eastern side of the park. Opened in 2011, the vibrant café has become the de rigueur meeting spot for families meeting up at the playground and is an excellent place to soak in the environs.

Precita Park Cafe serves cold drinks and hot meals.

Points of Interest

1 **Charlie's Café** 3202 Folsom St.; 415-641-5051 (no website)

2 **Moki's Sushi and Pacific Grill** 615 Cortland Ave.; 415-970-9336, mokisf.com

3 **Wild Side West** 424 Cortland Ave.; 415-647-3099, wildsidewest.com

4 **Bernal Star** 410 Cortland Ave.; 415-695-8777, bernalstar.com

5 **Esmeralda Slide Park** Esmeralda and Winfield Sts.; sites.google.com/site/esmeraldaslidepark, esmeraldaslidepark@gmail.com

6 **Precita Park Cafe** 500 Precita Ave.; 415-647-7702, www.precitaparkcafe.com

26 Glen Park and Glen Canyon
A Hillside Hamlet and a Rocky Outcrop

Above: *Glen Canyon's miles of wildflower-strewn trails and riverbanks seem far away from the city.*

BOUNDARIES: Bosworth St., Diamond St., Portola Dr., O'Shaughnessy Blvd.
DISTANCE: 2 miles
DIFFICULTY: Moderate (some hills, trails with loose rocks)
PARKING: Street parking on Chenery
PUBLIC TRANSIT: Glen Park BART station; 44, 52 Muni buses

San Francisco's urban continuity is frequently broken by hills topped by rock outcrops and mounds of soil yielding auburn grasses. In the case of Glen Canyon, the city gives way to a deep impression—a gash, really—where Islais Creek supports a rich riparian environment of arroyo willow, elderberry, blackberry, horsetail, monkeyflower, and eucalyptus.

The canyon is filled with birdsong and the dull jackhammering of woodpeckers. Red-tailed hawks are likely to swoop overhead, a harmless snake may cross your path, and a coyote may blend into the scenery while sunning itself on the canyon's grassy slopes. A rare example of native coastal scrub survives along the park's western slope. Making liberal allowances for the nonnative plants and the hush of unseen traffic on O'Shaughnessy Boulevard, a hiker in the rugged canyon might imagine San Francisco during the city's somnolent Californio days. Combine this with the hamletlike feel of the Glen Park neighborhood, and you've got a perfect urban walking blend. Grab some picnic fixin's in town and head for the canyon.

Walk Description

Our walk begins and ends in the pleasant Glen Park neighborhood, replete with mom-and-pop storefronts inviting window shopping and strolling. If you're coming via BART, the Glen Park station is at the corner of Diamond and Bosworth Streets. Follow Diamond Street north through the intersection of Chenery Street to find ❶ **Canyon Market,** a fabulous grocery that sells all manner of sandwiches and salads to create a picnic. Heading left on Chenery, the warm and inviting Rick and Nada Malouf have been running the ❷ **Cheese Boutique** since 1993, and it is *fantastique*. They will let you sample cheeses and craft a sandwich on the spot. Originally from Lebanon, the Maloufs also sell a homemade hummus that garners rave reviews.

Across the street, ❸ **Bird & Beckett Books and Records** is one of the coolest independent book and record stores in San Francisco. Not content to just offer a great selection of new and used books, they also stock vinyl records and often play host to jazz bands and poetry readings. You may want to save this spot for after our walk, as once you head in, you're sure not to want to leave. Instead, cross Chenery and follow your nose to the sweet and simple ❹ **Destination Baking Company** at the corner of Castro Street, where pies, breads, and pastries are baked daily, and café tables beckon for a little crossword puzzle work over a cup of steaming coffee.

Departing the small retail strip, our walk now takes us up Castro Street and then almost immediately left on residential Surrey Street. Look for the small stairway between houses 24 and 30 on Surrey Street that will connect you with the utterly charming Penny Lane, a country road that was once a 19th-century carriageway. Follow the rutted dirt road past sweeps of bougainvillea to its end at Diamond Street.

Turn right on Diamond and continue uphill; then turn left on Sussex. Halfway up the block, look for Ohlone Way, another mostly unpaved lane that will lead you behind gardens and homes before coming out at Surrey Street. Turn right to follow Surrey Street to Chenery. Turn right again to reach Elk Street and the entrance to Glen Canyon Park. You've surely figured out that we haven't taken the most direct route to the park but instead wound through the backcountry lanes that are such a unique treasure to this neighborhood.

Crossing into the park, you should have the playing fields on your left and the children's playground on your right. Skirt the playground and head past the tennis courts on your right to the wide Gum Tree Girls Trail that follows Islais Creek and is named for three women in the 1960s who lobbied to keep a four-lane freeway from running through the park. Condescendingly nicknamed the Gum Tree Girls, owing to the blue gum eucalyptus that were slated for removal due to freeway construction, the women had the last word as they successfully kept their urban oasis green. Shortly after leaving the playground behind, you'll come to a steep set of wooden stairs leading up to the right. Follow these to access the Coyote Crags Trail, following signs toward Christopher Playground. You'll traverse slopes covered with bunch grasses and oat grasses (green after sus-

Fragrant flowers and mostly forgotten country lanes greet the urban explorer.

tained rains, golden brown in the summer); rocky outcrops of crumbling chert; spreads of bramble, coyote brush, and poison oak; and clumps of trees. Down among the rock crevices hides a rare and shy native, the San Francisco alligator lizard. At dawn and dusk, it's not unlikely to see a coyote.

Don't follow the set of wooden stairs that end up at Christopher Playground, but instead stay straight to remain on Coyote Crag Trail. The trail eventually becomes a shaded path, completely closed in on either side by dense, low trees. This path ultimately rises to meet Portola Drive, so look for the sign pointing left to Islais Creek to return back down the canyon among the cool shade of the creekside trees. Brooks such as this once ran throughout San Francisco, each one filled in or diverted through culverts as natural terrain was converted to cityscape. Islais Creek is a rare, though not unique, survivor. It is fed primarily by natural springs within the canyon itself.

Past the boardwalk, the trail widens to accommodate service vehicles, and a nursery school appears in a dense eucalyptus grove to the right. The trail leads out of the canyon to some softball fields. Exit the park and turn right on Elk Street, then left on Chenery Street, which leads back to the neighborhood's small shopping district. Here you can refortify yourself over a sturdy breakfast or lunch at ❺ Tyger's Coffee Shop, at the corner of Diamond and Chenery. A half block south on Diamond toward the BART station, ❻ Gialina is sought after for its inventive takes on Neapolitan pizza.

Glen Park and Glen Canyon

Points of Interest

1. **Canyon Market** 2815 Diamond St.; 415-586-9999, canyonmarket.com
2. **Cheese Boutique** 660 Chenery St.; 415-333-3390, facebook.com/cheeseboutique
3. **Bird & Beckett Books and Records** 653 Chenery St.; 415-586-3733, birdbeckett.com
4. **Destination Baking Company** 598 Chenery St.; 415-469-0730, destinationbakingcompany.com
5. **Tyger's Coffee Shop** 2798 Diamond St.; 415-239-4060 (no website)
6. **Gialina** 2842 Diamond St.; 415-239-8500, gialina.com

27 Upper Market and the Castro
Rainbow Pride and Victorian Beauties

Above: The rainbow flag, designed by activist Gilbert Baker, first flew at the Gay Freedom Day Parade in 1978; today, it remains a vibrant emblem of gay pride.

BOUNDARIES: Market St., Octavia St., Douglass St., 20th St.
DISTANCE: 1.5 miles
DIFFICULTY: Easy
PARKING: You might try your luck along Guerrero or Valencia St. Off-street parking is available at the Market and Noe Garage.
PUBLIC TRANSIT: F streetcar

The Castro District, or the Castro for short, proudly celebrates its distinction as one of the first and most recognized gay meccas in the United States. But in addition to being at the forefront of civil rights as it pertains to marriage equality and gay, lesbian, bisexual, and transgender inclusion, it is also a treasure trove of lovingly maintained architectural gems, with unbroken strings of beautiful Victorian houses along many blocks.

An enclave of Eureka Valley, the Castro was known in the early 1900s as Little Scandinavia for the all the working-class immigrants from Norway, Sweden, Denmark, and Finland who settled here, bringing dairy farms and half-timbered architecture. During World War II, the military dismissed thousands of gay servicemen from the Pacific, and they found themselves landing in San Francisco's port.

The Polk Street area (see Walk 13, Tenderloin, page 88) was the city's original "gayborhood," but couples began drifting inland toward Castro Street in the early 1970s. They were most likely drawn by the well-priced Victorian houses and the winning location, with streets terracing up the eastern slope of Twin Peaks (see next walk), which on most days shields the Castro from the fog. The neighborhood's quiet residential streets reflect the refined tastes of its denizens, who are by and large established professionals.

Castro Street between Market and 18th Streets is the busy commercial hub, with Upper Market taking on much of the spillover. This tour will take in both sides of the district: the elegant homes as well as the bars and clubs that reflect the Castro's flamboyant social side. (The Twin Peaks walk explores the western part of the neighborhood, which climbs the western slopes of the prominent hills.)

It's hard to miss the welcoming purple exterior of the SF LGBT Center.

Walk Description

We'll begin our tour well east of Castro Street, at the corner of Market and Octavia Streets. Here, at 1800 Market, the vivid purple **1** **SF LGBT Center** stands as a welcoming portal to the neighborhood, with rainbow flags flapping proudly from each window. It offers services and programs for lesbians, gays, bisexuals, and trans people, including career counseling, youth mentorship, and healthcare resources. The center is architecturally interesting, as it consists of a historic Victorian that segues into a strikingly modern wing of tinted glass panels that meet at oblique angles. It's a suitable introduction to the neighborhood, where appreciating the old doesn't preclude embracing the new.

Heading west on Market Street, a few blocks up, on the same side of the street, you come to the

Slide into Cafe du Nord for local musical acts and an old-school cocktail lounge vibe.

2 **Mint Karaoke Lounge,** a little neighborhood dive that gets its name from the nearby U.S. Mint, which can be seen soon after you pass the bar. The Mint is a popular nightclub that draws a fairly mixed crowd, though it appeals mostly to hammy would-be singers eager for their turn at the mic. The U.S. Mint, up on the hill, is a foreboding structure that looks more like a futuristic military installation than a place that produced money. It no longer creates currency, but it does still churn out commemorative coins that are highly collectible.

Up Market Street a couple of blocks west, just before the corner of Sanchez Street, is **3** **Cafe du Nord.** The name is French, the architecture is Scandinavian, and the classy below-street-level joint is pure swank with a hip, modern edge. The onetime speakeasy is a mainstay on San Francisco's small-venue live-music scene, with a regular lineup of independent acts, many local and mostly worth catching. Upstairs, the Swedish American Hall is no meatball parlor but another excellent live-music venue. It has the look and feel of a Masonic lodge, with heavy Alpine woodwork. Events are scheduled here infrequently, though.

Across Market Street, at the corner of Noe Street, **4** **Cafe Flore** is a celebrated hangout where the patio tables are highly coveted on sunny days. As you can see, in construction it resembles a gardener's shed, though on a much larger scale. Potted greenery contributes to the effect. But Cafe Flore is about coffee, beer, light meals, seeing, and being seen. A block up is **5** **Catch,** a well-regarded seafood restaurant and also an official city landmark, as it's where the original AIDS Memorial Quilt was first conceived by activist Cleve Jones. Now considered the world's largest community folk-art project, the quilt began as a way to honor those who died of AIDS but were denied funerals or recognition due to social stigma. You are welcome to enter the restaurant to see a small section of the quilt displayed just inside the front door.

The corner of Market and Castro Streets, where you turn left onto Castro, is naturally one of the principal crossroads of the neighborhood. A huge rainbow flag flaps in the wind from a pole high above **6** **Harvey Milk Plaza,** at the southwest corner. Named for the assassinated city supervisor, the cramped little plaza is tucked between a building and the entry to the Muni station, but its size did not prevent it from being a mobilizing point for countless civil rights rallies and some rather raucous dance parties. It was here that Harvey Milk stood on an overturned box with a bullhorn to

Twin Peaks Tavern earned landmark status for being the first Castro watering hole with clear glass windows, doing away with the shame and secrecy of being seen in a gay bar.

motivate support, and it was here that tens of thousands gathered in the wake of Milk's death for a spontaneous candlelit march to City Hall in 1978. The vigil is repeated every year.

Just beyond the rainbow flag, wedged on the busy intersection between 17th Street and Market, is **7** **Pink Triangle Park,** the nation's only memorial to gay and lesbian servicepeople who were killed in World War II. The memorial comprises 15 stone columns, each representing 1,000 fallen soldiers and each topped with a pink triangle—the symbol that the Nazis forced gay and lesbian concentration-camp inmates to wear on their uniforms.

On the opposite side of Castro Street, across from Harvey Milk Plaza, **8** **Twin Peaks Tavern** attracts an older crowd of regulars. The bar has historic charm but has come a long way from its 1935 blue-collar roots. The neighborhood's biggest landmark is the **9** **Castro Theatre,** a few doors up Castro Street from the Twin Peaks Tavern. There aren't many movie palaces of this sort left anywhere in the country, which is why the Castro is treasured by all San Franciscans. The programming is eclectic, featuring a mix of independent films, bawdy sing-alongs, and screenings of camp classics such as *Mommie Dearest* and *Valley of the Dolls,* as well as pristine prints of iconic movies. The show is often preceded by an artful performance on the house organ, and on occasion the Castro screens silent films with a live pit orchestra. Several film festivals take place here as well. The building, a Moorish flight of fancy, is particularly dramatic at night, when the marquee is lit up. It was built in 1922, and the plans were drawn by architect Timothy Pflueger.

A couple of doors farther along, **⑩ Cliff's Variety** is the neighborhood hardware store, although that moniker hardly does it justice. In business since 1936, the Asten family that ran Cliff's was open to the changing neighborhood and was one of the first straight-owned stores to hire gay employees. Along with the usual plumbing and electrical fixtures, you can also stock up on feather boas, diamond tiaras, games, and housewares. On the same block, **⑪ Dog Eared Books** is an independent bookstore that hosts an LGBT book club and a regular series called Perfectly Queer Reading; they also specialize in small-press books and local publications.

The bookshop is just a few paces from the rainbow crosswalk corner of Castro and 18th Streets, which is considered the nexus of the neighborhood. There are restaurants and hangouts in either direction along 18th Street; turn right and walk half a block to reach the **⑫ GLBT History Museum,** one of few of its kind in the world. The museum is tiny, but $5 gains you access to a variety of audio recordings, photos, and historical information. It's closed on Tuesdays.

Retrace your steps to continue up Castro. At No. 575, Harvey Milk ran Castro Camera during the 1970s; today it's the **⑬ Human Rights Campaign Store**. A bronze plaque on the sidewalk commemorates Milk's contributions to the local community, and you can see a painted Harvey smiling down from the window of the upstairs unit where he once lived. The **⑭ Anchor Oyster Bar** next door, family owned since 1977, is a local favorite for fresh seafood dishes. The cioppino (seafood stew) is highly recommended.

The Castro Theatre is a beloved neighborhood movie house.

Just past 19th Street, Castro Street turns residential, with an impressive row of Victorian apartment buildings stacking up along the incline. Turn left on Liberty Street, which looks much as it would have more than a century ago. Immaculate single-family homes, nearly uniform in character, line both sides. These were middle-class homes originally but are worth six and seven figures today. From here, you could continue down Liberty Street (there's a staircase) and head toward Dolores Park and the Mission, or you can return to the Castro and window-shop along 18th Street.

Upper Market and the Castro

Points of Interest

1. **SF LGBT Center** 1800 Market St.; 415-865-5555, sfcenter.org

2. **Mint Karaoke Lounge** 1942 Market St.; 415-626-4726, themint.net

3. **Cafe du Nord and Swedish American Hall** 2174 Market St.; 415-471-2969, swedishamericanhall.com

4. **Cafe Flore** 2298 Market St.; 415-621-8579, flor415.com

5. **Catch** 2362 Market St.; 415-431-5000, catchsf.com

6. **Harvey Milk Plaza** Market and 17th Sts.; 415-500-1181, friendsofharveymilkplaza.org

7. **Pink Triangle Park** 2454 Market St.; pinktrianglepark.org (no published phone number)

8. **Twin Peaks Tavern** 401 Castro St.; 415-864-9470, twinpeakstavern.com

9. **Castro Theatre** 429 Castro St.; 415-621-6120, castrotheatre.com

10. **Cliff's Variety** 479 Castro St.; 415-431-5365, cliffsvariety.com

11. **Dog Eared Books** 489 Castro St.; 415-658-7920, dogearedbooks.com

12. **GLBT History Museum** 4127 18th St.; 415-621-1107, glbthistory.org/museum

13. **Human Rights Campaign Store** 575 Castro St.; 415-431-2200, shop.hrc.org/san-francisco-hrc-store

14. **Anchor Oyster Bar** 579 Castro St.; 415-431-3990, anchoroysterbar.com

28 Twin Peaks
Epic Views and Secret Gardens

Above: *Skyline vistas spur you on as you make your way to the top of Twin Peaks.*

BOUNDARIES: Market St., Danvers St., Corbett Ave., Twin Peaks Blvd.
DISTANCE: 4 miles
DIFFICULTY: Strenuous
PARKING: Market and Noe Center, 2284 Market St. between 16th and Noe, has off-street parking.
PUBLIC TRANSIT: F streetcars (street level); K, L, M streetcars (underground); 22, 33, 37 Muni buses

Twin Peaks has an allure that dates back at least to Spanish times, when the peaks were known as Los Pechos de la Choca, which is typically translated as "The Breasts of the Maiden" (or sometimes "The Breasts of the Indian Girl"); the more-subtle current name has become iconic to the point of overstatement. Scholars suggest that the Ohlone people may have once planted medicinal and ceremonial plants here. Certainly the vantage point was useful as a lookout. And indeed the view is magnificent—but so is the journey.

Climbing from the Castro flats, we explore colorful Victorian architecture, ferret out hilltop parks with a locals-only feel, and traverse magical secret garden stairs and slides. Keep your eyes peeled for the endangered Mission Blue butterfly, which can often be seen flitting about this windy perch. This walk requires some climbing on loose trails, so wear suitable shoes and expect to get some exercise.

Walk Description

A walk up to Twin Peaks is an excuse to explore the Castro's back streets. Starting from the corner of Castro Street, turn left and head west up Market Street on the south sidewalk. After several blocks, just after crossing Douglass Street, turn down the pedestrian stairs onto Ord Street; then turn right on 18th Street. Turn left to follow Danvers Street to Caselli, cross Caselli, and continue on the alleylike back street, which is still Danvers. At 19th Street, turn left again.

This part of the Castro may be San Francisco's most finely composed neighborhood. It has an ideal hillside setting and a solid collection of attractive, though not spectacular, Victorian residences. Eureka Valley, as the Castro is still sometimes referred to, was long a working-class neighborhood with immigrants from Scandinavia, Ireland, and Germany. But Little Scandinavia, as it was once called, is now more associated with rainbow flags celebrating gay pride than half-timbered homes. That said, the neighborhood is architecturally consistent. Whereas the imposing estates of Pacific Heights were surrounded by large lots on which 20th-century apartment buildings would be built, the Castro's kit Victorians were put up, and remain, side by side, almost uninterrupted. The grid bends to the terrain here, giving the neighborhood a European feel while also making it possible to switchback up and down.

Press on 19th to the corner of Yukon, where you will see ❶ **Kite Hill,** a scraggly open parkland with no apparent entrance. Continue a little way on the right side of 19th Street until you reach the first private garage, at which point a dirt trail should be plainly visible. Head up the trail, through gardens which rapidly yield to a wild, grassy mountaintop. Kite Hill seems a bit neglected, but it's more appealing for that fact. People live in San Francisco for decades without ever discovering this spot. For those who do make their way here, the views—of Castro rooftops and the downtown skyscrapers on one side, of a canyonlike neighborhood squeezed between Kite Hill and Twin Peaks on the other—are a big payoff. Regardless of the weather below, it's very gusty up top, and one can instantly understand the name. A kite would surely soar high over the city from here. If all you want to do is sit and absorb the view, you'll find a bench where you can do just that.

From the top of Kite Hill, look for the gravel path—the lower of two paths exiting the hill—near an SF REC AND PARK sign to make your way to Corwin Street. After walking a few hundred feet, you'll see a well-established community garden on the corner of Corwin and Acme Alley. These are dry gardens, well worth a lengthy pause to admire the impressive array of drought-resistant plants. Proceed downhill through the gardens until you reach a small patio that is actually half of ❷ **Seward Mini Park.** Yes, the odd concrete structures you see before you are a pair of slides. They look as slick and curvaceous as an Olympic luge run, not to mention kind of dangerous. The slides were built in 1973 following the guidelines set by a 14-year-old Seward Street resident, Kim Clark, who won a Design a Park competition at her local public school. Presumably these slides are for kids, but no one would fault an adult for taking this quick route the rest of the way down to Seward Street. The slides are closed on Mondays and after 5 p.m. all other days, with locked gates preventing renegades from sneaking a ride.

At Seward, turn right and stay on the elevated sidewalk, along the right side of the street. It's a beautiful block with lots of planting. At the end of the block, turn right onto Douglass. At 20th, Douglass hits an incline too steep for cars and the street turns into a concrete stairway for pedestrians. Walk up the steps, through another hillside garden, and at the top, continue along Douglass Street, on the right-hand side through another well-planted block. By now, you might have come to the reasonable conclusion that this is San Francisco's Garden District.

Turn right to return to Romain Street. Sutro Tower stands directly ahead, though it's still some distance off. Head two blocks up to Market Street. This part of Market, an extension that dates to the 1920s, forms a rampart, cutting off the Castro from streets such as Corbett and Clayton, on Market's upside. The divide turned out to be advantageous for the Castro, making the neighborhood feel more sheltered and complete.

Cross Market on the Romain Street pedestrian bridge, continue west up Romain, and make a left on Corbett Street. After you pass Rooftop Alternative School, turn right at Hopkins Street and then left onto Burnett Avenue. Here, the neighborhood takes an unexpectedly bland turn. It's evident that in the 1960s, Burnett Avenue and Gardenside Drive were handed over to developers of very little imagination. Adjacent to the drab apartment complexes that proliferate here, concrete public stairways lead upward—we'll take advantage of these now and

The slides of Seward Mini Park provide a thrilling means to go downhill.

Almost there: the final push to Twin Peaks

follow a more scenic route back down. The steps, intermittently signed as VISTA LANE, lead all the way up to Parkridge Drive. Here you'll see a signpost pointing left towards STEPS TO TWIN PEAKS. Turn left and cross the street to follow Vista Lane's steps upward; then cross Crestline Drive to the clearly marked SF REC AND PARK trailhead. A stepped, unpaved trail leads us out of apartment-land, past low shrubs and brambles, up to Twin Peaks Boulevard and the peaks themselves.

It must be said that the peaks aren't overly impressive when you first lay eyes on them from Twin Peaks Boulevard. In fact, the boulevard, which forms a figure eight around the two peaks, is largely the problem. The road, paved in 1934, has unsightly waist-high concrete shoulder barriers that may dissuade a dispirited walker from continuing all the way up to the peaks' blustery tops. But slide on over the barrier and forge upward.

The views from the tops of both peaks are spectacular, and if you scale both hills, the effect is almost stereoscopic. From the south peak, named Noe, Market Street appears as a prominent seam through the central city, leading the eye to downtown skyscrapers. Pan to the left for an attractive vantage of the Golden Gate Bridge and the Marin Headlands beyond. You can see the south peak's twin and glimpse Alcatraz just behind it to the right. Panning to the right along the bay, you'll see Treasure Island and the Bay Bridge. South of Market Street are Potrero Hill, Bernal Hill, Candlestick Point, impressive San Bruno Mountain, and, beyond that, the northern reaches of the Santa Cruz Mountains. To the west is Mount Davidson, San Francisco's highest peak, its giant cross poking up above a surrounding grove of eucalyptus. On a cloudless day you can see the surf at Ocean Beach, which from this distance appears to break in supreme slow motion. On days of crystalline clarity, you can even see the Farallon Islands, more than 25 miles away.

Looking immediately about you, the crumbling rock outcrops on which you stand obviously make a harsh habitat for plant life, but you'll notice ankle-high coast strawberries, blue wild rye, monkeyflower, and yarrow. At times, pesky poison oak shrubs tend to run a bit wild until the parks department cuts them back. (If you brush against poison oak—be on the alert for the small, scalloped green leaves, which turn reddish in summer—you can expect an unpleasant itch and rash.) From up here it's often possible to look down on red-tailed hawks as they survey lower slopes for prey.

Descend the south peak along the same trail you came up, cross Twin Peaks Boulevard, and head up the north peak, Eureka, where the view of downtown and the bay is closer but also somewhat obstructed by radio towers immediately to the east. As you will notice, from this vantage the Ferry Building lines up perfectly at the foot of Market Street. To the northwest, you'll have an unobstructed view of Sutro Tower, the giant three-pronged antenna that brought television to much of the city when it was completed in 1973. The awkward orange-and-white antenna still has its detractors, who were quick to object to its sci-fi implications back in the '70s, and it also has its fans, who are obviously unconvinced that Twin Peaks would be prettier without it.

The trail over the north peak continues down the other side. Follow Christmas Tree Point Road, which might easily be taken as a third rung in the figure eight formed by Twin Peaks Boulevard. Christmas Tree Point Road curves around the radio buildings, and along it is a popular viewpoint that's accessible to motorists. The overlook has parking and benches, and the view of downtown is excellent.

At the end of Christmas Tree Point Road, turn right on Twin Peaks Boulevard and follow it down. There's no sidewalk as the road hurtles downward, so be on your guard for cars. A sidewalk does materialize as the road becomes residential. You'll continue on Twin Peaks as it takes a sharp right turn at a small pocket park with a bench at Clarendon. If you still have any juice left, look for a wooden staircase heading up to your right directly across from Crown Terrace that leads up to ❸ **Tank Hill**. Although several hundred feet shorter than Twin Peaks, Tank Hill still affords amazing views and has the luxury of being relatively unknown to tourists. You'll often find locals on the hill at sunset. While the namesake water tank is long gone, it's now a favorite spot for neighbors to watch Fourth of July fireworks when the fog complies.

Once you've had your fill, return the way you came, cross the street, and descend Crown Terrace to enter another picturesque hillside enclave. The lane crooks past Edwardian houses with Spanish revival details and finishes. Turn right to descend the picturesque ❹ **Pemberton Steps,** an attractive brick stairway flanked by hillside plantings that include a number of young Japanese maples. This top section is the oldest, and the moss-covered stairs have a secret-garden feel to them. The lower stairs have been redone, complete with benches and water fountains, and the neighboring homes boast particularly vibrant gardens in spring.

Continue down the stairs all the way to Clayton. Cross Clayton Street—use caution!—and cut through the little rock-and-cactus garden fashioned with care from a triangular street corner. Turn left onto Corbett Avenue and follow it down to Danvers Street, which leads back to Market Street and your starting point at Market and Castro.

Twin Peaks

Points of Interest

1 **Kite Hill** Yukon and 19th Sts.; 415-831-6331, sfrecpark.org/destination/kite-hill

2 **Seward Mini Park** 30 Seward St.; 415-831-2700, sfrecpark.org/destination/seward-mini-park

3 **Tank Hill** Clarendon Ave. and Twin Peaks Blvd.; 415-831-5500, sfrecpark.org/destination /tank-hill-natural-areas

4 **Pemberton Steps** 1 Pemberton Pl.

29   Westside Cordillera
Corona Heights, Buena Vista Park, and Alamo Square

Above: The Painted Ladies preen for the paparazzi.

BOUNDARIES: 16th St., Central Ave., Golden Gate Ave., Steiner St.
DISTANCE: 2.5 miles
DIFFICULTY: Strenuous
PARKING: Two-hour street parking is available around Corona Heights, especially on 16th St. near the Flint St. entrance. Two hours doesn't leave enough time, so Sunday (when parking is unlimited) is a good day to make this walk. Off-street parking is available at the Market and Noe Garage.
PUBLIC TRANSIT: F streetcar; K, L, M Muni trains; 24 Muni bus

The three hilltop parks in this tour are only a few blocks apart but couldn't be more different. Corona Heights is a rocky outcrop just above the Castro District. Buena Vista Park's densely wooded terrain sprouts abruptly from the Haight. Alamo Square is a grassy quadrant amid classy Victorian houses. All have sweeping views of San Francisco, each offering a unique perspective, but the real pleasure of taking in all three in one shot is in passing through such varied topography within a short space. Wear good shoes for hiking, and be prepared to traverse steep, unpaved trails.

Walk Description

Assuming you've either parked your car or disembarked from public transit down in the Castro, start by climbing from the corner of 16th and Flint Streets up to ❶ **Corona Heights Park.** From just about anywhere along upper Market Street, if you look to the west, you'll see the red, jagged cliff to which we're headed. Begin ascending to the right of the tennis courts. It's a pretty barren hill, with a few trees, grasses, and wildflowers.

The most distinctive feature of Corona Heights is the rock itself: the reddish stone is visibly cracked on the surface, and the trails are strewn with squared-off chips and chunks. Pick up a piece and look it over. This rock is chert, formed by plant and animal matter that settled on an ancient seafloor and became petrified before being thrust up here. Similar rock formations turn up elsewhere in the city, but Corona Heights is the most striking example. The hill is crested by dramatic, jagged pinnacles of rock, some of it spray-painted on by taggers. From here, take a look around and enjoy a broad view of the city—in addition to the downtown skyline and city hall, you'll see all of the South of Market area, the Mission, the Castro, Noe Valley, Twin Peaks, and, immediately to the north, Buena Vista Park (our next stop). At lower elevations of Corona Heights are a well-situated playground, the ❷ **Randall Museum,** and a patch of green where people can liberate their dogs from their leashes. The Randall Museum is an educational museum for kids that has a combined emphasis on nature and the arts. It was completely remodeled in 2018 and has a small café if you need a snack.

Descend the other side of the hill toward the dog area and exit the park onto Roosevelt Way at Museum Way. Turn right on Roosevelt and bear left onto Park Hill Avenue. A block up is Buena Vista Avenue, which rings ❸ **Buena Vista Park.** Cross Buena Vista and turn left. The sidewalk here runs around the base of the park's southern slope. Opposite, the large peachy building at 351–355 Buena Vista Ave. E. made a brief appearance in Hitchcock's *Vertigo*. Constructed in 1928 as ❹ **St. Joseph's Hospital,** this historical landmark is now condominiums. Once you're past it, look for a set of well-maintained stairs leading up next to a green REC AND PARK sign. In the 1960s, hippies frolicked here. Near the top, you'll reach an asphalt path that will serve you well the rest of the way. It winds to good lookout points along the north and east side of the park, and it also dips down into a shady gulch that's very sheltered. By now you are surely appreciating the size and varied topography of this inner-city park. Originally called Hill Park, it was set aside by the city in 1867 and is San Francisco's oldest park. Many of the trees were planted on behalf of Adolph Sutro, who annually observed Arbor Day by donating seedlings. John McLaren, who for half a century was superintendent of Golden Gate Park, also oversaw the forestation of Buena Vista Park. If you look closely in some of the trailside drainages, you may find yourself gazing on a Victorian headstone fragment. When the city moved nearly all of its cemeteries to Colma in the early 1900s, unclaimed headstones were reused for gutters, among other things, and this is one of the parks that benefited.

Find your way toward the western edge of the park. As you descend, look for a set of stairs just past a wooden railed overlook and turn left to descend them toward the exit near the end of Frederick Street. Turn right onto Buena Vista Avenue, which curves around the park and leads to Haight Street. Along the way, take note of the ornate gate by metalsmith E. A. Chase at **⑤ No. 731 Buena Vista,** commissioned by Graham Nash (of Crosby, Stills, Nash, and Young) when he lived here. Years later, singer Bobby McFerrin owned the home as well. Next door, the mansion at **⑥ No. 737 Buena Vista** was built in 1897 for Richard Spreckels, whose uncle was sugar magnate Claus Spreckels. In the house's early days, writers Ambrose Bierce and Jack London supposedly resided here briefly as well (some claim that London penned *White Fang* here). More recently, Danny Glover lived here for a spell.

Past Haight Street, Yerba Buena Avenue becomes Central Avenue. Follow it to the Panhandle, the strip of shady greenery between Oak and Fell Streets. Cross the park to the Fell Street side and turn right. Where the Panhandle ends, turn left at Baker, then turn right at Hayes Street.

The jagged rocks of Corona Heights Park afford stellar perches from which to take in the city skyline.

❼ Alamo Square Park is three blocks up. Enter midway, about where Pierce Street hits Hayes, and climb the gentle slope to the top of the park. It's fairly conventional as San Francisco parks go—a hilly lawn with a grove of trees at its center, a single fenced-in tennis court—but the view from the park is a classic. Head over the crest and down the eastern slope, and you'll spot the photographers. They're always here, snapping shots of the row of impeccable Victorian houses along Steiner Street, with the downtown skyline beyond. It's a surefire cover shot—you'll have seen the image on scores of guidebooks and in the opening montage to the popular 1990s sitcom *Full House*. The Victorian stars of this view, the **❽ Painted Ladies** at 710–722 Steiner St., are notable mostly for their near uniformity and for having changed little over the years. They're not the most beautiful Victorians in the city or even on Alamo Square. The house at 1198 Fulton St., on the other side of the park, is much more striking but lacks the dramatic backdrop.

Head down to Steiner Street and turn left. While crossing Fulton Street, look to the right and you'll see the street descends directly toward city hall. It's a perfect vantage point of the building's handsome, helmetlike dome. On the opposite corner, at 1000 Fulton, the huge house with the mansard roof is called the **❾ Archbishop's Mansion,** because it was built in 1904 for Patrick William Riordan, archbishop of the Roman Catholic Archdiocese of San Francisco. The building has since been everything from an orphanage to a psychiatric hospital and now operates as a co-living space run by Roam. You can rent a room through Airbnb; if you're lucky, maybe you'll get to snooze in the archbishop's old bedroom.

Continue on Steiner. At No. 1057, on the corner of Golden Gate Avenue, **❿ The Chateau Tivoli** is one of the city's most distinctive buildings. It jabs at the sky with a full complement of turrets and dainty weathervanes, the Victorian architectural equivalent of propeller caps. The building has some mighty alluring curves, especially around its bay windows. It was built in 1892 and has served in a variety of capacities, including as a rooming house during the 1960s and '70s. More recently it has been beautifully restored and converted into a hotel (with surprisingly reasonable rates). Walk on around the corner, where the adjacent apartment buildings (at 1409–1417 Golden Gate) are collectively known as the Seattle Block. The buildings went up at the same time as the Tivoli and are equally well preserved, and collectively they make a marvelous row.

Turn left and follow Golden Gate Avenue to Divisadero Street, where a left-hand turn brings you to the award-winning fried chicken at **⓫ Brenda's Meat and Three,** a solid soul food joint. For lighter but equally delicious fare, head farther down Divisadero to **⓬ Souvla,** a casual Greek spot that offers rotisserie meats tucked into pita or heaped on salads; be sure to leave room for some frozen yogurt with baklava crumbles and honey. Heading farther south on Divisadero will eventually get you back to the Castro.

Points of Interest

1 **Corona Heights Park** Roosevelt Way and Museum Way; 415-831-2700, sfrecpark.org/destination/corona-heights-park

2 **Randall Museum** 199 Museum Way; 415-554-9600, randallmuseum.org

3 **Buena Vista Park** Buena Vista Ave. and Haight St.; 415-831-2700, sfrecpark.org/destination/buena-vista-park

4 **St. Joseph's Hospital (former)** 351–355 Buena Vista Ave. (no published phone number or website)

5 **No. 731 Buena Vista (former Nash/McFerrin home)** 731 Buena Vista Ave. (private residence)

6 **Richard Spreckels Mansion** 737 Buena Vista Ave. (private residence)

7 **Alamo Square Park** Steiner St. and Hayes St.; 415-218-0459, sfrecpark.org/destination/alamo-square

8 **Painted Ladies** 710–722 Steiner St. (private residences)

9 **Archbishop's Mansion** 1000 Fulton St.; 415-563-7872, airbnb.com/rooms/24354841

10 **The Chateau Tivoli** 1057 Steiner St.; 415-776-5462, chateautivoli.com

11 **Brenda's Meat and Three** 919 Divisadero St.; 415-926-8657, brendasmeatandthree.com

12 **Souvla** 517 Hayes St.; 415-400-5458, souvla.com

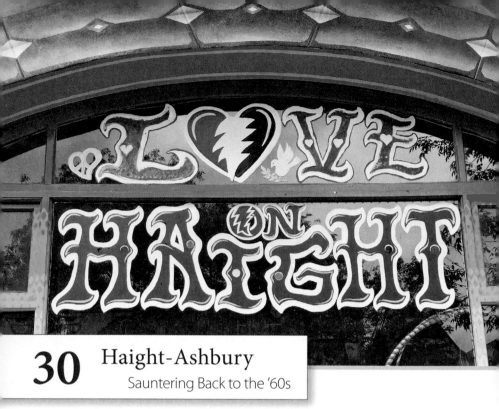

30 Haight-Ashbury
Sauntering Back to the '60s

Above: The counterculture vibe continues to pulse in psychedelic storefronts like Love on Haight.

BOUNDARIES: Scott St., Waller St., Fulton St., North Willard St.
PARKING: Unrestricted street parking can be found on Oak St., along the Panhandle.
DISTANCE: 2 miles
DIFFICULTY: Easy
PUBLIC TRANSIT: N Judah streetcar (get off at Duboce Park); 24, 71 Muni buses

Along with the gold rush, earthquakes, and gay liberation, the Summer of Love is one of San Francisco's iconic cultural moments. The intersection of Haight and Ashbury Streets is the city's most famous crossroads thanks to some craziness that occurred around this nexus from the mid-to-late-1960s. When North Beach became too expensive for artists and musicians, they found cheap rent and welcoming arms in the surrounding streets. While many hippies were simply indulging in the neighborhood's proliferation of drugs and sex, some idealistically saw the so-called Psychedelic

Revolution as hope for a better, kinder world. The neighborhood developed its own economy, spawned its own musical sound, threw outrageous parties in its streets and parks, and acquired a distinctive sartorial aesthetic. All in all, it was exciting, mind-blowing, and hilarious.

Today Haight-Ashbury does its best to live up to its rock-and-roll reputation, although some may argue that it's hypocritically cashing in on a political ideal of anticonsumerism. Whatever your point of view, the neighborhood is a satisfying blend of historical sites, exquisite Victorian architecture, and bustling counterculture commerce of the head-shop, tie-dye, and tattoo-den varieties. Several independent bookstores, loads of great places to eat, and a handful of social organizations still carry on the free-spirited vibe.

Walk Description

We'll start on a nondescript corner, where Scott and Page Streets meet. The building at 250 Scott, home of ❶ **Jack's Record Cellar,** played a significant role in the neighborhood's countercultural past. The upstairs flat was the home of poet Kenneth Rexroth, a central player in the San Francisco Renaissance. This home-grown literary movement attracted the likes of Jack Kerouac and Allen Ginsberg, thus bringing the Beat Generation to the City by the Bay. The cafés of North Beach were the big draw, but the serious salons took place in Rexroth's pad. Rexroth distanced himself from the Beats and moved back east, but thousands of students and poets subsequently moved into the Haight, looking for cheap rents and a bohemian atmosphere in the decade before the hippies. The record shop is rarely open—your best bet is Saturday afternoon—but if it is, step in. It's San Francisco's oldest purveyor of collectible 33-, 45-, and 78-rpm records, and the shop's walls are covered with concert posters from legendary jazz, R&B, and rock shows.

Head west on Page Street. On the corner of Broderick Street, at No. 1090, once stood the Albin Rooming House. According to rock historian Joel Selvin, this apartment building had a "ballroom" in the basement where Big Brother and the Holding Company and other bands frequently performed. There's nothing to see here, except in your imagination, so keep a-movin'.

At the corner of Lyon Street turn right. The attractive Victorian at ❷ **No. 122 Lyon** was the home of singer Janis Joplin during the Summer of Love. It was an apartment house in those days, and Joplin's room was on the second floor with the curved balcony off the front.

Head north one block to Oak Street and cross into the Panhandle, a shady, pencil-thin green that's ideal for dog-walking. Exciting events took place here during the '60s, including unforgettable free outdoor concerts. Jimi Hendrix once played here, so as you walk a block west in the park imagine his awesome sound reverberating off the apartment buildings along either side.

At the corner of Haight and Ashbury Streets, the time is always 4:20.

Following the Panhandle path west, turn left at Central Avenue, and at Haight Street turn right. On this block you'll see two relics of the Haight's radical past. ❸ **The Bound Together Anarchist Collective Bookstore,** at No. 1369, has been peddling radical treatises since 1976. ❹ **Pipe Dreams,** at No. 1376, is the oldest extant head shop on the strip. Stop by for bongs, hookahs, tobacco products, and groovy patches for your torn Levi's.

At the end of the block, the ❺ **Magnolia Pub & Brewery** is an attractive corner noshery that sells its own home-brewed ales. The facade has changed little since the '60s, when the site was the Drogstore Cafe. The name was an obvious appeal to the drug culture, with a twist in the spelling when the California State Board of Pharmacy objected. As the Drogstore Cafe, it was featured in the 1968 movie *Psych-Out,* featuring Jack Nicholson as the requisite stoner. The current owners pay homage to Magnolia Thunderpussy, an erotic bakery that operated in this space post-Drogstore. It was named after its owner, a burlesque performer (real name: Patricia Mallon) beloved for her free-spirited ways and her late-night delivery of desserts such as the Montana Banana. Today, Magnolia Pub produces some lovely cask ales in its basement; they're pumped up directly to the taps on the bar. The food is good too.

Across Masonic Avenue, ❻ **Love on Haight** is a psychedelic grotto of grooviness. The shop deals in everything you'll need for that '60s flashback you've been meaning to have, from handmade tie-dye shirts and incense to kaleidoscope sunglasses and glitter. If none of that's your bag, you can always admire the building's far-out exterior, with its columns shaped like Desi Arnaz congas and cartoony mural work on the window trim. Love on Haight walks the socially conscious walk as well; they have partnered with Taking It to the Streets, a nonprofit dedicated to helping San Francisco's homeless youth.

A block up, the corner of Ashbury is the epicenter of the neighborhood. Don't be afraid to snap some shots of the crisscrossing HAIGHT and ASHBURY street signs; everyone does it. In fact, the signs used to be stolen so often that the city stopped replacing them until they came up with the solution of hanging them extra high. On the northwest corner, note the wall clock that is perpetually stuck at 4:20 p.m.—cannabis-culture code for the correct time to smoke weed. (The term *420* derives from the time at which a group of Marin County teens would meet after school in the early 1970s to search for a supposed mother lode of marijuana growing on nearby Point Reyes.)

Hang a left and walk up Ashbury to ❼ **No. 635,** another place where Janis Joplin lived. Continue walking up Ashbury past Waller, as Joplin herself would have done to visit her friends at ❽ **710 Ashbury.** This Victorian was the home of the Grateful Dead as the band reached its prime (back in the days when bands conveniently lived together, like characters in a sitcom). Jerry Garcia, Bob Weir, and Ron "Pigpen" McKernan lived in the psychedelic frat house with managers Rock Scully and Danny Rifkin from 1966 to 1968. Take a moment to imagine the sounds and smells emanating from the house, now home to unfamous millionaires, and beat it on back to Haight.

Make a left on Ashbury and note the residential apartments at ❾ **1524-A Haight;** this is where Jimi Hendrix alighted for a while in his heyday. A little farther, at 1568 Haight, is ❿ **Michael Collins,** a standard-issue fake Irish pub. In the late '60s, it was the Pall Mall Lounge, where the so-called Love Burgers were very popular—most likely because if you didn't have any scratch, you could enjoy your burger free of charge. Turn right on Clayton to see the humble beginnings

Celebrated street artist Mel Waters pays homage to Jerry Garcia, the neighborhood's onetime house troubadour, with his Cole Street mural.

of one of the most important and ongoing positive social changes to come out of the Summer of Love, the ⑪ **Haight Ashbury Free Medical Clinic.** In 1967, David Smith, MD, a young faculty member at the University of California, San Francisco (UCSF) School of Medicine, was concerned by the alarming number of young people who had been lured to the city for its alternative lifestyle only to find themselves unprepared for some of its negative consequences: drug addiction, malnutrition, and sexually transmitted diseases, among others. Arguing famously that "healthcare is a right, not a privilege"—a sentiment that would later become the clinic's slogan—Smith began providing free medical care with the help of volunteers from UCSF and Stanford, and on its first day, the clinic treated 250 patients. Today there are more than 1,000 clinics around the country modeled after this one.

The Haight-Ashbury Free Medical Clinic's creed: "Health care is a right, not a privilege."

Returning to Haight Street, make your way to the ⑫ **Booksmith.** While the original Booksmith opened a few doors down in 1976, and hosted all manner of '60s icons like Timothy Leary and Allen Ginsberg, the current location stays true to its counterculture roots while also offering a celebrated series of author events and a collection that will satisfy any bibliophile. Across the street and just past Belvedere, you'll find ⑬ **The Red Victorian,** another standard bearer for the old neighborhood: a gorgeous old inn built in 1904 as the Jefferson Hotel. Peace activist Sami Sunchild took it over in the 1970s and designed the guest rooms to induce drug-free hallucinations. She hung more of her trippy art in a gallery off the lobby and hosted discussions about world peace every Sunday morning that were open to all. Sami lived here until she died in 2013 at the age of 88; because the rooms are still used as short- and long-term communal residential units, you need to make a reservation to poke around. Next door, Sunchild's Parlour, an eclectic vintage store, is doing its best to keep the vibe alive.

Vibrantly restored Victorians give the Haight much of its charm, and many once housed a veritable who's who of 1960s rock icons and their entourages.

Above the Red Vic, you'll see a graffiti rat gracing an exposed side wall. The original was done by renegade street artist Banksy while he was in San Francisco in 2010. Great controversy ensued when the art was cut out, removed, and displayed in various galleries (the San Francisco Museum of Modern Art refused to display it), which seemed contrary to the guerrilla art movement. A replacement popped up a decade later but has proved to be the work of imitators.

The **14** **Goodwill** store at the corner of Haight and Cole Streets was the site of the Straight Theater in 1967 and '68. Legendary shows took place here, and the Dead often used the hall as a rehearsal space. Across the street, at 1775 Haight, the Diggers (see Backstory, next page) kept a crash pad where anyone needing a free place to sleep could do so.

In the next block, in a converted bowling alley, is the immense **15** **Amoeba Music,** one of the city's best shopping stops for music. On many an early evening, free live shows are held in the store.

Turn right at Stanyan Street, walk along the eastern edge of Golden Gate Park, and turn left at Fulton Street. Look for the **16** **Jefferson Airplane mansion,** at No. 2400. It's a block up, at the

Backstory: Free Food and Tie-Dye—Can You Dig?

One of the more legendary but less known counterculture groups to take flight during the Summer of Love was the Diggers, a movement based on a society unencumbered by money. Taking its name from the 17th-century British Diggers, who didn't believe in private property, the group was formed by several members of the guerrilla theater group San Francisco Mime Troupe, including actor Peter Coyote. The Diggers' ideas manifested themselves in free bakeries (they were famous for their wheat bread baked in coffee cans), free crash pads, and free stores. They famously served free food in the Panhandle every day at 4 p.m., and they asked hungry takers to step through a giant yellow frame to receive their bowl of soup—a way to change their frame of reference, as it were. As more people grew their hair long and traded their button-downs for batiks, the free stores became inundated with cast-off white dress shirts. Digger Luna Moth Robbins (*née* Jodi Palladini) recommended tie-dyeing them—a then-innovative technique she'd learned in Vermont. The shirts flew off the shelves (for free) and were seen gracing the backs of Janis Joplin and Jerry Garcia—thus, a hippie fashion trend was born.

corner of North Willard, the end of your walk. It's a truly impressive three-story manse with a neoclassical columned entry. Members of the band moved here in 1968, painted the place black, and stayed through the 1970s. Along the way, the Airplane was converted into a Starship. Lead singer Grace Slick left San Francisco for a bigger galaxy (Los Angeles) in the early 1980s, saying she was tired of being a big fish in a small pond.

Points of Interest

1. **Jack's Record Cellar** 254 Scott St.; 415-431-3047
2. **Janis Joplin Home No. 1 (former)** 122 Lyon St. (private residence)
3. **Bound Together Anarchist Collective Bookstore** 1369 Haight St.; 415-431-8355, boundtogetherbooks.wordpress.com

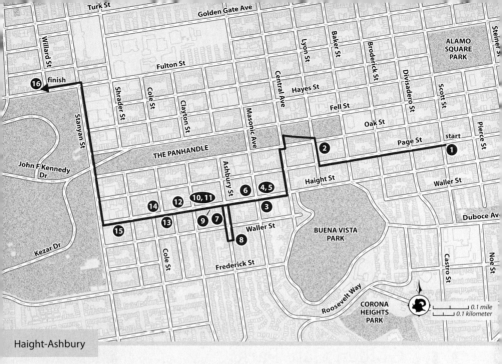

Haight-Ashbury

4 Pipe Dreams 1376 Haight St.; 415-431-3553, facebook.com/smokeshoponhaightt

5 Magnolia Pub & Brewery 1398 Haight St.; 415-864-7468, magnoliabrewing.com

6 Love on Haight 1400 Haight St.; 415-817-1027, loveonhaightsf.com

7 Janis Joplin Home No. 2 (former) 635 Ashbury St. (private residence)

8 Grateful Dead House (former) 710 Ashbury St. (private residence)

9 Jimi Hendrix Apartment (former) 1524-A Haight St. (private residence)

10 Michael Collins (former Pall Mall Lounge) 1568 Haight St.; 415-861-1586, michaelcollinsirishbar.com

11 Haight Ashbury Free Medical Clinic 558 Clayton St.; 415-746-1950, healthright360.org/agency /haight-ashbury-free-clinics

12 Booksmith 1644 Haight St.; 415-863-8688, booksmith.com

13 The Red Victorian 1665 Haight St.; redvictorian.com (no published phone number)

14 Goodwill (former Straight Theater) 1700 Haight St.; 415-738-5606, sfgoodwill.org

15 Amoeba Music 1855 Haight St.; 415-831-1200, amoeba.com

16 Jefferson Airplane Mansion (former) 2400 Fulton St. (private residence)

31 Golden Gate Park
A Sprawling and Sophisticated Backyard

Above: Pagodas and peaceful ponds punctuate the Japanese Tea Garden.

BOUNDARIES: Stanyan St., Fulton St., Lincoln Way, Great Hwy.
DISTANCE: 4.5 miles
DIFFICULTY: Moderate—no great hills, but it's a long, indirect route through a huge park.
PARKING: Street parking is easier to find on weekdays than on weekends. The underground lot by the de Young Museum is reached via the Eighth Ave. entrance, on the north side of the park.
PUBLIC TRANSIT: N Judah streetcar; 6, 33, 71 Muni buses

Golden Gate Park is a celebration of nature—only there's really nothing natural about it. The 1,000-acre urban parkland, among the nation's largest, is a series of groves, gardens, and lakes, all seeded, shaped, and constructed by human hands and machinery. When the city set aside the land, in 1870, it was a windswept expanse of sand and shrubs that few thought could be tamed for the leisurely enjoyment of the local citizenry. William Hammond Hall, the park's surveyor and first superintendent, planted barley and then lupine, both of which rooted and spread across the sands, holding it down and making it possible for further planting to take place. Within 10 years, natural-looking woodlands had been established across the once-barren land. The park also has historical buildings, museums, a boathouse, a bison paddock, and a classy brewpub. Plan on spending a few hours walking and exploring the terrain before enjoying a well-earned beer or meal.

Walk Description

Start at ❶ **McLaren Lodge,** near the convergence of Stanyan Street and John F. Kennedy Drive. Built in 1896, this gray-stone cottage with Moorish–Gothic overtones serves as the park's head-quarters (it offers only limited information to visitors, however). It bears the name of its one-time resident John McLaren, the park superintendent from 1890 until 1943—an astonishing run of 53 years that ended with McLaren's death at age 96. Credited with planting more than 2 million trees, this Scottish gardener was responsible for much of the greening of San Francisco. By all accounts a gruff and cantankerous man, McLaren nonetheless endeared himself to those who worked with him thanks to his tenacious commitment to beautifying the city.

Follow John F. Kennedy Drive into the park, and on the right-hand side you'll soon see the ❷ **Conservatory of Flowers,** a grand glass house constructed in 1876 and modeled after the Palm House in London's Kew Gardens. It's the oldest structure in the park. Making a brief visit is well worth the $9 admission charge to ogle the various exotic tropical plants contained within its humid interior. If you're walking in August or September, be sure to make your way to the Dahlia Garden just east of the conservatory. When in bloom, the garden is a riot of dahlias—San Francisco's official flower—some as large as dinner plates.

With the front of the conservatory at your back, head straight through the tunnel to cross under JFK. Turn right and look for the 12-foot-tall ferns. Veer right to follow the dirt path through this Jurassic-looking grove, veering left at the fork. You'll quickly reach the secluded Lily Pond, around which the trail loops partway as it leads to Nancy Pelosi Drive. Cross Nancy Pelosi Drive and turn left (east), looking for the entrance to the ❸ **National AIDS Memorial Grove.** Designated by an act of Congress, the grove is a reflective place where people can think of loved ones lost to AIDS. Memorial services are often held here, and a stone patio along the path, called Circle of Friends, has the names of some victims etched in an ever-widening spiral. From here, the path leads by a stand of young redwoods and through a grassy dell and alongside an artfully landscaped dry creek. Continue straight until you reach the meditative Circle of Peace and Fern Grotto. Look for stone steps to the left, and head up. When you reach the asphalt path, turn left and then stay left again where

Find your inner calm among the ponds and statues of the Japanese Tea Garden.

the path splits near a stone garden. Next, turn right where a dirt path heads downhill. (These directions should all be fairly easy to follow when you're actually on the trail.) Stick to the main path downhill, and a baseball field will come into view. Turn right and, with the fields at your back, head past the handball court building to return to Nancy Pelosi Drive, and turn left.

At Martin Luther King Jr. Drive, turn right and look for the ❹ **Shakespeare Garden.** Before following the sign to the garden, you may want to head straight a few paces and get in line for a scoop of handmade deliciousness at the ❺ **Twirl and Dip** truck, where organic soft-serve is paired with a fair-trade chocolate dip. Grab a cone or a fruit ice and enjoy it in the garden, where the plantings are all taken from references in the Bard's works. This is the most popular spot in the park for weddings.

Exiting the garden, turn right toward the California Academy of Sciences, and follow the path that veers left around it to reach the Music Concourse. If you spin in a circle on your heel, you'll see the new ❻ **Academy of Sciences,** the ❼ **de Young Museum,** the ❽ **Japanese Tea Garden,** and the huge band shell called the ❾ **Spreckels Temple of Music,** where the Golden Gate Park Band has been playing every Sunday at 1 p.m. (April–October) since 1882. Luciano Pavarotti and Jerry Garcia have also stepped behind the mic here.

The concourse area was laid out for the 1894 Midwinter International Exposition, which attracted more than 2 million visitors to the park. The city was eager to dig its way out of an economic depression and dazzle more-established bigwigs from the East Coast and Chicago. Newspaper publisher Michael de Young, who masterminded the plan, intended to lure people with California's gentler climes and wow them with the Golden State's boundless economic opportunities. Some 200 temporary structures filled the grounds, including an Eskimo village, an "erupting" Hawaiian volcano, and a simulated gold-mining camp, along with countless rides, daring acrobats, and trained animals doing tricks—nearly all of which would be deemed dangerous, offensive, and inauthentic by today's standards.

All that survives from the expo is the Japanese Village, now called the Japanese Tea Garden. After the expo, stewardship of the gardens was turned over to Makoto Hagiwara, who built a house on the grounds and lived here with his family. Hagiwara was fired in 1900 and rehired in 1907, and he stayed on until he was interned along with thousands of Japanese immigrants during World War II. Hagiwara's other contribution to the local culture was the introduction of fortune cookies, which were originally made as a unique snack to serve at the Tea Garden but are now ubiquitous in Chinese restaurants. (See Backstory in the Chinatown walk, page 37.) A stroll through the garden (admission $6, free before 10 a.m. on Monday, Wednesday, and Friday) is a favorite escape of many locals, and there's a lovely teahouse on a koi pond where you can order tea and Japanese snacks.

The California Academy of Sciences, a natural-history museum, aquarium, planetarium, and research center for sustainability and biodiversity, underwent a dramatic renovation in 2008. In addition to its excellent four-story rainforest and coral reef displays, the complex has achieved great fanfare for its state-of-the-art "living roof." A 2.5-acre rooftop garden helps provide insulation, captures storm water, and is home to abundant birds and butterflies. At $39.95, admission is steep, but this truly is a world-class museum where you could while away many hours.

The de Young Museum reopened in 2005 following damage from the 1989 Loma Prieta earthquake. The idea to replace the original Beaux Arts building with what you see now was not initially warmly embraced. San Franciscans are always a little suspicious of modern architecture, especially

Hop aboard a paddleboat to race with ducks on the tranquil waters of Stow Lake.

bold designs like this one, with its askew, 144-foot tower prominent above the park's treetops. It's clad in unprotected copper, which has begun to acquire a green patina that's very easy on the eyes. Admission is $15, which deters quick in-and-out visits, but you can take a ride up to the top of the observation tower for free without museum entry—just follow the signs to the tower elevator, where you will be whisked up to a glorious 360-degree view of the city. The crack you see on the ground leading from Music Concourse Drive up to the museum entrance is not the result of shifting fault lines, but the *Drawn Stone* installation of artist Andy Goldsworthy, although the similarity is likely intentional. (See Backstory on Andy Goldsworthy in the Presidio walk, page 115.)

Turn left on Hagiwara Tea Garden Drive and walk back out to MLK. Across the street is the Friend Gate to the ❿ **San Francisco Botanical Garden,** 55 acres showcasing some 7,500 varieties of plants from around the world. Its labyrinth of paths, ponds, woods, and rolling lawns is tempting to get lost in, and the arboretum is another site worth a dedicated visit (admission is $8). Return to this gate and cross the street to resume our walk. Continue walking west on MLK Drive and look for stone steps on your right. These lead to Stow Lake, so head on up. At the top of the steps, turn left on the shaded path, which clings to the water's edge. The lake here is a narrow ring, looking like a calm stream looped around high Strawberry Hill. You'll see plenty of paddleboats and ducks. When you reach the rustic stone bridge, cross and turn right, following the inside of the curvature of the lake. If you want to access the vistas at the top of Strawberry Hill, take one of the paths leading up, circle to the view, and return the way you came. Soon after you pass the Chinese Pavilion, looking like a gazebo awaiting a tea party, you'll hear and then see Huntington Falls, a charming artifice. This is perhaps the only part of the park where the rush of city traffic is completely drowned out, making it worth pausing for a little break here. Continue along the trail to Roman Bridge, cross it, and head left toward the ⓫ **Stow Lake Boathouse,** where sandwiches and ice cream are sold. Behind the boathouse, a trail leads to JFK Drive. Turn left.

After crossing under Crossover Drive and over Transverse Drive, look for the footpath to the left of JFK. You'll be walking past a wooded area to the left and picnic grounds and large green meadows to the right. Hellman Hollow (formerly Speedway) Meadow has been the site of many an outdoor concert, including the immensely popular and entirely free Hardly Strictly Bluegrass Festival, which takes place every October. The trail leads to the Polo Field, which is surrounded by a "trotting track" for equestrians and a cycling track for those on two wheels. Golden Gate Park Stables are across the Polo Field. The field is not so much known for polo matches as it is for the cultural events that have taken place here. On the afternoon of January 14, 1967, the Summer of Love got off to an early start here, with the Gathering of the Tribes and Human Be-In. Some 30,000 hippies congregated here to follow Timothy Leary's call to "turn on, tune in, drop out."

Allen Ginsberg ranted, the Grateful Dead jammed, and the crowd tripped late into the night. When the Dead's Jerry Garcia died in August 1995, a spontaneous gathering took place in the Polo Field as fans instinctively came here to remember the keeper of the '60s flame.

With the stables to your left, head straight through the tunnel next to the bleacher stands to eventually make your way across JFK Drive and to Spreckels Lake ahead. Dedicated to model boat racing since 1904, the lake was built at the behest of the older still ⓬ **San Francisco Model Yacht Club,** established in 1898. If members are present (which is the case most weekends), visitors are welcome to peruse the Works Progress Administration–era clubhouse and gawk at the antique boat models.

Returning to JFK, turn right and you'll soon see the Bison Paddock. Golden Gate Park has no zoo and is more about flora than fauna, but a herd of buffalo has lived here since 1892. The original idea was that buffalo would add a Wild West flavor to the park.

Follow JFK around the golf course. Before the street ends at the Great Highway, a Dutch windmill overlooks the Queen Wilhelmina Tulip Garden. Wilhelmina, who ruled the Netherlands from 1890 until she abdicated in 1948, gave San Francisco the windmill in 1902 to assist with irrigating the park and transforming the sand dunes into the foliage we see today. March and April are the best times to see the tulips in full bloom. The windmill was restored in the early 1980s and still works. There's another windmill at the southwest corner of the park, but it's in a sad state of disrepair.

The ⓭ **Beach Chalet** stands at the corner of JFK and the Great Highway. Designed by Willis Polk, the restaurant opened in 1925. The downstairs lobby is covered with murals, painted in 1936 by French-born artist Lucien Labaudt. Upstairs, in a room dominated by plate-glass windows facing the ocean, the microbrewery is a lively spot for breakfast, lunch, or dinner. The beer is good, and on many evenings live jazz combos perform. Alternatively, immediately behind the Beach Chalet, the ⓮ **Park Chalet** features small-plate California cuisine, indoor/outdoor seating, and often shorter waits for a table.

This windmill has proved both beautiful and useful in irrigating Golden Gate Park.

Golden Gate Park

Points of Interest

1. **McLaren Lodge** 501 Stanyan St.; 415-831-2700, goldengatepark.com/mclaren-lodge.html
2. **Conservatory of Flowers** 100 John F. Kennedy Dr.; 415-831-2090, conservatoryofflowers.org
3. **National AIDS Memorial Grove** Nancy Pelosi Dr. and Bowling Green Dr.; 415-765-0498, aidsmemorial.org
4. **Shakespeare Garden** Martin Luther King Dr. between Nancy Pelosi Dr. and Music Concourse Dr.
5. **Twirl and Dip Truck** 335 Martin Luther King Dr.; 415-205-8261, twirlanddip.com
6. **California Academy of Sciences** 55 Music Concourse Dr.; 415-379-8000, calacademy.org
7. **de Young Museum** 50 Hagiwara Tea Garden Dr.; 415-863-3330, deyoung.famsf.org
8. **Japanese Tea Garden** 75 Hagiwara Tea Garden Dr.; 415-752-1171, japaneseteagardensf.com
9. **Spreckels Temple of Music/Golden Gate Park Band** Music Concourse Dr. and Hagiwara Tea Garden Dr.; goldengateparkband.org
10. **San Francisco Botanical Garden** 1199 Ninth Ave.; 415-661-1316, sfbotanicalgarden.org
11. **Stow Lake Boathouse** 50 Stow Lake Dr. E.; 415-702-1390, stowlakeboathouse.com
12. **San Francisco Model Yacht Club** John F. Kennedy Dr. and 36th Ave.; sfmyc.org (no published phone number)
13. **Beach Chalet** 1000 Great Hwy.; 415-386-8439, beachchalet.com
14. **Park Chalet** 1000 Great Hwy.; 415-386-8439, parkchalet.com

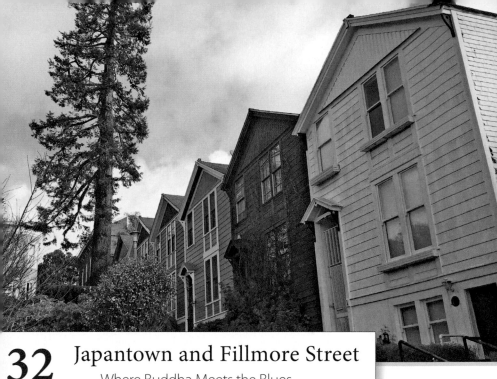

32 Japantown and Fillmore Street
Where Buddha Meets the Blues

Above: The Victorians of Cottage Row escaped the wrecking ball of redevelopment in the 1960s.

BOUNDARIES: Fillmore St., Geary Blvd., Pine St., Octavia St.
DISTANCE: 1.5 miles
DIFFICULTY: Easy
PARKING: There is a parking lot beneath Japan Center. Street parking is often available on
   Webster St., south of Geary Blvd.
PUBLIC TRANSIT: The 22 and 38 Muni buses stop at the corner of Geary Blvd. and Fillmore St.

Japantown and the Fillmore District are two odd and interesting neighborhoods. Japanese immigrants began settling here after the 1906 earthquake and were unjustly moved from their homes and relocated in internment camps during World War II. The African Americans who moved to the Fillmore were drawn by jobs in wartime industries, but 1960s redevelopment of the area caused yet another exodus as a sizable proportion of the neighborhood's housing was demolished to make way for the widened Geary Boulevard Expressway and for hotels and retail structures.

Although the Japanese had dispersed by that time, the redevelopment included construction of the Japan Center, along with some senior housing catering to elderly Japanese. So what we have now is a modern commercial district with a strong Japanese flavor but only a very small remnant of the Japanese community. Similarly, Fillmore Street retains hints of the area's African American past. Amid the modern hotels and condominiums are some gorgeous Victorian homes that were spared the midcentury wrecking ball. The neighborhood is pleasant for walking, but the chief interest here is inside the Japan Center itself. We'll end up there.

Walk Description

Start at the southwest corner of Geary Boulevard and Fillmore Street, at the ❶ **Fillmore Auditorium,** legendary for its rock shows during the 1960s. The elegant hall predates rock and roll by several decades, however. Built in 1912 and originally dubbed the Majestic Ball Room, it had a brief stint as a roller rink among other things, but in the early 1950s it once again provided music to the masses as the Fillmore. Very likely some of the most remarkable shows to ever take place in the building were by jazz and R&B performers during the heyday of the black Fillmore District: Count Basie, Billie Holiday, and a young James Brown electrified audiences here. Rock promoter Bill Graham put on shows here from 1966 to 1968. All the local bands—the Grateful Dead, Jefferson Airplane, Big Brother and the Holding Company—took the stage on a regular basis, and out-of-town guests included Jimi Hendrix, The Doors, and The Velvet Underground, with the psychedelic posters lining the walls to prove it. The Fillmore reestablished itself as one of the city's preeminent rock venues in the 1990s and remains an intimate venue where top-tier talent performs in a variety of musical styles. And in a nod to Graham, a barrel of free apples is still available to those who want them.

The Boom Boom Room is a longtime Fillmore nightlife staple.

Cross Geary Boulevard to reach the ❷ **Boom Boom Room,** a Fillmore District stalwart. This classy little cinderblock dive was for many years known as Jack's and was one of the first nightclubs in the neighborhood to cater to African Americans. It's a loungelike inner-city juke joint with a black-and-white-checkered linoleum floor, padded booths, and a small stage where blues artists perform nightly. During the late 1990s, the club was partly owned by bluesman John Lee Hooker, who for many years lived in Redwood City, just south of San Francisco.

Cross Fillmore Street at Post Street and continue up to Sutter Street; then turn right on Sutter and walk on the north (right) side of the street. Before reaching Webster Street, head up the path to ❸ **Cottage Row Mini Park.** The six two-story cottages along this little pedestrian block were built in 1882 and are on the National Register of Historic Places. Cottage Row ends at Bush Street. Turn right and then right again on Webster. At No. 1737, the John J. Vollmer House is one of the neighborhood's better-preserved Victorians; built in 1885, it was moved here in the mid-1970s. It was evidently a tight fit—part of the house had to be sliced off to get it into the narrow lot. Nevertheless, the trim, with flowers carved into the woodwork, is some of the city's finest.

Adjacent to the Japan Center, the Peace Pagoda is a symbol of Japanese–American friendship.

Turn left on Sutter and, if you have a sweet tooth, make your way to ❹ **Yasukochi's Sweet Stop,** a tiny bakery inside the unassuming Super Mira Market. You'd never know it simply from passing by, but the Yasukochi family has spent near half a century providing San Franciscans with their beloved coffee crunch cake. A signature special occasion treat of the long-defunct Blum's pastry shop, the Yasukochi's replica is so authentic that the retired Blums allowed them to use the name upon tasting it. The alternating layers of whipped cream, sponge cake, and crushed coffee candy regularly make lists of things to eat in San Francisco before you die, and the cakes sell out before closing every day.

Turn left on Laguna Street. At 1909 Bush St. is the ❺ **Konko Kyo Church,** where members of a Shinto sect worship. The church, built in a simple yet graceful Japanese style, went up in 1973.

Turn right on Pine Street. Just off the corner of Octavia Street, at 1881 Pine, the large structure with the stupa on the roof is the home of the ❻ **Buddhist Church of San Francisco.** The temple was built in 1937, but the Jodo Shinshu congregation began worshiping here, in an earlier building, in 1914. Hidden within the stupa are relics of the Buddha, given to the congregation by the king of Thailand in 1935.

Turn right on Octavia Street. At Bush, the corner lot behind the row of eucalyptus trees on the Octavia side is of historical interest. In the 1860s a woman Mary Ellen Pleasant built a mansion here and planted the trees you see. A plucky entrepreneur who embellished her life story—she may or may not have been born a slave in Georgia, and she may or may not have been the granddaughter of Virginia governor James Pleasants—Pleasant arrived in San Francisco with an inheritance from her first husband already in her pocket. She saw the flophouses that men were living in (and at that time the city was nearly 85% male) and saw an opportunity. She amassed a fortune—at one point estimated at more than $500 million in today's dollars—operating a string of boardinghouses and investing in the stock market and real estate; she also built a career as the go-to event planner for San Francisco's elite, catering lavish meals and organizing parties and balls. The house she built on this spot became known as the House of Mystery after her business partner and assumed lover, a younger man named Thomas Bell, died here under suspicious circumstances. The local newspapers imbued Pleasant with an unsavory reputation, spreading rumors that she was a voodoo priestess and a madam, and they nicknamed her Mammy Pleasant—a moniker that she despised ("I am not mammy to everybody in California," she once groused). What is known for certain is that she used her wealth to aid the escape of slaves on the Underground Railroad. After a legal battle with Bell's family over his estate depleted her fortune, Pleasant died in poverty in 1904, and her mansion was demolished in 1927. A memorial plaque is embedded in the sidewalk amid the eucalyptus trees.

Continue on Octavia and turn right on Sutter Street. At Buchanan turn left into the Buchanan Street Mall, a pedestrian shopping strip that echoes the Asian emphasis of the Japan Center, to which the street directly leads. Stop in at unassuming bakery and coffee shop ❼ **Benkyodo,** one of the oldest family-owned-and-operated businesses in Japantown. Its first store opened in 1906, but its real claim to fame was supplying so-called fortune tea cakes to the Japanese Tea Garden, thus birthing the fortune cookie (see the Backstory in the Chinatown walk, page 37). The shop was closed during Japanese internment but reopened following the war and has been churning out fresh *manju* and *mochi* (traditional sweets made with buckwheat flour and rice flour) ever since. While the ambience screams "diner," the handmade confections are the real Japanese deal and have a loyal neighborhood following.

Crossing Post Street, you'll enter the plaza of the Japan Center. Built in the 1960s, architecturally it reflects the style of the era but with distinct Japanese overtones. It was designed by Minoru Yamasaki, who went on to achieve greater heights by designing the ill-fated World Trade Center in New York. Crossing Post Street, you'll find a 100-foot pagoda in Peace Plaza, a stark concrete slab where the elderly sometimes take in some sun. If you're facing the pagoda, to your left is the East Mall, home to the fashionable ❽ **Hotel Kabuki,** a very hip hostelry, in which the rooms have sleek Japanese stylings. To the right is Kintetsu Mall. Go on in.

The mall has the meandering feel of an airport, with food courts and narrow stores selling the same sorts of cultural curios you'd find in duty-free shops. If the impulse strikes you, you might wind up with a new silk kimono while here. Of more likely interest is the ⑨ **Kinokuniya Bookstore,** where several aisles are devoted to Japanese art books, manga comics, DVDs of anime films, and a smattering of Godzilla classics. Studio Ghilbi fans take note: there are all sorts of books, videos, plushies, and decor dedicated to the Tokyo film studio's works at the bookstore. On your way there, you'll pass through restaurant row, where the decor really lays it on with the movie-set Japantown feel. The windows all have artfully arranged plastic meals on display to lure you in. ⑩ **Marufuku Ramen,** touted by *Zagat Survey* as one of "8 Must-Try Ramens in the Bay Area," is an excellent place to try traditional Hakata-style *tonkatsu* (pork) ramen, characterized by a rich broth and ultrathin noodles. To capture your Japantown experience on film, head across from the bookstore to ⑪ **Pika Pika,** where campy photo booths await. Styled after the print clubs popular in Japan, Pika Pika lets you enlarge your eyes, add makeup, and embellish your printable sticker photo with a pet, crown, confetti, and the like—think Instagram filters on steroids. For another J-town (as locals call it) novelty, head to ⑫ **Chocolate Chair** to sample some Dragon's Breath dessert balls. While not necessarily a Japanese experience, the chance to blow smoke out your nose and mouth after ingesting these liquid nitrogen–soaked treats (they taste like fruity cereal) is hard to resist. If you'd like to linger longer, Kintetsu Mall also has several cafés, a posh movie theater, and karaoke bars.

Back on the street, at the corner of Post Street and Webster Street, be sure to drop by the ⑬ **Nijiya Market,** a supermarket in miniature, with tiny carts and narrow aisles stocked with Japanese foodstuffs. Just past the registers, an aisle is stocked with a huge selection of bento lunches neatly packed in plastic trays.

Continue down Webster and make a right on Geary. Toward the end of the block, ⑭ **Kabuki Springs & Spa** offers the perfect antidote to urban grit. For $25, you can enter this serene sanctuary and enjoy communal baths (hot pool, cold plunge, sauna, and steam room) in the tradition of Japan's public baths. Designed to instill harmony and relaxation, this is an oasis of calm. Sunday, Wednesday, and Friday, the baths are open to women; Monday, Thursday, and Saturday are reserved for men; all days are clothing-optional except Tuesday, when the baths are coed and bathing suits are required.

Tasty bowls and bento lunches tempt hungry shoppers.

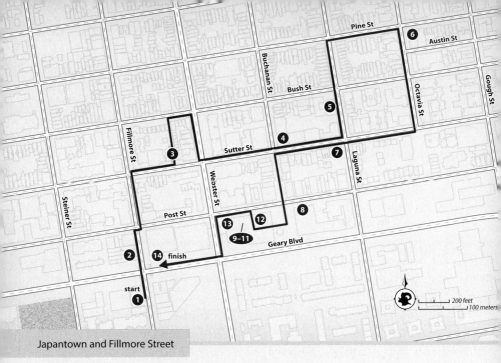

Japantown and Fillmore Street

Points of Interest

1. **Fillmore Auditorium** 1805 Geary Blvd.; 415-346-6000, thefillmore.com

2. **Boom Boom Room** 1601 Fillmore St.; 415-673-8000, boomboomroom.com

3. **Cottage Row Mini Park** Fillmore and Sutter Sts.; 415-831-2700, sfrecpark.org/destination /cottage-row-mini-park

4. **Yasukochi's Sweet Stop** 1790 Sutter St.; 415-931-8165, tinyurl.com/yasukochi

5. **Konko Kyo Church** 1909 Bush St.; 415-931-0453, konkofaith.org

6. **Buddhist Church of San Francisco** 1881 Pine St.; 415-776-3158, buddhistchurchofsanfrancisco.org

7. **Benkyodo** 1747 Buchanan St.; 415-922-1244, benkyodocompany.com

8. **Hotel Kabuki** 1625 Post St.; 415-922-3200, jdvhotels.com/hotels/california/san-francisco/hotel-kabuki

9. **Kinokuniya Bookstore** 1581 Webster St.; 415-567-7625, usa.kinokuniya.com

10. **Marufuku Ramen** 1581 Webster St.; 415-872-9786, marufukuramen.com

11. **Pika Pika** 1581 Webster St.; 415-673-7898, pikapikasf.com

12. **Chocolate Chair** 1737 Post St.; 415-567-9255, chocolatechair.com

13. **Nijiya Market** 1737 Post St.; 415-563-1901, nijiya.com

14. **Kabuki Springs & Spa** 1750 Geary Blvd.; 415-922-6000, kabukisprings.com

PIROSHKI
WITH CABBAGE
$3.00

PIROSHKI
WITH POTATO
$3.00

PIROSHKI
With Beef & Cheese
$3.00

TRIANGLE WITH BAKERS
CHEESE & RAISINS
$3.75

Poppy Seed
Roll
$7.25

Apple Turnover
$3.75

Cherry Turnover
$3.75

Apple Strudel
$3.75

Donut With Custard
Cream
$2.50

SMALL CHALLAH
BREAD WITH RAISINS
$1.25

Round Challah
With Raisins
$1.25

CHALLAH BREAD
$1.25

33 Richmond District
An International Culinary Stroll

Above: In this bakery, Russian piroshki share a display case with Jewish challah and apple strudel.

BOUNDARIES: Arguello St., Clement St., Geary Blvd., 25th Ave.
DISTANCE: 1.5 miles
DIFFICULTY: Easy
PARKING: Street parking is metered, with 2-hour limits. Parking is very difficult to find
   on weekends.
PUBLIC TRANSIT: 1, 38 Muni buses

Clement Street in the Inner Richmond District will always be "New Chinatown," even though
Chinese immigrants have been operating businesses here since the 1970s. The area naturally
invites contrast with the old Chinatown, and indeed there are interesting similarities and differ-
ences. Being out in San Francisco's Fog Belt, Richmond has always attracted more than its share
of immigrants, and there's plenty of evidence of many waves of newcomers, some of whom are
obviously still here. To be sure, along Clement you'll find roasted ducks hanging in windows,

along with steamed pork buns, produce stalls, and bargain bazaars to rival, if not surpass, those of the old Chinatown. But in the mix you'll also encounter the city's best used-book store, Russian bakeries, Korean barbecue joints, Irish bars, Israeli delis, bohemian cafés, and loads of Southeast Asian restaurants. This walk is sort of an eating and shopping excursion that needn't involve maxing out your credit card. The main idea is to snoop around a bit to see what sorts of intriguing items you might find along Clement, one of the city's more interesting streets. Unlike much of gentrified San Francisco, the Inner Richmond allows an authentic glimpse into the waves of immigrants who have made the city their home.

Walk Description

As much of this walk concentrates on culinary delicacies, it makes sense to begin a few steps north of Clement Street on Arguello at ❶ **Arsicault Bakery,** named *Bon Appétit*'s Bakery of the Year in 2016. A hole-in-the-wall establishment with just a few tiny tables, Arsicault has lines that invariably extend out the door for croissants described as "impossibly tender and buttery on the inside" by the magazine's seasoned tasters.

Head west on Clement. If the fog is blowing the other way, you'll know you're headed in the right direction. If it's daytime, the ❷ **Plough and the Stars** pub, at No. 116, will be closed, which is just as well as we aim to get a little walking done. Note that this is no fake Irish pub, which should be apparent from the bar's exterior, which doesn't bother to project a St. Paddy's Day party atmosphere. Instead, the place has genuine spirit. Irish musicians perform here every night, and many of the patrons come to do a little fancy steppin'.

Passing numerous Chinese and Vietnamese restaurants, many of which may merit a visit, make your way to No. 309, the much-lauded ❸ **Burma Super Star.** Despite the glamorous implications of its name, Burma Super Star is a tranquil place that serves a type of cuisine not commonly found in the United States. The food of Myanmar is spicy and aromatic, with rich curries and sizzling vegetables bringing together the influences of both East and South Asia. Sure enough, this little joint is very popular.

On the next corner, ❹ **Toy Boat Dessert Cafe** is an ice cream parlor. While you're waiting for your server to scrape your scoops, check out the store's amusing array of toys and novelty items, such as Pez dispensers and Teenage Mutant Ninja Turtle dolls.

Down Clement at No. 525–547, ❺ **Kamei Housewares and Restaurant Supplies** takes up two buildings, each filled to the rafters with utilitarian crockery, knives, bamboo placemats, chopsticks "for special guests," soup bowls, rice bowls, clay pots, and teapots. Across the street, ❻ **Green**

Chinese markets sell a variety of unusual foods that aren't widely available outside of Asia.

Apple Books and Music is a large emporium of new and used books. It's a densely packed series of rooms both upstairs and down, with additional space a little ways down the block—some patrons have been known to simply disappear here, never to be seen again. The beloved seller opened in 1976 with 750 square feet of space; today Green Apple takes up more than 8,000 square feet, its devoted loyalists ensuring that it isn't squeezed out by online sellers thanks to its robust lecture and events series.

⓻ **New May Wah Supermarket,** at No. 719, is exactly the sort of place you expect to find in a Chinatown-ish nabe. It has an endless aisle devoted to Asian snacks—shrimp puffs, Pocky (think KitKats on sticks), and the like—and other rows fully stocked with bean sauces, fish sauces, and canned tropical fruits of the kind that aren't widely grown in the States: rambutan, durian, soursop, and lychee, among others. Take a gander at the impressive butcher and fish market as well.

Wander out past Park Presidio Boulevard, and you're committing yourself to a fairly long walk extending into the Outer Richmond District. You could hop on a No. 38 bus for the return trip, but if you're up for more exploration, making your way down Geary will give you a glimpse into Little Russia, which makes for an interesting contrast with New Chinatown.

Make a left on Funston Street before cutting across it to take the greenbelt through Park Presidio. At 300 Funston, in a former Christian Science Church, the ❽ **Internet Archive** is quietly creating the world's largest digital library. The nonprofit brainchild of Brewster Kahle, an early internet developer and advocate of "universal access to all knowledge," the Internet Archive heads such projects as the Wayback Machine and the Open Library. Thrilled to find a new home that matches its logo (which is based on Egypt's Alexandria Library), the archive welcomes visitors. Next, follow the Park Presidio greenbelt south toward Geary and turn right. ❾ **Kabuto Sushi,** at 5121 Geary, is a nondescript-looking sushi joint that faithful fans swear is the city's finest. A block farther, ❿ **Russian Renaissance Restaurant** has been serving up hot borscht and sweet blini since 1959. This stretch of Geary and environs, extending toward the golden onion domes of the Russian Orthodox Church, is home to nearly 100,000 Russian Americans who have been arriving in waves since the 1920s when anti-Communist Russians fled the Revolution. As you walk, look for bakeries, tearooms, and bars sporting Cyrillic-lettered signage.

After crossing 18th Street, cross the street to where ⓫ **Joe's Ice Cream** has been scooping up deliciousness under the same pegboard sign since 1959. They also have an old-school lunch counter and swivel chairs for a trip back in time. A few blocks farther and across the street, ⓬ **Ton Kiang,** at No. 5821, prepares outstanding dim sum in an unfrenzied atmosphere—select your dim sum from a menu, and it's prepared to order. ⓭ **Tommy's Mexican Restaurant,** at No. 5929,

The serenely handsome San Francisco Columbarium is one of the few places within the city limits where one can commune with the dearly departed.

Backstory: San Francisco's Deepest Sleep

While you're exploring Clement Street in the Inner Richmond District, take a quick detour to check out the **1a San Francisco Columbarium.** It's one of those places that locals hear about but never get around to visiting, and it's just a couple of blocks from where this tour begins.

A columbarium is a building divided into compartments in which the ashes of the dead are kept. (You could say that columbaria are old folks' homes for folks who are a wee bit beyond old.) The word derives from the Latin *columba*, meaning "dove," and is a reference to tightly arranged coops built for domesticated doves and pigeons. The San Francisco Columbarium, built in 1898, is a particularly elegant example. It's a gorgeous piece of historic architecture, with beautiful tiling and graceful glass enclosures rising three stories above the main floor.

San Francisco is a city nearly devoid of cemeteries. Only two graveyards remain in the city: one in the Presidio and another behind Mission Dolores. Large cemeteries formerly covered much of the Inner Richmond, and the Columbarium was within the 167-acre Odd Fellows Cemetery. During the early 20th century, all of these graveyards were moved south of San Francisco to the city of Colma, where the dead vastly outnumber the living (and the official motto is "It's Great to Be Alive in Colma"). Thus, for the most part, San Francisco keeps the dearly departed at arm's length. The Columbarium was spared, even though cremation was for several decades outlawed in the city. The facility was restored in the late 1970s.

The Columbarium is the only place within the city limits where a civilian can hope to rest in peace. Vaults are privately owned, and their value rises and falls (mostly rises) with more energy than San Francisco's housing market. Annually, the Columbarium throws a cocktail party for people who own but do not yet occupy vaults. It's a way for future neighbors to get to know each other before they meet their makers!

The Columbarium is just a few blocks from Clement and Arguello Streets. On Arguello, walk two blocks south, past Geary Boulevard, and turn left onto Anza Street. Turn left onto Lorain Court, a cul-de-sac that ends at the entrance to the Columbarium. Open to the public, it's a peaceful place to walk amid the touching memorials to loved ones on display, complete with photos, treasured mementos, and the occasional bottle of booze. Many local celebrities, Harvey Milk among them, are honored here.

is as well known for its margaritas as it is for its fine Yucatecan cuisine. The drinks are prepared by hand—no mixes—with high-quality tequilas and fresh ingredients. The food goes down mighty easy after one or two of 'em. Nearly next door, **14 Khan Toke Thai House** is an opulent oasis of calm that is frequently touted as one of the most beautiful Thai restaurants in the city. Slip off your shoes, settle yourself on a cushion, tuck your feet under the table, and prepare to be transported. Take a peek in back to see their beautiful garden.

Crossing Geary at 25th, head to the other side and peer in the window of ⑮ **Paul's Hat Works,** where master milliners have been blocking and crafting custom hats since 1918. If they're open (hours are infrequent), pop in and you'll be greeted by the latest apprentices to have taken over the business, which has been passed down since Napoleon "Paul" Marquez first set up shop. The latest incarnation is owned by two young women who have breathed fresh life into the craft while still retaining all the old techniques. One of their handmade beaver-felt fedoras even graced the head of Barack Obama during his second presidential term (he received it as a gift from a supporter while in town for a fund-raiser).

Tiki bars are all the rage around the Bay Area these days. They're throwbacks to the 1930s, when mainlanders first discovered ukulele music and longed for the easy life under South Seas palm trees. ⑯ **Trad'r Sam,** at No. 6150, is no throwback. It's been operating out here in the fog since before World War II. It has all the atmosphere of Thurston and Lovey Howell's hut, and the fruity drinks prepared by hardworking barkeeps resemble Carmen Miranda's hats. Show up in the afternoon if you want to avoid the just-turned-21 crowd.

If you need to repent for any rum-based sins, our walk ends under the protective shadow of the ⑰ **Holy Virgin Cathedral,** the largest Russian Orthodox Church outside of Russia. Also known as the Joy of All Who Sorrow, the church is a hand-painted jewel box of chandeliers and stained glass. If the doors are open, you are welcome to step in and delight in the stunning interior. Services take place twice daily, and most women don head scarves. Parishioners largely stand for services, hence the lack of abundant pews.

Points of Interest

❶ **Arsicault Bakery** 397 Arguello Blvd.; 415-450-9460, tinyurl.com/arsicaultsf

❷ **The Plough and the Stars** 116 Clement St.; 415-751-1122, theploughandstars.com

❸ **Burma Super Star** 309 Clement St.; 415-387-2147, burmasuperstar.com

❹ **Toy Boat Dessert Cafe** 401 Clement St.; 415-751-7505, facebook.com/boatdessertcafe

❺ **Kamei Housewares and Restaurant Supplies** 525–547 Clement St.; 415-666-3699, facebook.com/kameisf

Richmond District

- **6** Green Apple Books and Music 506 Clement St.; 415-387-2272, greenapplebooks.com
- **7** New May Wah Supermarket 719 Clement St.; 415-221-9826 (no website)
- **8** Internet Archive 300 Funston Ave.; 415-561-6767, archive.org
- **9** Kabuto Sushi 5121 Geary Blvd.; 415-752-5652, kabuto-restaurant-san-francisco.sites.tablehero.com
- **10** Russian Renaissance Restaurant 5241 Geary Blvd.; 415-752-8558, rr.restaurant
- **11** Joe's Ice Cream 5420 Geary Blvd.; 415-751-1950, joesicecream.com
- **12** Ton Kiang 5821 Geary Blvd.; 415-752-4440, tonkiangsf.com
- **13** Tommy's Mexican Restaurant 5929 Geary Blvd.; 415-387-4747, tommystequila.com
- **14** Khan Toke Thai House 5937 Geary Blvd.; 415-668-6654, khantokethaihouse.com
- **15** Paul's Hat Works 6128 Geary Blvd.; 415-221-5332, hatworksbypaul.com
- **16** Trad'r Sam 6150 Geary Blvd.; 415-221-0773 (no website)
- **17** Holy Virgin Cathedral 6210 Geary Blvd.; 415-221-3255, sfsobor.com

Backstory

- **1a** San Francisco Columbarium 1 Loraine Ct.; 415-771-0717, neptune-society.com

34 Lands End
Where Raw Beauty and Culture Hug Coastal Cliffs

Above: *Try your hand at balancing rocks on windswept Mile Rock Beach.*

BOUNDARIES: 48th Ave., Geary St., and the edge of the continent
DISTANCE: 4.75 miles
DIFFICULTY: Moderate (some stairs; a bit hazardous in spots)
PARKING: Street parking on 48th Ave. near the end of Geary or Anza has no time limit.
PUBLIC TRANSIT: 38 Muni bus

On a sunny day, locals know that there's no better way to wow visitors than taking them along the windswept trails of Lands End. Ocean vistas appear at every turn, Golden Gate Bridge views are framed by wildflowers and dramatic cypress trees, and secluded beaches and labyrinths invite exploration.

San Francisco is oriented toward its bay, but to overlook the coastal trails that run along the cliffs at the city's western edge is to miss out on some of the city's most striking natural scenery.

Trails, some of them slim and rocky footpaths, follow the coastline and then bend back to landmark buildings such as the Cliff House and the Palace of the Legion of Honor. The area's intriguing history manifests itself in captivating ways. The washed-out remnants of Sutro Baths are a modern ruin looking much like the leavings of a long-gone civilization. And the vast and forgotten grounds of Adolph Sutro's former estate hint at a one-time Shangri-la. Plus, always, there is the ever-changing surf. If you're lucky, you may even spot some sea lions, whales, or dolphins cavorting in the distance.

Walk Description

Begin at the ❶ **Lands End Lookout and Visitor Center,** where maps, a small café, bathrooms, a bookstore, and amazing views greet you. From the adjacent parking lot, a trail leads down to the ❷ **Sutro Baths,** one of San Francisco's more fascinating historical sites. Walk all the way down into the cove, where long-abandoned swimming pools have become desolate duck ponds. You'll have to use your imagination (and refer to more old photos) to get an idea how incredible the Sutro Baths were when they opened in 1896. While walking—carefully—among the ruins, see if you can picture a massive steel framework supporting a glass dome overhead, with several large pools, slides, three restaurants, and a grandstand that seated 3,700. The water in each pool was a different temperature, and some pools contained salt water while others had fresh water. The baths were exceedingly popular initially, but by the late 1930s attendance had declined and the facility was converted into an ice rink. It closed in 1952 and burned down in 1966.

From the baths, follow the trail that wends uphill to your left to reach ❸ **Point Lobos,** aka Seal Rock. Early Spanish explorers noted the abundant sea lions—*lobos marinos,* or "sea wolves" in Spanish, hence the name. Seafaring was no easy business in this neck of the woods due to the strong surf, dense fog, and shallow rocky coastline. In 1936 the SS *Ohioan* met a watery fate running aground near Seal Rock. No crew members were lost, but rescue attempts became quite a spectator sport, and it's rumored that one gawker had a heart attack from watching the proceedings. The boat was deemed unsalvageable, subsequently caught fire, and was eventually broken into pieces by relentless surf over the years.

Continue uphill along the Sutro Baths Upper Trail to reach the Coastal Trail and turn left. The flat grade here is partly thanks to Adolph Sutro (see Backstory, next page) who built the Ferries & Cliff House Railroad to carry passengers from downtown to Cliff House and environs. The narrow-gauge steam train hugged the same seaside cliffs that we are, which made for quite a thrill.

Keep your eyes peeled for the small sign pointing left toward ❹ **Mile Rock Beach.** Follow the wooden stairs down to a secluded beach strewn with balancing rock formations. New ones are

Backstory: Silver-Lined Pockets, Starry-Eyed Ideas

Adolph Sutro (1830–1898), a native of Prussia, moved to San Francisco in his 20s during the gold rush. He made his fortune on the Comstock Lode and became one of the era's most successful entrepreneurs. He was an engineer, and his ticket to glory was in developing a tunnel that drained and ventilated the deep silver mines around Virginia City, Nevada. When Sutro sold his tunnel in 1879, he turned his attention to real estate in the rapidly growing city of San Francisco. He bought nearly 10% of the land within the city limits, most of it undeveloped at the time. Using his wealth to create an urban playground, Sutro's estate was a vision of lavish landscaping and European statuary. He also built the world's largest indoor swimming complex, transformed the Cliff House into a seven-story French château with a restaurant and museum, created an amusement park (Sutro's Pleasure Grounds) along Merrie Way, and managed a steam train to ferry visitors from downtown. Sutro served one term as the city's mayor, from 1894 to 1898. He termed himself the "anti-octopus" candidate, referring to the power of the Southern Pacific Railroad, which at the time was a many-tentacled political force.

added daily, and the protected cove strewn with logs—perfect for a picnic seat—has a hidden-pirate-lair feel to it. During low tide you can see the remains of shipwrecks. The most tragic occurred in 1901 when the passenger steamer SS *City of Rio De Janeiro* hit a nearby rock on a foggy night and sank completely within minutes. The sinking was so fast that more than 100 people drowned, but nearby Italian fishermen were able to save a few passengers clinging to floating refuse. Small, white Mile Rock Lighthouse, visible in the distance, was added in 1906 to try and curb the number of shipwrecks along this stretch. The lighthouse tower was removed in the 1960s, and the remaining base is now used as a helicopter platform.

When ascending from the beach, eschew the stairs and take the sandy trail to your left to wind up toward the ❺ **Lands End Labyrinth,** a magical meditation circle with a commanding view of the Golden Gate Bridge. Constructed in 2004 by artist Eduardo Aguilera, the labyrinth was initially a renegade and anonymous labor of love. But the delightful secret soon got out, and now it's even featured on area maps. The maze has been vandalized a handful of times but is always rebuilt quickly by the artist and a team of devoted volunteers. It's particularly popular on solstice evenings.

Return to the Coastal Trail and continue east. You may notice that some parts of the trail pass through cleared land—this is because of a Golden Gate National Recreation Area program that is removing nonnative plants in order to encourage a return of native species. Just past ❻ **Eagle's Point Overlook,** you'll reach a junction with El Camino del Mar. Our walk loops back to our start, past museums, memorials, and some historical structures, but you could also hit a couple of beaches rather than visit the museum.

To get to China Beach, take the Coastal Trail to McLaren Avenue and into the Richmond District. Follow it as it curves to the left and then hits Sea Cliff Avenue. You'll see some steps leading down to the beach. China Beach, so named for the camp of Chinese fishermen based here prior to the 1906 quake, has swimmable surf—that is, swimmable if you don't mind the cold temperatures. Farther down Sea Cliff, where the street ends, a footpath, actually a continuation of the Coastal Trail, leads into the Presidio and to Baker Beach. This is the city's prime sunbathing spot, with a spectacular view of the sea and the Golden Gate Bridge. Swimming is discouraged due to dangerous riptides, but the far end of the beach does tend to be clothing-optional. From here you can walk the sands almost all the way to the bridge.

Our route, however, turns right to follow the paved road through the Lincoln Park Golf Course. On your right, you'll pass the **7 Memorial for Peace,** a carved stone with neighboring benches placed in 1984 to honor the continuing quest for world peace. Further up the road as you cross toward the museum, artist George Segal's haunting **8 Holocaust Memorial,** also called *The Survivor,* is a vivid and moving depiction of Nazi concentration-camp life. The artist asserted that sometimes "it's more painful to be standing and surviving." The bodies include a number of religious and allegorical references, including a Christlike figure.

The Palace of the Legion of Honor houses an impressive collection of fine art.

Rodin's *The Thinker* contemplates life outside the Palace of the Legion of Honor.

Through the parking lot, it's impossible to miss the ❾ **Palace of the Legion of Honor,** one of the city's biggest art museums. Intriguingly, the building is a replica of a replica. The 1915 Panama Pacific Exposition included a French Pavilion, modeled on the Palais de la Légion d'Honneur in Paris. The French Pavilion showcased French art during the expo but was torn down afterwards. Alma de Bretteville Spreckels, wife of sugar magnate Adolph Spreckels (you can read more about her in Backstory, Walk 4, page 31), missed the pavilion and had this more permanent version built (it opened in 1924). The museum's holdings include many 20th-century European masterpieces. You don't need to enter to have a look at Auguste Rodin's *The Thinker* in front—it's a bronze cast, but Rodin oversaw its production. Some memorable scenes from Hitchcock's *Vertigo* were shot here too.

From the museum, continue west on Camino del Mar through a narrow parking lot and eventually past a yellow barricade to a pedestrian-only path. Stay left to follow the trail, and make your way to the ❿ USS *San Francisco* Memorial, which pays homage to the World War II heavy cruiser that played a dramatic role in the decisive naval battle at Guadalcanal in 1942. More than 100 lives were lost, and the memorial is partly constructed from the bridge of the ship that shows signs of the furious battle.

Continue along the road and cross Point Lobos Avenue. To your left, ⓫ **Seal Rock Inn** is a budget-friendly (for San Francisco) seaside motel that Hunter S. Thompson famously holed up in while writing the feature "Fear and Loathing on the Campaign Trail" for *Rolling Stone.* He likened the barking of the sea lions through his open window as "like living next to a dog pound." Head right and pass between the sentry lions that were once part of the elaborate gateway entrance to ⓬ **Sutro Heights Park** and the estate of Adolph Sutro (see Backstory, page 228). Sutro, an unusually civic-minded millionaire, fashioned his gardens into a grand park open to the public. He had the grounds landscaped in the style of an Italian garden, and although some cracked wise about Sutro's unrefined tastes, San Franciscans seldom objected to the plaster nymph statues that peered out between the trees and shrubbery. All is gone now, save for some cypress trees, lovely rolling lawns, and what appears to be the broken footprint of Sutro's old manor house, which fell into disrepair after his death and was demolished in 1939.

Loop around the ruins and look for a small, sandy path next to a bench on the southern end of the loop trail, which eventually leads down a sandy set of stairs to Balboa Street. Between 1920 and 1972, stretched out before you would have been Playland at the Beach, a 10-acre amusement park complete with roller coasters, bumper cars, and funhouses; it was also the birthplace, in 1928, of one of San Francisco's most delicious and enduring treats: the It's-It ice cream sandwich, which was available only at the park until it closed (and is now sold nationwide and online at itsiticecream.com).

Cross the Great Highway and make your way up the hill to the **⓭ Cliff House.** There have been several Cliff Houses on this site, beginning in 1863. The first was owned by a retired sea captain known as Pop Foster, and for a time, Foster's Cliff House was a house of ill repute. Adolph Sutro bought the remote resort in the 1890s; it burned down in 1894, but Sutro had it rebuilt two years later. Sutro's Cliff House was the magnificent, cliff-hanging Victorian beauty so often featured in historical photos—the most familiar of which, sadly, is the 1907 shot of the building going up in flames. The current Cliff House, completed in 1909, is much less comely from the

street, but after a recent remodel it has become a fine-looking restaurant and bistro, with exotic Casablanca decor and picture windows making the most of the sea view.

If you're not eating, walk on through, find your way to the veranda overlooking the cliffs, and spend $3 to take a gander at the **⓮ Camera Obscura** for a large 360-degree view of the scenery. A holdover from the aforementioned Playland at the Beach, the big camera is remarkable mostly as a relic of archaic technology. It represents a link in the chain of inventions that led to photography; Leonardo da Vinci drew up plans for such a device in the 15th century, and this same technology was used to create Jan Vermeer's painting *Girl with a Pearl Earring*.

Back out on the sidewalk, amble north to **⓯ Louis' Restaurant.** It's a casual and friendly

Cypress-lined coastal trails provide a natural escape from city traffic.

Sweeping ocean views are never far from sight along Lands End Trail.

diner with the same exceptional views you'd enjoy at the much more expensive Cliff House. Opened on Valentine's Day in 1937 by Greek immigrant Louis Hontalas, the restaurant remains in the Hontalas family to this day. In the 1930s, Louis and his wife, Helen, used to lug a popcorn machine out to the sidewalk to sell snacks to passersby. At one point the National Park Service, which now owns the land that the eatery occupies, considered turning it into open space, but a postcard campaign by more than a thousand devoted fans of Louis' changed their minds.

Just up the street is the Lands End Lookout and the conclusion of our walk.

Points of Interest

1 **Lands End Lookout and Visitor Center** 680 Point Lobos Ave.; 415-426-5240, nps.gov/goga /planyourvisit/landsend.htm

2 **Sutro Baths** 1004 Point Lobos Ave.; 415-426-5240, nps.gov/goga/planyourvisit/cliff-house -sutro-baths.htm

3 **Point Lobos** Lands End Trail, N37° 47.095' W122° 30.486'; 415-426-5240, nps.gov/goga

4 **Mile Rock Beach** Lands End Trail, N37° 47.266' W122° 30.342'; 415-426-5240, nps.gov/goga

5 **Lands End Labyrinth** Lands End Trail, N37° 47.294' W122° 30.301'; 415-426-5240, nps.gov/goga

6 **Eagle's Point Overlook** Lands End Trail, N37° 47.206' W122° 29.704'; 415-426-5240, nps.gov/goga

7 **Memorial for Peace** 1142 El Camino del Mar; 415-426-5240, nps.gov/goga

8 **Holocaust Memorial (*The Survivor*)** Lincoln Park, Legion of Honor Drive at El Camino del Mar; 415-831-2700, sfrecpark.org/destination/lincoln-park

9 **Palace of the Legion of Honor** Lincoln Park, 100 34th Ave.; 415-750-3600, legionofhonor.famsf.org

10 **USS *San Francisco* Memorial** 415-334-0263, usssanfrancisco.org

11 **Seal Rock Inn** 545 Point Lobos Ave.; 415-752-8000, sealrockinn.com

12 **Sutro Heights Park** 846 Point Lobos Ave.; 415-561-4323, nps.gov/goga/planyourvisit/sutro-heights-accessibility.htm

13 **Cliff House** 1090 Point Lobos Ave.; 415-386-3330, cliffhouse.com

14 **Camera Obscura** 1096 Point Lobos Ave.; 415-450-0415, giantcamera.com

15 **Louis' Restaurant** 902 Point Lobos Ave.; 415-387-6330, louissf.com

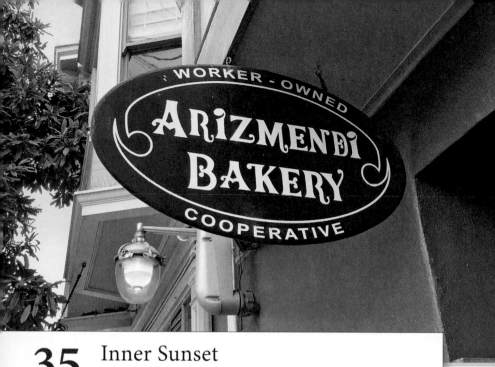

35 Inner Sunset
Flatland Dining and Colorful Steps to Grand Views

Above: *Cooperative bakeries, artisanal ice cream, and fresh-from-the-sea sushi are just some of the culinary delights you'll find along Ninth Avenue.*

BOUNDARIES: Lincoln Ave., 16th Ave., Moraga St., Ninth Ave.
DISTANCE: 2 miles
DIFFICULTY: Strenuous (many sets of uphill stairs)
PARKING: Metered 2-hour street parking plentiful.
PUBLIC TRANSIT: 44 Muni bus; N Judah

While it lacks iconic landmarks like a golden bridge or a soaring tower, the Inner Sunset District has an appeal that lies in its unassuming charm. At one point, this area was covered by vast sand dunes and was known as the Outside Lands; considered inaccessible and uninhabitable, it was a relative no-man's-land until the late 1800s. Shortly after World War II, developers changed all that when they started throwing up the stucco row houses that we see today to house working families and immigrants who called, and still call, the area home.

There is some disagreement on how this fog-swathed neighborhood came to be known as the Sunset. It appears to have been a marketing term first coined by real estate developer Wendell Easton, who waxed poetic in an 1889 edition of the *Alta California,* one of the newspapers of the time: "The golden hued sun, as it bids good day to this western slope and dips itself gracefully into its evening bath in the placid Pacific, throws its last kisses prior to its final dip upon these, the truly Sunset Heights." While this description may be a bit over the top for an area that's frequently enveloped in thick coastal mist, the restaurants are amazing, the community vibe is robust, and there are great parks with tremendous views not mobbed by tourists.

Our adventure begins and ends around the commercial hub of Ninth and Irving, where coffee shops, breweries, bakeries, and all manner of restaurants reflect the multicultural makeup of the neighborhood. Strolling past pastel-hued homes, we'll gradually make our way up, up, up along mosaic-graced stairs to a nearly 360-degree view of the city before descending to the flatlands again. Pack a windbreaker, grab a cup of coffee, and prepare to enjoy the quiet allure of one of San Francisco's hidden gems.

Walk Description

We begin our journey at the epicenter of Inner Sunset gastronomic glory: the corner of Ninth and Irving. You'd be well advised to fuel yourself with a cup of java from ❶ **The Beanery Inc.,** where beans are roasted on-site and neighbors stop to have a chat. You'd be well advised to pair it with a savory cheese roll from ❷ **Arizmendi Bakery.** A worker-owned cooperative, Arizmendi has been delighting the neighborhood since 2000 with fresh-baked goods and pizzas. If you begin your walk on a Sunday morning, head to the community gathering spot of the ❸ **Inner Sunset Farmers' Market,** around the corner on Eighth Avenue. Here you'll find fresh fruits, produce, and local artisanal wares from 9 a.m. to 1 p.m.

Head west toward the ocean on Irving Street, the main commercial heart of the Inner Sunset. Mom-and-pop stores outnumber chains here, and there's a gentle hum to the neighborhood. That hum gets louder when you approach seemingly nondescript ❹ **San Tung,** a restaurant whose dry-fried chicken wings have achieved a near cult following: they made *Food & Wine* magazine's list of best chicken wings, and they are absolutely worth the inevitable wait for a table.

Make a left on Funston Avenue to admire the Romanesque revival architecture of ❺ **St. Anne of the Sunset,** a Catholic church completed in 1931. The elaborate frieze above the front entrance was created by Sister Justina Niemierski, who spoke infrequently and preferred to express herself through art. Originally from East Prussia, Sister Justina graduated from the Academy of Art in Berlin before moving to the Bay Area in 1912 to aid German immigrants.

These beautiful tiled stairs are a resplendent display of community action at work.

Turn right on Judah Street and then left on 16th Avenue to begin our climb. Crossing Kirkham Street, you'll see a colorful tile sign welcoming you to the ❻ **Hidden Garden Steps,** the newer of two spectacular sets of mosaic stairways in the neighborhood. Local artist Colette Crutcher and Irish ceramicist Aileen Barr were commissioned after a vigorous grassroots fundraising effort in 2013 to help design and complete this 148-step mosaic staircase, replete with butterflies and flowers plus a giant salamander artfully winding up the stairs. This is the second set of stairs completed by the duo and a whole host of generous neighbors who volunteered tirelessly to make the project come to fruition. The first project, the ❼ **16th Avenue Tiled Steps,** was completed in 2005—we'll reach it shortly.

When you crest the top of the stairs, turn right on Lawton Street, which eventually becomes 16th Avenue. The brightly colored homes here help combat the frequent gray fog that often shrouds this part of the city. Follow 16th to reach the intersection with Moraga Avenue and the original 163 tiled steps. More than 300 community members contributed to this inaugural neighborhood beautification project, and you can see their names reflected in many of the tiles. The motif here is from sea to sky. Be sure to stop frequently so you can turn around and enjoy increasingly expansive views of Ocean Beach behind you.

Once you reach the top of the stairs, your journey isn't over. Cross the street to reach the wooden stairs beckoning farther upward to reach aptly named ❽ **Grandview Park.** Many locals refer to this spot as Turtle Hill, and from afar, the mound does, indeed, resemble the shell of a wayward turtle heading back to the ocean. The park itself isn't much to look at, consisting mostly of coastal scrub on top of chert that was once part of the sea floor, but the view is arguably one of the city's best. Plant yourself on a bench—we hope you brought a jacket!—and drink in the vista. Depending on fog levels, you should be able to pick out a Golden Gate Park windmill, Seal Rock, the Golden Gate Bridge, the downtown skyline, and more.

When you're ready to descend, follow the trail that skirts the top and then head down the stairs in the opposite direction from which you climbed. Cross 14th Avenue and keep descending the sets of stairs along Moraga Avenue, which we'll follow until we reach Ninth Avenue again.

As you turn left on Ninth Avenue, pass between the brick pillars denoting Windsor. This short stretch of both Eighth and Ninth Avenues between Moraga and Lawton, called **❾ Windsor Terrace,** features the grandest homes in the neighborhood. Note that you don't see any garages; this is because they're all tucked behind the homes and accessed by Auto Drive, a narrow road between the two avenues. Not much is known about the Windsor Terrace designation, which has likely been a real estate ploy from the get-go, but photo archives date the pillars at least back to 1910. Those who grew up in the Sunset claim it's always the best area for trick-or-treating.

As we return to our Ninth-and-Irving starting point, we suspect that you've worked up an appetite for some local grub. Always topping lists of best Bay Area sushi restaurants, **❿ Ebisu** has been slicing up the region's freshest fish for more than three decades. Across the street, relative newcomer **⓫ San Francisco's Hometown Creamery** has quickly amassed a loyal following for its small-batch ice cream in flavors ranging from strawberry-balsamic to peanut butter–chocolate fudge. Brothers Adar and Saadi Halil went so far as to obtain a pasteurizer's license to ensure that they could make everything completely from scratch.

Also notable on this block is one of the last remaining magic stores in the city, **⓬ Misdirections Magic Shop.** Catering to professionals and amateurs alike, founder and magician Joe Pon prides himself on creating a community that includes lectures and workshops from visiting magicians and other sleights of hand. Across the street is the Inner Sunset outpost of the beloved **⓭ Green Apple Books.** Author events and readings are frequent at this location.

Our walk ends with a step back into history at **⓮ The Little Shamrock,** the city's second-oldest bar (after the Saloon, which is featured in our North Beach Bars jaunt; see Walk 8, page 57). Originally opened in 1893 to cater to the workers creating the California Midwinter exposition in Golden Gate Park, the "Sham" has somehow survived two earthquakes and Prohibition without closing its door or losing its license. Look for the wooden clock that stopped ticking after the '06 quake as you belly up to the bar. Recent additions include backgammon, board games, and darts. Vintage couches, a fireplace, and stained glass chandeliers add to the cozy, unpretentious charm of this historic watering hole.

Inner Sunset

Points of Interest

1. **The Beanery Inc.** 1307 Ninth Ave.; 415-661-1255, facebook.com/thebeaneryinc

2. **Arizmendi Bakery** 1331 Ninth Ave.; 415-566-3117, arizmendibakery.com

3. **Inner Sunset Farmers' Market** 1315 Eighth Ave.; 925-825-9090, tinyurl.com/innersunsetfm

4. **San Tung** 1031 Irving St.; 415-242-0828, santung.net

5. **St. Anne of the Sunset** 850 Judah St.; 415-665-1600, stanne-sf.org

6. **Hidden Garden Steps** 16th Ave. between Kirkham and Lawton Sts.; hiddengardensteps.org, hiddengardensteps@gmail.com (no published phone number)

7. **16th Avenue Tiled Steps** Moraga St. between 15th and 16th Aves.; 16thavenuetiledsteps.com, 16thavenuetiledsteps@gmail.com (no published phone number)

8. **Grandview Park** Moraga St. and 14th Ave.; 415-831-5500, sfrecpark.org/destination/grand-view-park

9. **Windsor Terrace** Eighth and Ninth Aves. between Moraga and Lawton Sts.

10. **Ebisu** 1283 Ninth Ave.; 415-566-1770, ebisusushi.com

11. **San Francisco's Hometown Creamery** 1290 Ninth Ave.; 415-682-4977, sfhometowncreamery.com

12. **Misdirections Magic Shop** 1236 Ninth Ave.; 415-566-2180, shop.misdirections.com

13. **Green Apple Books on the Park** 1231 Ninth Ave.; 415-742-5833, greenapplebooks.com

14. **The Little Shamrock** 807 Lincoln Way; 415-661-0060, facebook.com/thelittleshamrock1893

Appendix: Walks by Theme

Architecture
Financial District (Walks 1 and 3)
Nob Hill (Walk 10)
Golden Gate Bridge to Sausalito (Walk 17)
Pacific Heights (Walk 18)
Potrero Hill and Dogpatch (Walk 24)
Market Street (Walks 1 and 27)

Arts and Culture
Union Square and the Theater District (Walk 4)
Civic Center and Hayes Valley (Walk 12)
Embarcadero South (Walk 19)
SoMa (Walk 20)
The Inner Mission (Walk 22)

Dining, Shopping, and Entertainment
North Beach (Walks 7 and 8)
Tenderloin (Walk 13)
Mission Bars (Walk 23)
Potrero Hill and Dogpatch (Walk 24)
Glen Park and Glen Canyon (Walk 26)
Upper Market and the Castro (Walk 27)
Haight-Ashbury (Walk 30)
Japantown (Walk 32)
Richmond District (Walk 33)
Inner Sunset (Walk 35)

History
Market Street (Walks 1 and 27)
Barbary Coast (Walk 6)

Urban Parks
Marina and Cow Hollow (Walk 15)
The Presidio (Walks 16 and 17)
Bernal Heights (Walk 25)
Glen Park and Glen Canyon (Walk 26)
Twin Peaks (Walk 28)
Westside Cordillera (Walk 29)
Golden Gate Park (Walk 31)
Lands End (Walk 34)

Stairways
Telegraph Hill (Walk 9)
Russian Hill (Walk 11)
Twin Peaks (Walk 28)
Inner Sunset (Walk 35)

Index

Page references followed by *m* indicate a map.

About the Authors

Photo: Eric Doherty

Kathleen Dodge Doherty is a San Francisco–based free-lance writer, adventurer, and lover of all things outdoorsy and literary. For more than two decades, Kathleen has been writing, editing, and reading about San Francisco—climbing hills, downing burritos, paying too much for coffee, and ferreting out speakeasies in the name of research. She is the author (with Jordan Summers) of *Day & Section Hikes: John Muir Trail* (Menasha Ridge Press) and has also written for Fodor's, Lonely Planet, Moon Handbooks, *Afar Magazine, AAA Via Magazine,* and many websites. A one-time researcher, developer, and leader of bicycling and hiking tours worldwide, Kathleen largely runs after her kids and jumps in local puddles these days. A swashbuckler at heart, Kathleen is continually surprised by the never-ending treasures that await in her city by the bay.

Tom Downs grew up in the Santa Clara Valley, south of San Francisco. He has lived in Los Angeles, New York City, Oakland, and Berkeley, as well as in Chinatown and the Mission District in San Francisco. He is a travel writer who has authored books and articles about New Orleans, Hanoi, and the West of Ireland for Lonely Planet, BBC Studios, and a host of magazines, newspapers, and websites. His photography has appeared in publications including *National Geographic* and *The New York Times.* In 2007 his post-Katrina *Lonely Planet New Orleans* was honored with the Lowell Thomas Award, granted by the Society of American Travel Writers, for Best Guidebook.